750

D1615322

DOWN
IN P

DOWNING STREET
IN PERSPECTIVE

DOWNING STREET IN PERSPECTIVE

Marcia Falkender

Weidenfeld and Nicolson
LONDON

To Timothy and Daniel
to help secure their future

Copyright © Lady Falkender 1983

First published in Great Britain by
George Weidenfeld & Nicolson Ltd
91 Clapham High Street, London sw4

ISBN 0 297 78107 3

Printed in Great Britain by
Butler & Tanner Ltd, Frome and London

Contents

Illustrations

Acknowledgements

To Anne de Courcy, without whose endeavour and good humour this book would never have been written. Her hours of encouragement and co-operation made my task far easier. This warrants my deepest gratitude.

To Ella Wright, who so patiently and painstakingly typed both early and later manuscripts, and to Susan Utting, who helped in this. To my sister who transcribed some of the tapes, helped with all the tedious jobs involved in putting a book together and was always able to see the real perspective. To Barbara Twigg for the research she did for the early manuscript.

ONE

Resignation

On the morning of Tuesday, 16 March 1976, I arrived at the office early. There was the same smooth daily routine as usual, with the policeman on duty pressing the discreet bell beside the black front door as he always did when staff arrived at Number 10. As usual, too, the door was open by the time I reached the step, where I greeted the doorman before walking to my office beside the Cabinet Room, at the end of the corridor.

From then on, nothing was as usual. Harold Wilson, four times Prime Minister, an ambitious man who loved politics and was in the pink of health, able not only to endure but to enjoy the physical and mental strain of the highest office in the land, announced his resignation that morning.

It hit the nation like a bolt from the blue. The first intimation to the general public was the news flash with which ITN broke into a news bulletin. In his own constituency the shock was, of course, greatest: in its schools, for example, classes were interrupted by those who had heard the news. Neither teachers nor pupils could believe it. Here is how Sean Hughes, prospective parliamentary candidate for Harold Wilson's constituency of Huyton, describes that moment:

> I was teaching a fourth year O level set on the events in British politics after the First Reform Act of 1832. While I was speaking, one of the caretakers appeared at the classroom door and beckoned me out. He obviously thought Harold had resigned completely and suggested I should go home and change into a suit. When I asked him what he was talking about, he said 'Harold's spewed it', which I remember the *Guardian* translated as Liverpool slang for 'Harold has resigned'.

In the House of Commons, the reaction was similar. Although the House was not sitting, there were various committees in session. In some cases, the doors of the rooms in which they were meeting were flung open without ceremony by clerks, with cries of 'Wilson has resigned!' Momentarily, there was silence, as everyone tried to work out whether this was some lesser-known Wilson of whose activities they should be aware but were not, whether the messenger who bore the news was a madman, or whether the Prime Minister was, in fact, stepping down. The reaction in Huyton, expressed by Sean Hughes, summed up the general feeling of disbelief and, indeed, sadness. 'People of my generation had not known the Labour Party without Harold as Leader, and found it difficult to envisage a Labour Party without him at its head.'

As the words sank in, the committee rooms emptied and groups gathered in the corridors and round the ticker-tape machines, which chattered out both the news of the resignation and the reasons for it given by the Prime Minister: in brief, that he had held this office for a total of almost eight years – enough for any one man – and that, as he had always urged his own Ministers to retire at sixty, he should do the same himself.

Despite the logic of this explanation, the surprise caused by the announcement was such that, with the passage of time, few people believed that it represented the truth. 'It's completely out of character for a man who so clearly enjoys being Prime Minister' was about the most non-committal reaction; others ranged from a belief that some hidden scandal was about to break to the theory that the Prime Minister was suffering from an illness as yet unrevealed.

But the Prime Minister's health was excellent (I should mention that the cancer for which he was operated on in 1980 and which necessitated a restful convalescence was first diagnosed by his doctors four years after his resignation); and no scandal surfaced either then or subsequently. Yet Parliament and the country at large still found it difficult to accept both his resignation and his explanation for it.

His own Party could hardly believe that their Leader could, so to speak, suddenly down tools and go; as for his opponents – here was a man whom they had only been able to defeat once, who had returned to win against them twice in succession, who had more or less forced them to change their own Leader on three occasions, a man who, in sum, had dominated politics during the 1960s and 1970s, simply walking out of the arena. It seemed incredible.

Nevertheless, the official explanation was the correct one, as those who were close to Harold Wilson well knew. There were one or two additional minor reasons, not least that Mary Wilson hoped he would take an early retirement.

Even as far back as the early 1960s, I had learned of his view that there should be a limit to the amount of time anyone remained in high office. In the late 1960s, he had already indicated that if he won a further election, he would want to stay as Leader and Prime Minister for a further two years only. Those close to him, therefore, knew that if Labour had been returned in the election of 1970, he would probably have resigned in 1972; when they went into Downing Street with him in 1974 they were equally aware that his intention was to resign in 1976 – unless prevented by crisis. This was a key phrase; some who knew of his plan believed that he might be persuaded to stay on longer if he thought this was necessary for the country or Party.

While it was true that the Common Market Referendum had been carried successfully in 1975, inflation – brought about by the oil crisis and by the Heath incomes policy with its built-in inflationary aspects – had soared. Here Harold Wilson (who had set up a Counter-Inflation Unit at Number 10) felt that his major task was to bring inflation under control within a year. Indeed, in a television talk to the nation on this subject in the summer of 1975, he had urged people to 'Give a year for Britain' by making an extra effort.

I seized upon this phrase in 1975, using it to enforce my argument when he began to refer once again to the question of his resignation. There still seemed so much to be done. I remember saying, 'You have asked the nation to "Give a year for Britain". If you resign, you yourself will only be giving six months. Don't go now – at least carry through with your "Year for Britain", and then leave.'

As early as July 1975 he had set a target date of October. He had wanted to announce his resignation at the Party Conference in Blackpool. Here, I was able to influence him: by pointing out, as we sat discussing it in the garden at Chequers after his Helsinki visit, that Harold Macmillan had announced his resignation in the middle of the Tory Party Conference – and that it had almost destroyed the Tory Party.

A similar announcement from Harold Wilson would have had the same effect, with the Conference dissolving into an electioneering jamboree and candidates making vote-seeking speeches rather than concentrating on Party policy or setting out what action the Government had taken on inflation, incomes and prices. Accepting this, he first suggested

Christmas as a possibility; again I demurred – as anyone whose responsibility is carrying through decisions knows, national holidays cause difficulties and delays, and people dislike interruption at these special family times. He finally said: 'As you know, I have always taken the view that Ministers should retire at sixty, while they are still young enough for another job within the political arena; also, when you have been a long time in office, you inevitably become a little stale.' With the same problems coming up again and again, he continued, both a Government and its Chief Minister lose their original vigour and freshness, and though resolution is still intact, a certain enthusiasm disappears. 'I think, Marcia,' he concluded, 'that the announcement should be made at the time of my sixtieth birthday.'

From then on we all accepted that this was what would happen although, for my part, I continued to argue against it right until the last moment. I thought the nation would be stunned and shocked at the sudden disappearance of this man whom they had come to regard as a permanent fixture in their lives – right or wrong, agree or disagree, Labour or Tory, Harold Wilson was *there*. I felt that it was something that should happen more gradually, and at a time when things were easier.

There were clouds ahead. A three-month moving average for the General Index of Retail Prices showed the index in July 1975 as running at an annual increase in excess of 7.2 per cent, but 26.3 per cent up on the same figure for July 1974.

Until the very last moment, I hoped that Harold Wilson could be persuaded that he was the right person to stay in charge – not least because he was a good Cabinet chairman who had been in power long enough to understand all the current difficulties and anticipate those ahead. He himself was quite aware that he might be forced to change his mind because of, say, a run on sterling or the need for a vote of confidence in the House.

On Sunday 14 March, I said to him at Chequers, 'All this time, while you've been saying you will resign and I've been trying to talk you out of it, you haven't actually told me your intended date!' He replied, 'The 16th March – the day after tomorrow.'

This was the first time I heard from him the actual resignation date, although I knew it had been suggested because Mary Wilson had pencilled it into her diary four or five months earlier, marking it 'D-Day' in very large letters.

Harold Wilson had informed the Queen well in advance – on 9

December, in one of the weekly audiences he had with her – saying that he was thinking of retiring and explaining the reasons. He had also told friends at a dinner party at Lord Goodman's; but although rumours to the effect that he was going began to circulate after this, nobody believed them. Apparently, it was considered 'one of Wilson's tricks', possibly to lure the Opposition into some move that would give him an advantage over them.

It was important not only from the point of view of courtesy but from that of procedure that Harold Wilson should notify the Palace well in advance of his decision to resign: there was no precedent for a Prime Minister resigning voluntarily (apart from compelling reasons of health), and certainly no precedent for the resignation of a Prime Minister from a Party where the Leader was elected rather than selected.

The Queen, therefore, could not do what she did after the resignation of Harold Macmillan: that is, after consultation, send for the person she thought the Tory Party would choose. With the Labour Party, if there was no clear-cut result after the first election for the Leadership, it could be a question of waiting for another one or two weeks while subsequent elections took place. So on the day of the resignation itself, Harold Wilson's audience with the Queen was not the final departure ceremony – which could not take place until Her Majesty had a new Labour Leader to send for – but to state formally words to the effect that: 'I am announcing my resignation, which will take effect as soon as a new Leader is elected.'

This audience took place at 10.15 a.m. on the morning of Tuesday 16 March. Three-quarters of an hour later, the Cabinet was due to meet. I have often been asked how many of the twenty-two members of the Cabinet knew what they were about to hear. The answer is: probably only three or four. Four or five others were, I suppose, aware that Harold Wilson's resignation was imminent, but the others were taken completely by surprise.

Just before the Cabinet met, and immediately after his return from Buckingham Palace, the Prime Minister had brief informal meetings with Ted Short (Leader of the House and Lord President of the Council) and Jim Callaghan, to inform them officially of the announcement he would be making in Cabinet. Jim had actually been told about it formally on the evening of Harold's birthday five days earlier, but as his two closest aides were also extremely close to Harold Wilson's aides it would be naïve to suppose that they had not received some indication of what was to happen considerably earlier. Denis Healey had been told the day before; Eric Varley knew in advance. Apart from the few who knew what was about to 'break', there was total ignorance of the fact that a new paragraph was to be written into parliamentary history.

From my room next to the Cabinet Room I could hear the Cabinet beginning to gather. Among them, of course, would be Peter Shore, with whom I had a luncheon appointment. I went out to look for him, thinking that he would want to cancel it: why should a busy Cabinet Minister spend time on this of all days having lunch with someone who wouldn't be around in another three weeks?

As I moved through the gathering of Ministers, keeping what I hoped was an expressionless face, the reactions were varied and interesting. Some cast me sympathetic looks, others smiled at me in total ignorance, still others looked away, unwilling to be involved in any conversational interchange in case, presumably, they said the wrong thing. When I reached Peter, I said, 'I suppose we won't be lunching today?'

'Why on earth not?' he replied. Each of us looked at the other in astonishment, he because of the seeming irrelevance of my question, I because I was surprised that he did not know of Harold's resignation. I pulled myself together and said, 'Well, in view of Harold's statement.' 'What's that?' he responded; when I told him, he stood there quite speechless.

Almost immediately, the Cabinet went in. Harold, sitting in his usual chair in the centre, read out his prepared statement, which was greeted by silence – a stunned silence from those not previously 'in the know', a silence of perplexity from those who had known but were not quite sure how to handle this new and unprecedented situation.

By 11.15 – a scant quarter of an hour after it had begun – the meeting was over. In contrast to the aftermath of 'ordinary' Cabinet Meetings, these moments too were quiet. Normally, even after a hostile meeting, or one that has been convened to deal with some depressing or difficult crisis, the exit from the Cabinet Room is the signal for a general 'unwinding' process: there is a lot of back-slapping, noisy jokes, a rush for the Gents' loo next to my room, a few shouted remarks, Ministers in a hurry to return to their Departments – in general, quite a din. Today, all was subdued; everyone left the building quickly; many clearly wanted a chance to talk this happening over with other people as soon as possible.

The Prime Minister himself had a series of official meetings with, amongst others, Jack Jones of the Transport Workers and Len Murray, the General Secretary of the TUC. Just after midday, he was giving an exclusive interview to the *Daily Mirror*. After a brief lunch, he went to the House: business had to go on as usual.

Back in Number 10, the atmosphere was strange, almost unreal. We were still working for the Head of Government, but 'The King is dead, long live the King!' Meanwhile the Prime Minister's Agent in Huyton, Arthur Smith, received a phone call from Albert Murray at Number 10, which consisted of one line from the song 'The Party's Over'.

Who would be the new King? When would be the Prime Minister's last day – and when would we ourselves be physically leaving Downing Street? All these thoughts passed through my mind as I joined Peter Shore, who had insisted on keeping our date. We sat opposite each other, saying very little at first, in Lockets Restaurant, which was buzzing as usual with parliamentarians and gossip. What remarks we did make were confined to the 'What an extraordinary day!' variety. After a while we talked about the economic situation, and what effect the resignation would have on the counter-inflation policy and how it was pursued by the Government.

At four o'clock, Harold Wilson went to a large press conference at the Ministry of Defence, where everyone was extremely warm and complimentary to him. Most of the journalists present had been around since he was elected; all of them enjoyed his repartee. The world's press, too, were there in force.

Afterwards, back at Number 10, a semblance of normality briefly supervened. The Prime Minister did routine governmental work – chiefly going through his boxes – and went out to dinner later that evening with George (now Lord) Weidenfeld. I too was present; I had been interviewed for the BBC's *Nationwide* programme that evening, and George had taken me to the BBC in his car. Harold Wilson was already at George's flat when we arrived back from Shepherd's Bush, and we all dined round a small table in a window alcove overlooking the river. It was a calm, pleasant, almost muted occasion. George Weidenfeld's flat, with its high-ceilinged rooms, superb paintings, striking chocolate-brown walls, book-lined drawing room and – in those days – brilliant sofas and side tables in reds and burnt oranges, is a place designed for entertainment on a grand scale. That day, in contrast, our small table in the alcove had an air of peace and intimacy.

Our conversation at the end of this dramatic and exhausting day was similarly low-key. We talked, I remember, mainly about Harold Wilson's future: not simply what would happen over the next few weeks but about his long-term plans in the way of writing.

For me, the impact of the resignation announcement began to make itself felt the following day, when the job of working out the arrangements for the Prime Minister's departure began. As, owing to the way the new Leader would be elected, we did not know exactly when this would be, we worked on the assumption that 'D-Day' would be two weeks ahead. As things turned out this gave us the bonus of a week in hand.

The whole of those first two weeks seems, in retrospect, to have been taken up with packing cases. Packing cases for books, packing cases for office equipment, packing cases for family and personal possessions. The files – of which there were an enormous number – stayed in their filing cabinets because they were moved with the PM. As for accommodation, after a talk with the Chief Whip this was resolved by the allocation of two rather nice large rooms in Abbey Gardens, which looked out over the back of Westminster Abbey Gardens; Harold Wilson himself was also allocated a small room in the House of Commons.

Before leaving Downing Street and moving into the new offices there was plenty to be done, from organizing the actual departure to arranging certain important farewell parties. It had been intimated that Her Majesty the Queen would accept an invitation to a private dinner in Downing Street as a farewell to her longest-serving Prime Minister; and we also had to organize a dinner for the Cabinet. The work of planning for, in particular, these two parties and for the smooth transference of Harold Wilson's office into its new habitat all took place against the background of the event that made it possible for Harold to leave: the election of the new Leader – a drama which, for once, we could watch as outsiders though endowed with inside knowledge.

The dinner party for the Queen on 23 March had a happy, relaxed air about it right from the moment Her Majesty arrived at Downing Street, where staff were gathered in the corridors or looking down from the stairways so that they could see her entrance. The messengers and custodians got the first glimpse of her, as they stood in the entrance hall. It was only the second time (the first was with Winston Churchill) that she had dined with a Prime Minister to bid him farewell. Her clothes, as always, were perfectly in keeping: she wore a dark, multi-coloured dinner dress with a silk shawl, rather than the glittering dresses, the diamonds and the furs in which she dresses for State occasions. As for the guests, most were senior members of the Cabinet, former Prime Ministers, high officials, and their wives or escorts. The Queen made a charming speech about the Prime Minister; his, in return, was in the same relaxed, informal mood. I remember her amusement when he said that she had now seen five Prime Ministers off these premises and would doubtless see off many more before her reign came to an end. After dinner, we left the great State Dining Room and went back into the Drawing Room where the Queen circulated amongst the guests – including the rest of the Private Office staff and some of the Press Office, who had organized their own dinner upstairs and then came down and joined everyone afterwards. She stayed until midnight.

The State Dining Room was also the setting for the Cabinet dinner party. If the one for the Queen could be described as relaxed, this affair was positively end-of-term. Barbara Castle sat almost opposite me, punctuating the entire dinner with questions about Harold's resignation. She would give me a fierce look and say, 'Come on, Marcia – *you* must have known for a very long time,' or, 'Come on, Marcia – who else knew?' Then there would be a pause and we would all start chatting again to our neighbours – mine were John Silkin and Sir Douglas Allen (then Permanent Secretary to the Treasury) – and suddenly I would hear Barbara's voice from her seat opposite John Silkin, 'Now, Marcia, you'll tell us who knew – you *must* know who'd been told!'

I did my best to dodge these bullet-like questions that occurred all through dinner, though slightly distracted the while by Tony Benn's attempts to take photographs. Meanwhile, there were the speeches, all lighthearted and amusing with the exception, oddly enough – he is usually extremely funny and witty – of Tony Benn: he got very political, which did not fit in with the mood of the evening – nor, indeed, with his photographic efforts.

The last party was much the quietest. I had discovered that nothing had been arranged for the Prime Minister's last day in Downing Street. It ought not to pass without being marked in some way, I thought, so suggested a small luncheon. Only those closest to him in his working life were invited on this final day: apart from Harold and Mary Wilson themselves, there were only senior members of his staff – Kenneth Stowe, his Principal Private Secretary, Joe Haines the Press Secretary, the Assistant Press Secretary Janet Hewlett-Davis, his Senior Policy Adviser Bernard Donoughue, his Special Policy Adviser Andrew Graham, Albert Murray, my sister Peggy and myself. As was to be expected, we spent most of the time reminiscing and laughing about things that had happened in the past; it was a very happy occasion.

This last luncheon put the final full stop to our Downing Street period. We were literally ready to leave: I had spent the whole morning helping with the packing of the last of our things. Later, I regretted that I had taken no photographs on that day, but Janet Hewlett-Davis took some in the Pillared Room before the party broke up.

Afterwards, Harold Wilson went straight over to the House of Commons, returning briefly to Downing Street in order to be ready to leave for his 5.15 appointment with the Queen, at which he would formally resign; after which Jim Callaghan would go in his turn to the Palace, kiss hands on his appointment and come to Downing Street to be clapped and cheered in by the staff.

Before that first applause, so thrilling to a new Prime Minister, rang in Jim's ears, much had happened behind the scenes. The past three weeks had seen the battles of the Leadership election campaign.

Uninvolved for once, I watched the teams mobilizing for their respective candidates: Merlyn Rees emerging as campaign manager for Jim Callaghan, Bill Rodgers for Roy Jenkins. It seemed curiously familiar, the only difference being that – unlike the 1963 campaign, which became, towards the end, unpleasant and vicious – this one was conducted almost totally without personal malice. Instead there was much more hard argument about why each particular candidate, and his supporters, felt that he should be *the* one. Not so colourful, certainly, but much more adult. Perhaps this was to be expected, as the candidates were all substantial figures – apart from Jim and Roy, Tony Crosland, Michael Foot and Tony Benn all stood. Harold himself took great delight in working out what he thought the vote would be, believing that the final result would be quite close. As it was, Jim came much nearer to defeat than Harold himself had done in 1963. Disappointed by his showing on the first ballot, Roy Jenkins did not wish to be accused of upsetting the Party still further by subjecting it to the inevitable long delay which more balloting would have caused, and decided to withdraw his candidature. By the third ballot on 5 April Jim Callaghan, as had seemed probable all along, became the new Leader and entered Number 10 as Prime Minister on the evening of that day.

Well before his arrival I had taken myself off, leaving almost immediately after Harold Wilson had departed as Prime Minister for the last time. After he had left for his final audience with the Queen at 5.15 p.m., he drove straight on to Chequers, where he and Mary Wilson, according to tradition, were staying the night – every outgoing Prime Minister is invited to stay at Chequers after his resignation.

The car I had booked to take me home was parked, as usual, well away from the front door of Number 10, in order to keep this clear. I remember that the policeman on door duty that day – a lovely man – rang through to say that he had asked for it to be brought right up to the door, so that I did not have a long walk to it in front of all the photographers and reporters clustered outside. Even with a clear view, however, they wouldn't have been able to spot whatever it was they were looking for on my face – happiness, gloom, shock or hilarity – because I was feeling curiously emotionless.

The whole day had also been strangely emotionless. Now that the final day had actually come, it was difficult to take in, especially as there was no high point to it, no grand drama. Low key is perhaps the best way to describe it; certainly Harold Wilson himself was registering no emotion at all. Indeed, for the past week or so he had had the air of a man walking through a dream, as though, now that he had finally taken the decision, he could hardly believe that it was all happening.

I cannot now accurately recall my own feelings as I came quickly out of the door of Number 10, after saying goodbye to everyone inside. But I remember my policeman friend giving me a goodbye kiss in the hall before the door opened for me for the last time, and I walked out of the house and away from almost eight years of my life there.

TWO

Return to Opposition, 1970

16 March 1976 was not, of course, the first time Harold Wilson, and therefore myself as well, had left Downing Street. Nor was it the most traumatic: I recall with particular vividness the difficulties of setting up the Office of the Leader of the Opposition in 1970.

In part, these were psychological, in part physical. In 1970, we had expected to win – more, at the beginning of the campaign we were *sure* that we would win. We were quite unprepared for defeat.

It had been a hot election campaign in every sense. The weather was warm, the sun had shone most of the time, and Polling Day itself – 18 June, Waterloo Day – was sultry. We ourselves were cheerful and optimistic: all the polls had given Labour a clear lead, and even those who thought that we had chosen the wrong date for Polling Day – coming as it did at the end of what was virtually a five-week campaign – were still confident of the outcome.

That we were all of us completely wrong is now history. Those early polls that gave Labour such a massive lead were disastrously misleading; perhaps, if we had had a private opinion poll, a truer picture might have emerged, and we would at least have been prepared.

But even if we had been able to afford such a poll, I doubt if we would have believed any negative findings. So convincing were not only the regular opinion polls but the predictions that appeared in the national press that we disregarded until too late various small but significant pointers: the audiences that ranged from unresponsive to downright apathetic, the heckling that sometimes rose to physical abuse like egg-throwing. So unassailable was our confidence, so deep-rooted the idea of victory, that for months after the election we remained bemused;

speculation about what had gone wrong dominated our thoughts for many weeks after that conclusive defeat.

Paradoxically enough, one major factor responsible for the defeat was the seemingly popular 'In Place of Strife'. Though this piece of intended legislation was undoubtedly welcomed by the average voter – who by this time had become increasingly fed up with strikes and disruption generally – even such a mild attempt to curb union power was deeply resented by the Labour movement.

Even though 'Strife' in its final form had lost much of the bite of the original concept envisaged by Harold Wilson, it was still seen by committed Party members as an attack on their own people by their own Government. Hurt and offended, Party activists throughout the country lost heart; and their support, in physical as well as mental terms, fell away. There were fewer people to knock on doors, deliver leaflets, organize meetings, canvass the undecided, impress on the solid Labour voter the importance of getting to the poll. For a poor Party, as Labour had always been, losing voluntary workers is like losing valuable blood.

Another blow to the now-weakened Party was Edward Heath's electioneering tactic of combining the bribe of promised tax cuts with a last-minute scare that if a Labour Government were to be re-elected they might devalue the pound a second time.

Labour's backbone has always been the working man – the chief sufferer under policies devised to ease economic difficulties. The working man was, as always, the person hit hardest by the Statutory Prices and Incomes Policy; after devaluation, he was able to afford even less. The years of restraint, necessary though they were to return the economy to good shape, acted on him financially with the rigidity of an iron corset. No wonder he was fed up – and what a familiar cycle it has now become.

As we sat in the comfort of the Prime Minister's first-floor room in the Adelphi Hotel, Liverpool, on that scorching June day in 1970, we knew we had lost when the Guildford result, with its swing to the Tories of 5.3 per cent, flashed on to the screen. The nightmare began.

What we were seeing was the power of the female vote: it was the women of this country who put Edward Heath in office. But we were in no mood to appreciate the niceties of the historic fact that, all over the country – while their husbands were at work and therefore unaware that their wives were for the first time voting Tory – the women were going to the polls in the afternoon. Labour supporters traditionally vote early in the morning or after they have had their suppers before the poll closes in the evening.

When the Guildford result came in, I looked at Harold Wilson and he looked at me. Nothing was said, but both of us knew what had happened.

What you do, how you act, what you say, in the face of crushing, unexpected defeat, is the stuff of which politics is made. Harold Wilson was impassive, though obviously downcast; he sat alone on an enormous sofa, looking isolated and enigmatic.

Everyone had their own formula for coping with the shock: it was only afterwards that I learned that one Downing Street girl had managed to enjoy a brisk discussion about Uganda with a visiting journalist on the sofa in my sister's office while everyone else was watching the election results on a nearby television.

During the early hours of the morning of 19 June we returned to London by car, arriving exhausted at Downing Street around 6.00 a.m. Immediately, the problems began – problems which had to be faced in the main by the Wilsons' staff, as they themselves were occupied in playing out their respective roles in the final scene of this particular drama.

First and most pressing was the question of somewhere for them to live. Unlike a retiring American President, a Prime Minister has to leave immediately, with scant ceremony, though he is always assured of a final weekend at Chequers in which to rest after the rigours of hard campaigning up and down the country, and come to terms with the bitter disappointment of defeat.

Although the Prime Minister conceded defeat in a television interview at midday, it was not until 6.30 p.m. that he actually drove to the Palace to tender his official resignation. (The Queen, who had already decided to spend that day, Friday, at Windsor, so that she could go racing at Ascot, returned to London in the late afternoon to receive the Prime Minister.) After this short, sad journey – as usual, his driver was the faithful Bill Housden – the Wilsons went immediately to Chequers.

Ironically, the weather was still wonderful and the garden at Chequers looked glorious, so that when those who could, I suppose, be described as the Prime Minister's inner circle – since they always seemed to be near him at times like these – came over to discuss what had gone wrong, the *post mortem* was held over tea in the garden. It seemed strange to be sitting there, in the splendour of that marvellous June day, in the spacious and leisured surroundings that none of us thought we would ever see again, conducting our own private inquest and discussing plans for our future in Opposition.

Our tea party was, as usual, in the familiar setting of the rose garden. There was a scent of lavender from the border near the house, the red bricks of the Elizabethan wall (now replaced by an enormous swimming pool) glowed mellow in the sunlight, the table around which we sat stood on a paved terrace.

Thomas Balogh had come over from Oxford, Peter Shore and Gerald Kaufman had motored down from London. As for the tea, as usual everything was home-made and delicious: the scones, the strawberry jam, the little angel cakes with their two 'wings' stuck into fresh whipped cream. The pot of Indian tea, under its knitted tea-cosy, stood ready to pour into the delicate Minton teacups.

Although I cannot recall the conversation with any precision, I do remember that even before coming to Chequers that Friday Harold had made one important decision and one prophetic announcement (the latter to his staff in the study at Number 10). Both were an indication of how to behave politically during the early months in Opposition.

'We'll have to play things quietly during their honeymoon period' were the tactics he laid down for future action. As for the 'honeymoon' itself, he forecast that even this supposedly pleasant period 'would not really be as enjoyable for them as for some people'. In pursuance of his strategy of giving the Opposition the centre of the stage in which to make their mistakes, he explained that he himself intended to make only two major speeches in the near future: one during the debate on the Queen's Speech and the other at the Party Conference in Blackpool at the end of September.

Prior to that final weekend at Chequers (which some have compared to the last breakfast given to the condemned man) a home had had to be found for the Wilsons. Unlike most Prime Ministers and their families, they had nowhere to go and – so sure were we of victory – had not really given the matter much thought. The problem was immediate: ex-Prime Ministers have to disappear from the scene in hours rather than days.

How to set about finding a home overnight? I asked two of the staff to telephone Harrods to see if they had any furnished accommodation available near Westminster. This time luck was with us: the first attempt brought the perfect answer. Film producer Jerry Epstein, close colleague and friend of the late Charlie Chaplin, wanted to let his beautiful house in Vincent Square in which he and his girl-friend Bernice had been living; their plan was to move into the basement flat beneath the house.

When the Epsteins realized who their new tenants would be, they promptly had the whole house redecorated. They also decided that their own situation needed regularizing before the Wilsons moved in, so made arrangements to get married. I always wondered if this was the first time an ex-Prime Minister had 'caused' a wedding!

Another of their kindnesses was to offer Harold Wilson the use of their driver. As Bill Housden had had to go back into Government service to be reallocated to someone else instantly the Chequers weekend was over, and as Harold Wilson himself had not driven for years, this was a real boon. The Epsteins' chauffeur drove Harold until the early autumn.

All these arrangements took place within a matter of days, but it was only years afterwards that we learned from the Epsteins just how Labour's defeat had transformed their lives.

THREE

Reorganizing Life in Opposition and the Private Office

Even the dust seemed familiar. Nothing had changed in the Opposition Leader's Room in the Palace of Westminster since I had seen it last over five years before. That day, Friday, 19 June 1970, as I stood looking around it I saw that not only was the furniture the same, but it was still arranged in much the same way. However, a great deal had changed in the role of the Leader himself; and this in turn required a change in the size and scope of the Private Office that serviced him.

This change had its roots in the days of Harold Macmillan, with the introduction of a presidential-style approach to the premiership – a style that found its own apotheosis in the Kennedy era, its personality cult, brilliant use of the media, image-building, and mind-bending ability to achieve personal popularity.

But even before Kennedy – and his glamorous family – reached the White House, Harold Macmillan was already inaugurating a new style of 'politicking' in Great Britain. True, he became Prime Minister at just about the moment when television was finding its way into every home in the country so that he was the first television 'fireside' Prime Minister, though without a presence to match this could have been a disadvantage. As it was, his mastery of the medium was superb. Like the great actor-managers of the past, he managed to look the aristocrat but speak in clear, direct language that could easily be understood by everybody. Not only this, what he said was what they wanted to hear. His success on the 'box' transformed politics and it has never been the same since: we still – even though unconsciously – rate our politicians as much on their ability to 'perform' as on their policies.

Against Macmillan, this marvellous performer and brilliant politician with his sense of occasion, flair, dash and communication with the general public, what had we in the Labour Party got? The answer was: Hugh Gaitskell.

Even Hugh's friends admitted that however inspired a communicator he might have been in private life or within a small political circle, this did not extend more widely, and certainly not to television – the twelve-inch arena to which the emphasis had now been shifted. We had arrived at the day of the television interview, the triumphant foreign visit whose highlights were caught so crisply, the reassuring, almost intimate chat on the nation's affairs – in short, the whole business of the presentation of politics in the living-room of every home in the country. And here Macmillan shone.

Harold Wilson quickly recognized this. When he succeeded Hugh Gaitskell as Leader of the Party on 14 February 1963 after Hugh's death, he realized that his first job was to organize himself to compete with Harold Macmillan on this new and vital territory – territory on which Macmillan had already staked out a prior claim.

The task ahead was difficult not only because Macmillan was a formidable opponent, but also because of the differences in the back-up machinery available to the two Leaders.

In those days, a Conservative Leader, though he did not necessarily have the large Private Office of today at the House of Commons, had all the resources of the rich Tory Central Office to call on. Lack of money was never a brake on Harold Macmillan's plans.

Harold Wilson, by contrast, had to operate on a shoestring. In the days of Clement Attlee or Hugh Gaitskell, when a comparatively small volume of work passed through the Leader's Office, this would not have mattered so much. When Clem Attlee was Opposition Leader, he had one Private Secretary only – a girl who had been an Executive Branch civil servant in his private office when he was in Government. She coped single-handed with all his work, from taking dictation and typing letters to arranging his engagements, setting out his speeches and generally running his working life. Research, briefing for debates, speeches and parliamentary questions, and liaison work with the Party was carried out by the General Secretary of the Parliamentary Labour Party (PLP), his deputy and staff, in conjunction with the Research Secretary and staff at Party Headquarters.

When Hugh Gaitskell succeeded Clem Attlee, this popular and

invaluable woman continued to run the Leader's Office, this time with the help of an Assistant Private Secretary who did the more routine secretarial work. Soon after, she was joined by a Press Officer, John Harris (now Lord Harris of Greenwich), who was also a Gaitskell personal aide. (On Gaitskell's death, John Harris went to Transport House, where in due course he became Director of Publicity, in which capacity he worked under Harold Wilson a year later, in the 1964 election.)

Despite the fact that there were now three Private Office staff instead of one, there were still considerable limitations on the amount of work that could reasonably be done. When Harold Wilson took over, in the final flowering of the Macmillan era, the work to be done had not only increased but altered: as well as the considerable expansion in routine work, there was the task of making sure that the Labour message got across via every possible medium. Television exposure alone meant an enormously increased volume of mail.

This vital process of restructuring the Party's image, ensuring a viable modern and efficient focus and bringing general strategy up to date, had to take place in Harold Wilson's Westminster office rather than be left to Party Headquarters. The latter had neither the funds nor, I fear, the will to help him. Their attitudes were conservative with a small 'c' – indeed, we used to call any particularly blatant example of an out-of-date prejudice 'a bit of Eccleston Square mentality' (when the Party was first formed its headquarters were in Eccleston Square).

If the Labour Party were to survive after thirteen years of continuous Tory Government, let alone regain effective electoral control, change was essential, not least in the organization of the Leader's Office.

Now that almost twenty years have passed, all this seems self-evident. So does the fact that, with the whole of the Government now more public, the workload of Party Leaders has inevitably increased, and with it the need for an efficient support system. In those days, the idea that in order for democracy to work effectively HM Opposition, just as much as HM Government, must be freed of financial handicaps had never even been mooted.

Harold Wilson was the first Prime Minister not only to recognize this need of the constitutional machine, but to act on this knowledge. Since 1975, during his last administration, Opposition Parties in Parliament have been entitled to certain sums from public funds. In the Queen's Speech of March 1974, when Harold Wilson took office again, a promise was included for the 'provision of financial assistance to enable Opposition Parties more effectively to fulfil their parliamentary franchise'. A Resolution of 20 March 1975 made this entitlement a fact. The Labour Party, on becoming the official Opposition in 1979, received £165,000 per annum: £65,000 of this entitlement went to the Private Office of the Leader of the Opposition. Today the entitlement is £290,000, of which approximately £100,000 goes to the Leader's Office. Although the Labour Party does not devote the major part of the entitlement to the Leader's Office (it is also used to finance the PLP and, through it, various specialist groups and committees), it still leaves very substantial funds with which to recruit top-level staff for the Leader's Office and ensure them adequate financial security.

This provision of an adequate Opposition office financed by the Treasury was one of the best contributions made recently by anyone to the effective running of parliamentary democracy in this country. My own regret is that, excellent as this reform was, the Boyle Commission did not go even further and make a provision for the running of a Political Office at Number 10. There is a very strong argument that this also should be funded by the State. As Professor Jones of the London School of Economics has said in describing how at the top politics and administration are inextricably mingled: 'The Prime Minister is one Minister who stands on the peaks of both politics and administration.'

The subsequent proposal to finance political parties as such on continental lines was turned down, mainly by the Conservatives, who thought that if the political parties were released from the 'apron strings' of those who fund them, this would cut the cord between the Labour Party and the trades unions, and the Labour Party would thus lose one of its electoral handicaps – the appearance of being a puppet of the unions. Yet the case for funding is, in my view, extremely strong.

But at the time of which I am writing, June 1970, reformation of any kind was not much more than a glint in the Leader's eye. Harold Wilson was going back into Opposition with the added commitment of being an internationally known figure rather than the untried Leader of his first Opposition period; his Opposition Private Office had to reflect the greater expectations of the public as well as the new requirements. As an ex-Prime Minister, his own standards were now considerably higher; five and a half years in Downing Street, serviced not just by the Political Office but by the Civil Service – the world's most superbly efficient bureaucratic machine – had left him taking total efficiency for granted. But once outside an expensively maintained system, super-efficiency usually boils down to money.

Harold Wilson himself had no large cash reserve to dip into. Like all Prime Ministers before him, up to and including the very rich, he had left Downing Street with a bank overdraft. Contrary to the belief held by many, life at Downing Street is not completely funded by the tax-payer. Entertainment, for instance, is only put on the country's bill when the visitor has an official appointment; but there are many occasions when drinks, dinner or luncheon parties, though politic, are not strictly 'political' and therefore come out of the private purse of the Prime Minister.

So did the cost of Christmas cards: £2,000 worth of these, plus postage, represented a considerable sum. (When Harold Wilson returned to power in 1974, he discovered thankfully that Edward Heath had managed to establish that a large part of the list could be classified as 'official' and therefore by paid for by the taxpayer.) Using his official car (the only car the Wilsons had) on anything that had not an official purpose meant a bill, worked out on a mileage basis, from the Department of the Environment. And if he said, 'Have a glass of whisky,' to Cabinet colleagues who had unexpectedly dropped in, or if Mary had to drive to a luncheon, though these events both happened as a direct result of the premiership, because they were not government business both drink and drive were paid for by the Wilsons.

Which side of the line falls the nightcap given to the parliamentary friend who drops in for a chat but who winds up discussing an important piece of policy? Though it is obviously extremely important to avoid not only waste but extravagance, this splitting of costs on some arbitrary basis is needlessly worrying and time-consuming. There cannot be many other countries in the world where there is such a nit-picking approach to funding the office of Head of Government.

What Harold Wilson could afford in terms of a Private Office in 1970 and what he needed were two very different things. With no money in the bank, the only staff guaranteed us were those that Transport House were responsible for over the years since he had become Leader of the Labour Party: one or two secretaries or research assistants, sometimes a half-time helper, and occasional people seconded from time to time when additional help was needed. Perhaps I should mention at this point that I was always paid by Harold Wilson personally, since I started working for him in 1956; later he received the Member of Parliament's secretarial allowance for this purpose.

Though the Transport House staff worked in the Leader's Private Office in Westminster, they still remained to all intents and purposes

Transport House staff. Their salaries were paid by Transport House (we never knew what they were) and adjusted by their union, and they usually kept to all the rules of Transport House from hours of work to days off. They were, of course, absolutely correct and within their rights in so doing, but from our point of view it was often inconvenient, to say the least. As anyone in politics will tell you, working late comes with the job – and crises are no respecters of Bank holidays. But it was not just the fact that at 5.00 in the evening everyone could disappear. The Private Office needed more people than the few provided, in particular senior staff with specialist skills.

In addition, the Leader required a Press Officer, a job that in the early 1960s had been performed by the Publicity Officer at Transport House, who came over regularly for discussions with him at the House of Commons. In Harold Wilson's earlier years, the Publicity Officer had been John Harris and then Percy Clark, the Deputy Press Officer who succeeded him. The press side of the work had now expanded and Harold Wilson, having spent a number of years in Downing Street with a very good Press Office, also expected more. During most of his time at Number 10, the Political Press Officer was Gerald Kaufman (who later became a senior Minister and, in Opposition, a front-bench spokesman and member of the Parliamentary Committee of the PLP). Gerald had efficiently fulfilled a very special role in Downing Street, helping with political speeches, putting out statements, talking to the press all over the world, managing the whole complicated system of liaising with the press, and generally 'presenting' the Prime Minister in a political sense.

But Gerald had left the staff early in 1970 because of the demands of his own career: he was elected MP for Manchester Ardwick in that same disastrous election. We were now faced with the problems of having no Political Press Office and what to do with Joe Haines, the Number 10 Press Secretary, a man unlikely to be kept on at Downing Street, unlikely to be asked to join the Civil Service, and unlikely to accept if he were. He was also unlikely to get a good job straightaway in Fleet Street in the aftermath of defeat and failure.

Harold Wilson was very conscious that he had asked Joe to sacrifice the newspaper salary he was earning as the number two political writer on the *Sun* to come to him in Downing Street in 1969. We discussed the problem as a matter of priority on the morning after the defeat; it was decided that on balance the best answer was to take Joe into Opposition and appoint him Press Officer to the Leader of the Opposition. Accordingly this was done. It added a further substantial sum to the salary costs of the Opposition Leader's Office. Again, the problem was: how to fund this?

As well as a lack of cash, there was a lack of experience: apart from Harold Wilson himself, I was the only other person there who had worked within the Palace of Westminster in the Leader of the Opposition's Office. Working in Parliament for anyone is a completely new and different experience; to go in as a novice, after the cloistered life of Number 10 – where hours are regular and weekends are sacrosanct except for the occasional major political rally or big political speech, when one would be asked to take down and type out a speech – was a major experience. Yet here we were, going into a completely new environment with a Leader who had no money to finance us.

This chaotic situation was exacerbated by something impossible to mention – or admit – at the time: the tacit antagonism that existed between Transport House and Westminster. This had its roots in Transport House's belief that those in Parliament were merely the glamour end of the business: the real Party existed in Transport House and at grass-roots level around the country. I can remember sharing this feeling myself, when I worked there in 1955. The staff felt then that they were going into a dreary building each day, doing a nuts and bolts job without which those others would not be able to work in the corridors of power, hob-nobbing with Cabinet Ministers. Now I was at the so-called glamorous end – and the limelight that shone on political personalities and Parliament was brighter and more dazzling than ever.

Certain people at Transport House did not share this feeling of resentment, mainly those who were able to move back and forth freely between Transport House and Westminster: heads of department like Peter Shore (head of Research), Percy Clark (Publicity Officer), and David Ennals (head of the Overseas Department). They often went over to Westminster to brief leading Party members and attend joint meetings there. But many others lower down in the Party hierarchy, who did not get the best of both worlds, resented any attempt by the 'glamour side' to take funds away from Party Headquarters.

In 1970 we knew that without funds there would be a blank space in the centre of the now well-lit political stage. This was apparent to all of us from the moment we knew the election was lost. It was characteristic of Harold Wilson that his approach to the problem was from the standpoint of the ideal: first to assess what the Party needed from its Leader and then, somehow, to raise the required finance, rather than seeing what cash was available and tailoring the Private Office around that. He also recognized that an appraisal of that kind could not be carried out by the Leader himself, so a group of office management consultants, Hesketh, Hardy and Hirshfield, were called in. (Desmond Hirshfield had been accountant to the Party for many years.) The accountants followed the customary practice of looking at the work we were doing, carrying out time-and-motion studies, interviewing, questioning, and generally assessing how many staff were needed and how much this would all cost.

Unfortunately (through our fault, not theirs) they carried out their work at the wrong time. Because the matter of setting up the Opposition Private Office was so pressing, we invited them in immediately after the election. This was a joint decision by Harold Wilson and myself – and a disastrous error. In retrospect, it would have been far better had they spent October with us rather than July. It is in the autumn, when Parliament is assembling again, that the political season starts and the work escalates, whereas in August parliamentary work falls off and that of the Private Office also diminishes. We did not, unfortunately, realize this. When, for example, the number of letters dropped from the 2,000 a week of Downing Street days to 1,000 and then to 800, we assumed this was because we were now in Opposition. By October the figure had risen to 2,500 a week, thanks largely to a change in the political climate: as hostility to the Heath Government built up, so the consequent heightened political activity and interest naturally focused on the Labour Party – and its Leader. But by then Hesketh, Hardy and Hirshfield had been, gone and left us with an estimate of staff correct for our July needs – but grossly inadequate for the rest of the year. As for the money they assessed as necessary to finance the Leader's Office, they estimated the figure at £20–25,000 a year.

At that moment this was to all intents a minus quantity. Harold Wilson had, as I said earlier, emerged from Downing Street with a sizeable overdraft and, though he still had the money from the sale of his house in Hampstead Garden Suburb, this was needed to buy somewhere for the Wilsons to live. In the event, the Wilsons bought a house in Lord North Street, conveniently close to Westminster; they were also anxious to find somewhere in the country so that Harold could achieve a much-needed break at weekends, if possible in the countryside near Chequers which he had grown to love as Prime Minister.

Here my father was able to help. At Harold Wilson's request, he searched the Great Missenden–Chequers area over the next few weeks and was able, as a former small builder, to screen potential homes thoroughly. In a remarkably short time he found Grange Farm, which proved a happy choice. The Wilsons bought much of the furniture left there by the previous owners; and they turned the beautiful Elizabethan barn attached to the main house into a workplace for Harold, with an extension added on for the storage of his official papers. Anyone who sees the film *The Dambusters* will get a glimpse of Grange Farm in the opening shots; it was once the home of Barnes Wallis, who invented the bouncing bomb.

The first big step taken by Harold Wilson towards the improving of his financial situation was an agreement with Times Newspapers to write a lengthy and comprehensive history of his years in Downing Street. For this, he was to receive a very large sum of money.

The spoken as well as the written word became a source of income too. On three annual occasions Harold Wilson spent a fortnight of the summer recess on a lecture tour of the United States. So substantial were the fees for each lecture that a fortnight's speaking tour per year took care of Joe Haines's annual salary and other expenses.

But this still left the salaries of the secretarial staff and office expenses, from all the usual overheads to the tea, coffee and alcohol necessary to offer as refreshment to visitors, as well as all the miscellaneous expenses, from lunches and dinners to Christmas cards.

After some time the problem became apparent to those around him. The result was the idea of setting up a Trust Fund to help finance the office of the Leader of the Labour Party. Initially, of course, this was Harold Wilson, but should he retire or be ousted – and in 1970 his survival during the years of Opposition was not a foregone conclusion – then the next Leader would benefit in the same way.

The three chief organizers of this fund were Lord Wilfred Brown, who was to be its chairman, Lord Fisher of Camden and Lord Plurenden, who all worked closely with the lawyers and accountants in its setting up and administration. So discreet were they about the organization of the Trust Fund that, although Harold Wilson knew of its existence, neither he nor anyone else knew the full details about it. Certainly, it was rarely discussed. It operated quite separately from the Private Office, and we did not know at any one time exactly who contributed to it.

Wilfred Brown had been known to Harold Wilson for many years, both in Government and Opposition. Indeed, Harold Wilson had given Brown a key job in his Government. Brown himself was a long-standing member of the Party and former member, too, of the 1944 Association

– a group of wealthy businessmen who had supported Labour in the Attlee and Gaitskell years. When I first started work for the Party, in the General Secretary's Office, one of my responsibilities there had been secretarial work connected with the 1944 Association. Little was known about it publicly, though its membership was extremely impressive, including Leonard Machan, the millionaire businessman who lives in the Channel Islands, Raymond Mais, Wilfred Brown, Alan Sainsbury and many others. All the members were connected with flourishing businesses; all, I believe, made contributions to Party funds. Some became even better known later. A number were subsequently honoured – some by Harold Wilson during his first Government, others earlier by Clement Attlee and Hugh Gaitskell – for the contribution they had made to the Party and to public life.

All the members of the Trust Fund, apart from the chairman and Lord Plurenden, were introduced to the Leader by either the General Secretary of the Party direct, or by Lord Fisher of Camden.

When the Trust Fund itself was eventually set up it was, contrary to subsequent descriptions, extremely modest, partly because the two senior members of the Private Office, Joe Haines and myself, were not paid out of it, and partly because Transport House were providing two of their own staff for the Leader's Private Office. What was needed from the Fund to complete the office complement were salaries for four to five secretaries and research assistants, and an office junior. The reason for such a comparatively large staff was not just the volume but the hours of work: a shift system was necessary because Harold Wilson worked late into the evening and often wanted to dictate letters, speeches or memoranda late at night or perhaps at weekends. This meant that the office had to be covered from approximately 9.30 a.m. until 10.30 p.m., with weekends where necessary.

The original estimate by Hesketh, Hardy and Hirshfield was supposed to cover the various staff salaries as well as all office expenses from stationery, photocopying, duplicating, telephone bills, a direct outside line for more speedy calls than via the House of Commons switchboard, and the TV rental, some travelling expenses – everything right down to tea and coffee. Although we were as frugal as we could be – all the typewriters, for instance, except one, were the original ones allocated in 1963 – by the time we regained office in 1974 the cost of running an office had escalated so much that the original £20,000 per annum was less than adequate.

The result of being somewhat under-financed showed in the staff. We could not afford the sort of super-efficient secretary who could command a top salary; what we mostly got were bright, able and intelligent girls who often saw the job as an underpaid but useful stepping-stone on their way to something better – one went on to university, another became a GLC councillor, one the Conference Officer at Party Head-quarters.

The centre of all this buzzing activity was, as I have said, the same office that Harold Wilson had used in 1963 and 1964, a large and historic room just behind the Speaker's Chair in the House; off it was a tiny cell-like ante-room for his Principal Private Secretary and Parlia-mentary Private Secretary. Since those earlier days, however, there had been a slight improvement in terms of space: several more small 'cells', in a modernized part of the building some distance away and on a different floor, had also been allocated to him. The Press Office and secretarial staff used them.

His own room was like a piece of history on which the dust (literally) had settled. It was old-fashioned, but the aura of previous occupants, from Gladstone and Disraeli to Winston Churchill and Clement Attlee in this century, still hung about it, down-at-heel and shabby though it was. There was a desk for the Leader to use at one end, together with an armchair and a drinks cabinet at the other end, and two other leather armchairs in the window recess (all so much in the same places as when we were last there that I could have sworn there must be chalk marks beneath them).

Here the list of adequate furnishings ended. Instead of a conference table around which the whole Parliamentary Committee or Shadow Cabinet could sit, there were two less useful smaller tables for committee meetings which neither quite matched nor, when placed together, proved large enough. The carpet was a down-trodden patch in the centre of the room, with a linoleum surround. The curtains were faded, and the walls had not been redecorated since our previous occupancy – and the paint had not been new then. The whole room was drab and depressing, an effect which was not helped by a series of inexplicable telephone calls that we kept receiving. It was only after some time that it was discovered that the telephone in the ante-room was connected direct to Tory Central Office; and that there was another that went straight through to the Tory Whips. This turned out to be helpful on the whole, as it let us know that we, too, could have direct links installed to our Party Headquarters, something we had not enjoyed before in Opposition.

Minor facilities too were lacking. True, we had an electric kettle, but there were no shelves – let alone a cupboard – for cups, saucers, milk or tea. Washing-up was done by whoever volunteered to take the dirty china to the Ladies at the end of a long corridor and down to the floor below, or to the Gents along the same corridor and up a flight of steps. If the Leader wanted to change for some evening engagement, he had to turn his staff out and lock the door into the outside corridor, where the staff clustered until he had finished. Petty details, but nevertheless, I cannot think of any other large organization or company that would have expected its chief executive to work in these Heath Robinson conditions. For a man who had just left the country's top job, with its superbly functioning office and organization, it was doubly jolting.

No wonder, as we learned later, that Edward Heath used this room very little, preferring to operate from his set of chambers in the Albany, while his PPS – whose own secretary used the small ante-room – carried on here with any work that did not require Heath's actual presence. For Edward Heath, working at home or at the office was a matter of choice; for Harold Wilson it was not. The first home the Wilsons found after leaving Downing Street was rented accommodation and, in any case, Harold's family objected strongly if he brought home work on this scale: all of them disliked his job intruding into their home environment in such a direct way.

Today, things are very different. The Leader of the Opposition has a suite of rooms off Speaker's Court: they were originally a flat which belonged to one of the officials of the House, an Assistant Serjeant-at-Arms. They consist of the Leader of the Opposition's own room facing New Palace Yard, with adjacent kitchen, small additional room and an area for a Private Secretary. Then there is a Shadow Cabinet Conference Room, with adjacent lavatory, a Research Assistants' Room, two further small rooms for staff, and a bathroom on the mezzanine floor, which is part of the suite. The first Opposition Leader to use these rooms was Margaret Thatcher, to whom they were allocated during the Wilson years.

Despite the handicap of Harold Wilson's dismal and awkward office accommodation in 1970, one great improvement to the life of the Leader was just over the horizon. When Harold Wilson first became Opposition Leader in 1963 he drove his own car on the normal daily trips in and out of Parliament, using a hired car for any engagements to which he had not been invited officially as Leader of the Opposition (for these, he was allowed to book an official car from the Government Car Pool). Edward Heath, during his time as Opposition Leader, had a car provided for him by Tory Central Office, with a full-time chauffeur. When Harold Wilson returned as Opposition Leader in 1970, not only was there no official car, but since his previous years in Opposition he had got out of the habit of driving. When he said that he would go back to driving himself again, as before, we all shuddered. Even at the best of times he was an appalling driver. The intervening years had done nothing to mitigate this. Although the car he bought had an automatic gear-box, he still couldn't drive it. In the old days he would try to drive up a steep gradient like Haverstock Hill in Hampstead in third, or drive out of New Palace Yard in third, change up and attempt to circum-navigate Parliament Square in top gear. I remember once Nye Bevan sitting beside him, muttering, 'Go on boy, give the car a break – *change down!*'

The problem of Harold's safety and the car's continued existence was temporarily solved when Jerry Epstein let us borrow his chauffeur for a time. But the real breakthrough occurred in the form of a magnanimous and imaginative gesture from Edward Heath, who decreed that the Leader of the Opposition should be allocated a car and driver at Minister of State level. This meant that not only were a car and driver allowed, as before, for official appointments, but the same car and driver remained available at all times, personal and political use being paid for on a mileage basis.

When Edward Heath's letter offering this arrived, a terrific cheer went up – not least because it meant the return of a faithful friend. Bill Housden had been Harold Wilson's driver since 1947, except for a break during the years of Tory Government. Bill could turn his hand to anything, and frequently did. He packed Harold's suits, saw that his shoes were cleaned and repaired, his ties pressed, and in general filled a role that was part chauffeur, part valet and part nanny. With Bill back, not only was the sharp contrast between Downing Street and the Opposition Office lessened, but we no longer had the nagging worry that one day big black headlines would scream 'Leader of the Opposition in multiple Whitehall car crash'.

Though one potential source of nightmare was removed – and we were truly delighted at this piece of thoughtfulness by Edward Heath – a pervasive sense of gloom remained.

However you look at it, defeat is depressing. When you expect to win, it is particularly galling. *Post mortems* take on an added bitterness; because of the unexpectedness of being thrust into Opposition, adjustment is slower and more traumatic. If Harold Wilson had been spoilt by Government, so too had his colleagues. Gone, overnight, were their smoothly functioning offices, their efficient staff, their ministerial cars, the deference, the place in the spotlight. Some looked, and acted, shell-shocked. After a while, their increased and involuntary leisure bore unexpected fruit: old quarrels resurfaced, intrigue flourished, there was a hatching of plots and counter-plots to forward this or that political ambition.

But all that came later. At first, the effect of the 18 June defeat was almost that of a death in the family: the same mixture of shock and misery, coupled with the urgent conviction that it was essential to resume 'normal' life as speedily as possible in order to prevent those most deeply affected from sinking into a despairing lethargy. Though the analogy of death may sound over-dramatic, it is impossible to overstate the sense of shock which was felt in those post-defeat months, and its effect on politicians and staff alike, all of which had been aggravated by the long hours, sudden changes and extra workload of the campaign itself. Everyone felt both tense and let-down; all difficulties appeared acute, almost insuperable. The questions 'What went wrong?' and 'Why did it happen?' continued to dominate our thoughts for many months to come. We had been thrown into disarray and disorganization; the longer this was allowed to continue, the more difficult it would be for the wound to heal.

For me personally, this had meant organizing Harold Wilson back into Opposition, with an efficiently functioning office, as swiftly as possible. The first step towards this was ensuring that we actually had an office to go to, which, in turn, meant convincing Edward Heath's Office of the need to vacate the two main Westminster rooms *immediately*. Not unnaturally, they could not at first understand the desperate hurry, due to the fact that we had literally nowhere else to go, and that until we had a new home we ourselves could not vacate the Downing Street office rooms. Harold Wilson had no home, where files could have been stored on a temporary basis, and Transport House had no room for us – nor were they particularly anxious to have us, even as temporary tenants (this aspect would never have occurred to the Heath Office, who presumably would have had no such problem with Tory Central Office).

When, after a series of telephone conversations and explanations, they realized our position, Douglas Hurd and his colleagues became extremely co-operative and promised to speed up their departure from the Palace of Westminster to the extent of letting us have the rooms that evening.

By 6.30 on the day after Polling Day, everything from the Number 10 offices was packed, labelled and waiting in the basement to be moved out. Few of us were there to organize the removal. It was mainly carried out by myself, George Caunt from the Parliamentary Labour Party, two part-time helpers and my family, since Joe Haines, still a civil servant, had gone home for the weekend. It had been extraordinarily hard work, both mentally and physically.

There were plenty of petty problems and irritations during that last hectic day in Number 10, with all of us on a rather short fuse, thanks to the long hours we had been working throughout Polling Day, during election night, and on the next day (in my case this amounted to thirty-six hours non-stop). There were also one or two mildly hysterical episodes: at one point we 'lost' a newly joined member of the staff and searched for her for ages, getting gradually more and more worried. Finally she was found by Terry Lancaster, curled up fast asleep in the knee-hole of Gerald Kaufman's desk and hidden completely by the top.

The weekend was spent in exactly the same way: setting up the Private Office so that the Leader of the Opposition could, from 9.30 onwards on Monday morning, start all the work that was so necessary to restore the fortunes and repair the morale of the Labour Party. It was strenuous in the extreme; I do not think many people realize exactly how much hard physical work is involved in going into Opposition! In addition, there was the worry, which I found even more stressful: I had become responsible not only for the reorganization of the office but also for that of the Wilsons' private life as well, with the additional handicap of a much smaller staff.

To shield the Leader as much as possible from the inevitable chaos, I tried to ensure that the putting-in-order process spread outward from his own room, leaving the disarray in our second-floor offices until last.

Apart from getting my own little office – the ante-room – straightened out, the major need, I believed, was to have Harold Wilson's own office refurbished and redecorated so that it was as pleasant and comfortable as the one he had been used to in Number 10. The House authorities were very co-operative, but naturally laying new carpets, putting up new curtains, installing a proper conference table, all took time, and it was not until Conference week in the Autumn (which I spent at Westminster overseeing the main changes) that the room was finally completed.

At the same time I was helping the Wilsons find a permanent London home, mainly by contacting estate agents and doing a preliminary inspection of the houses to find out if they were worth the Wilsons even looking at them: often, too, I accompanied them on a second visit. It was easier for me to do this sort of reconnoitring than for Mary Wilson, as she did not drive. In any case, Mary Wilson was submerged under a sea of the Wilsons' belongings which were temporarily at Vincent Square and which needed sorting out for use or storage.

I should mention here that Edward Heath had been extremely courteous immediately after the defeat, making it clear to Mary Wilson that she did not have to speed the removal of the Wilsons' personal possessions from the flat at Number 10 until she was absolutely ready. This meant that she was able to sort their things out with the aid of the housekeeper, Mrs Pollard, over a two-week period. Nevertheless, it was still awkward and uneasy for the Wilsons, as by now – despite Edward Heath's kind offer – they felt like intruders at Number 10. Photographs taken at that time, showing them removing their belongings via the back door, also give that impression.

Monday, 22 June 1970, therefore, saw us installed in the Private Office at Westminster. Harold Wilson, who had spent the weekend at Chequers, was unaware of the frenzied work, the seemingly insurmountable problems, the sheer effort that had been involved during those two days in order to make the office operational for the Monday deadline. He came in expecting everything to work – and luckily, it did.

He himself had an immediate preoccupation: the writing of his book, *The Labour Government 1964-1970: A Personal Record*. Negotiations were quickly under way, organized by Lord Goodman, with Times Newspapers, Weidenfeld & Nicolson and Michael Joseph for the serialization rights. A satisfactorily large sum of money was in question – enough to clear his overdraft and make some provision for his future retirement, for staff pensions and for the Private Office.

On 24 July, Parliament returned and we had to swing into action politically. I do not think the difficulties of becoming operational politically in those days have ever been fully realized.

Today, with an office that runs smoothly from the day after defeat, no financial worries and therefore a continuity of staff, the new Opposition Leader has much more time in which to concentrate on the political aspects of the current situation. In 1970, it was not so. More, too, was expected from Harold Wilson than from previous Leaders, owing to his success in building up the 'presidential image' of Party Leaders; and the machinery of government and the complications of political life were also greater than they had been ten years earlier.

But the success of the Downing Street Political Office during Harold Wilson's Prime Ministership of 1964-70 had somehow to be continued in Opposition. The Leader of the Opposition needed exactly the same servicing as Her Majesty's First Minister, but now he no longer had the aid of the highly efficient Civil Service machine via the Number 10 Private Office. All his needs were now dealt with by his own people; and by now his role had been considerably developed. A typical day in the life of the Leader of the Opposition would, in range and scope of work, be very similar to a typical day in the life of the Prime Minister.

Admittedly, the Leader of the Opposition did not come to his office until about 10.00 a.m., but for the next twelve hours (when the House was sitting), it would be his base. He would issue from it for meetings, luncheons and press conferences; in it he would receive visiting overseas leaders, just as the Prime Minister does at Number 10, and reply to any mail that had not been processed by the office.

As the one who ran this office, I was responsible for organizing his day and ensuring that he was fully briefed on everything from the political background of a visiting Foreign Secretary or Prime Minister to the afternoon's big economic censure debate, which would have meant advance work for a week or two, and the aid of researchers at Party Headquarters.

The majority of the 2,500-odd letters that arrive at the Private Office every week do not, of course, need referring to the Leader and are dealt with by the staff, but even handling these requires considerable organization because they are of such variety. They range from the problem or complaint of an individual, which can be siphoned off and sent to their own MP, to some complicated question on nuclear missiles, which will be passed to the Overseas Department of Party Headquarters. Important letters, together with relevant information from various sources, are laid before the Leader, who can then say what action he wants taken. Information to, and from, the press must also be organized.

The Private Office is also responsible for keeping the Leader in touch with everyone from his own constituency workers, regional and local organizations all over the country, to senior officials in the trades union movement. Then there are the Parliamentary Questions.

Here, although a great deal of help is given by the Parliamentary Labour Party (the Assistant General Secretary of the Parliamentary Labour Party or one of his colleagues acts as special adviser to the Leader, in particular on Parliamentary Questions), much of the work falls on the Private Office. In this context, it is vital that anyone working in or running a Private Office should know the rules of the House – how a Ten Minute Rule Bill goes through Parliament, how private members ballot for their place in introducing a Private Member's Bill – as well as being conscious all the time of what has happened in the House or is going on in the Chamber at that particular moment, so that you are alert the whole day as to anything that may happen in Parliament which will require the Leader's presence. For this purpose, in each of the rooms of the Opposition Leader's Office there is an annunciator with a small TV screen, which shows who is on their feet, what subject is being debated and the time.

The first step towards active Opposition came, I suppose, with Harold Wilson's re-election as Leader of the Parliamentary Labour Party on the very Monday he entered his new Private Office for the first time: 22 June 1970. Thereafter, the other posts in the PLP were up for re-election too, and a great deal of intra-Party political warfare broke out.

It was already clear that Roy Jenkins would be the major candidate for the Deputy Leadership. Barbara Castle wanted to stand against him and Harold Wilson had to dissuade her from this, or there would have been an immediate Party split on lines related almost solely to the issue of the Common Market. Eventually, after long hours of talk (mostly late at night) he persuaded her against it, though two other figures of far lower political stature at that time did stand: Fred Peart and Michael Foot (Michael was still very much an outsider, regarded as a left-wing Bevanite by his parliamentary colleagues and so far untried in office).

One curious incident occurred that took Harold Wilson very much by surprise. Out of the blue, Tony Benn decided that he wanted to stand as a candidate for the office of Chief Whip. The idea, presumably, was that the Left should have candidates for all the positions up for election. Tony, in fact, gave up this idea (Bob Mellish was re-elected); but as well as the known battle lines of the Marketeers versus the anti-Marketeers, there was already emerging again the Left–Right confrontation that has now grown to such damaging and dangerous proportions.

FOUR

Common Market Problems

In the late 1960s and early 1970s the Common Market roused passions that seem almost unthinkable today, but which could return. Certainly Labour is likely to play the Market card fairly strongly in any campaign.

In the early 1970s, there was an almost religious fervour in the dedication of the Marketeers, as in the hostility of those against the idea of going into Europe, that produced the most unlikely bedfellows. The majority of the Conservative Party was in favour, while most of Labour was against; the issue dominated the 1970–4 Parliament.

The Common Market was the most difficult problem Harold Wilson had to handle. One of the greatest tributes to his powers as Leader and manager of the Labour Party was that he kept the Party united through three and a half years of Opposition, despite the large and vociferous minority whose views were in complete contradiction to those of their colleagues.

The Conservative Party were convinced, too, after their surprise victory in June 1970, that the Market would be *the* issue of the new Heath Parliament. This much was clear even from gossip between respective staffs as possessions were moved from Downing Street to the Opposition offices in the House of Commons that the Heath people were vacating. They told us that they thought the Market was probably going to be the most difficult of all the problems they would have to handle; and they were not a little worried at the prospect.

On the Labour side, part of the reason why the Market issue appeared so difficult was because of the fanaticism it aroused on both sides of the argument. The media did not help with descriptions of those who ran counter to the accepted Party line as 'men of integrity who put principles before the narrow considerations of Party' and so on. Today even those who were then most fervent would regard such an approach to the whole Market philosophy as slightly absurd.

In those days it was, to say the least, not a light-hearted matter, but one on which everyone was expected to declare where he or she stood. For Harold Wilson, this meant ensuring that the large pro-Market group led by Roy Jenkins (this included the other three members of the later so-called 'Gang of Four') remained within the framework of the Labour Party – which by definition meant ensuring that Party policy could accommodate their uncompromising views.

As for the then Left, generally speaking they were anti-Market, although Party lines were crossed here too.

To this cats' cradle of political and Market views was added the already complicated history of the British Government's attitude to Europe; thus the task of ensuring that the Labour Party emerged at the end of the Heath Parliament as a united, fighting political party able to offer a credible alternative Government appeared truly formidable.

In the Shadow Cabinet, views broke down on unexpected lines. Tony Crosland, for instance, who belonged to the Right, was anti-Market (though adhering to the Party line once a middle-of-the-road course had been decided upon). Tony's stance sprang partially, I suspect, from his closeness to Hugh Gaitskell, who himself had made two u-turns over the Market: originally Hugh Gaitskell had been very much in favour of our entering Europe but found, when Party Leader, that this viewpoint made it difficult to preserve the necessary Party unity. Gradually, Hugh had swung round; by 1962 he was making a passionate speech at the Party Conference in Brighton declaring the Party to be pro-Commonwealth and in favour of the widening of trade ties with the rest of the world (including the Eastern bloc, in particular Poland, which he had just visited). For his loyal disciple, Tony Crosland, the Market was never, I suspect, to be the Utopia Roy Jenkins and his friends saw it as.

Denis Healey took more or less the same view as Tony but for rather different reasons. Along with Harold Wilson, Denis and other leading Labour figures had supported the Labour Government's 1967 application to join the Market that had been vetoed by De Gaulle. Once in Opposition it seemed more natural to revert to an anti-Market stance: the Labour Party, with its international socialist links, has always seen itself in an international context and therefore as transcending barriers locking it into one area alone. Although the Conservative Party, by contrast, has a more limited viewpoint, a number of anti-Market Tories, such as Enoch Powell, Derek Walker-Smith and John Biffen, were going to cause the Heath Government trouble during the next few years.

Jim Callaghan had also supported Labour's application to join the Market during the years in Government; once in Opposition his increasing ties with the trades union movement and his own solid position within the Party caused him to take a robust anti-Market line. Nevertheless, he supported Harold Wilson in formulating an agreed policy.

Edward Heath's own commitment to Europe was so profound and so passionate that he tended to dismiss the fact that a close connection with Europe is not something that the British necessarily view with great joy. Our historical tradition is confrontation, if not actual conflict, with Europe, and though as a nation we were adept at forming alliances in order to keep the peace, we were also skilled at keeping ourselves uninvolved. We have, in short, always been suspicious about considering ourselves as Europeans.

So Edward Heath's dogmatic line and dramatic tactics, with their assumption of acceptance, gave Harold Wilson the opportunity he needed. The legislation Heath introduced was brief, not to say simplistic: the Bill to take us into Europe had few clauses; little time was allowed for discussion of details on the floor of the House. Eventually he made the suggestion of a free vote in the Commons.

However, all these factors combined to help not Edward Heath but Harold Wilson. Although Heath was successful – in the sense that he was the one who made the application – in taking Britain into Europe, he did this on terms that were even then unsatisfactory, and today would be described as 'impossible'. It is a monument to his determination that he succeeded in pushing this Bill through Parliament, though the haste and inflexibility with which this was done, resulting in the aforesaid poor terms, left the British people hostile to the European idea for some considerable time.

Because of this, Harold Wilson as Opposition Leader was able to say at the outset, 'The terms you have negotiated are not terms which we would accept, and therefore a Labour Government will want to re-negotiate them before agreeing whether or not we should stay in Europe.' Towards the end of the Opposition years the subsidiary thesis emerged: 'If we as a Party renegotiate successfully, we should then want to put these new terms to the British people for their agreement, or dissent, on this vital step.'

This, of course, is exactly what happened, with Harold Wilson's declaration in the 1975 Parliament that terms had been renegotiated, and that the whole nation would have the right to decide in a referendum whether we remained in Europe or withdrew.

That in the Referendum of June 1975 there was an overwhelming vote for staying in the Common Market is now history. But that 'Yes' vote, it seems to me, was based not so much on the straightforward question: 'Are you in favour of being part of Europe?', but on the belief that an economic fairy godmother was lurking just around the corner, ready to wave her magic wand the instant the word was given.

'Market' was the word that keyed us in. During debates for or against remaining in Europe, none of the argument took place on the political implications; all the emphasis was laid on the economic benefits or, in the case of anti-Marketeers, how these would cut across Commonwealth or other trading links.

Pro-Marketeers presented the country with a picture of a Market so enormous that British goods would sell in great numbers, exports would thrive and home industries therefore flourish – and everyone would prosper. The Conservative Party, spearheaded by Edward Heath and his principal Cabinet colleagues, believed this; along with the Jenkins group they united in what the Government described as the Festival of Europe (organized by, among others, the then Sir George Weidenfeld and Lord Goodman). This was in effect an enormous publicity campaign, aimed at convincing the British people of the tremendous adventure of now being 'Europeans', with the prospect of breaking out of the old vicious circle of economic weakness and the inflationary spiral.

The campaign was extremely well orchestrated; the result was that virtually the entire press, including pro-Labour newspapers like the *Daily Mirror*, took the Market line, pro-Marketeers like Roy Jenkins receiving a far better handling in their columns than the Labour Leader himself. Nothing is more convincing than something you want to believe – and who does not want to believe in a rosier future?

For Harold Wilson in 1970, the whole Market question was extremely complicated, not solely because of the differing shades of opinion and various cross-loyalties in Parliament, but also where the country was concerned. At constituency level, most of the Labour Party was very strongly anti-Market. So, too, was the trades union movement in general – though not so passionately as many trades unionists thought. A large proportion of the right wing had strong political views about Europe, reinforced by strong links with the various European trades union organizations, with whom many of our own unions had already established good working relationships. In Parliament, there was the

comparatively small but powerful pro-Market group around Roy Jenkins opposing the main body of opinion around the Leader. Harold
Wilson had the problem of keeping these disparate elements together
and, indeed, of so organizing them that the Market debate did not
dominate the whole of the rest of that Parliament.

As it was, although both Labour and Conservatives believed that the
success or failure of the Heath Government would hinge on the Market,
its downfall came from a different direction. Edward Heath's undoing
came from his relationship with the trades union movement.

FIVE

The Trades Unions in Opposition

Although the direct cause of the downfall of the Heath Government in 1974 was the confrontation with the National Union of Mineworkers, this immediate point of impact was not, of course, the whole story; indeed, trades union relationships with the Government in the context of the 1970-4 Parliament cannot be understood without referring back to earlier Wilson years.

During 1966-7 Harold Wilson had been forced into applying a statutory wages and incomes policy, which had abraded his relationship with the trades union movement. The economic difficulties necessitated sacrifices on the part of the unions; in particular, they felt that the social policies essential both to their future negotiating position and their confidence were being undermined. As a result, they became less and less co-operative.

As well as this increasing toughness of attitude, there were unofficial but overt acts of defiance from the rank and file, much of it no doubt inspired by extremist elements: the spate of 'wildcat' strikes which were at their height during the winter of 1968-9. The point was finally reached when Harold Wilson decided that action must be taken to restore the country's confidence in the Government's ability to control the situation generally, no less than the Trades Union Congress's ability to keep a hold over its own members.

The Prime Minister decided, therefore, that an Industrial Relations Act bringing much of union behaviour within the framework of the law was necessary. On the unions' part, their hostility to the idea that their freedom of action could be subject to restraint, and their anger that the Government was prepared to legislate against them, was to cause great difficulty to Harold Wilson – and later, more dramatically, to Edward Heath.

The fact that a Labour Government was prepared to legislate against its 'own' was to a large extent the fault of the trades union movement itself. For many years it had promised, but not carried out, reforms that would have obviated this crisis of confidence: a reduction in numbers of trades unions within a particular industry, and more power in the Trades Union Congress as the central co-ordinating and representative body for the movement as a whole. Had not George Woodcock, then General Secretary of the TUC, promised exactly this?

The reasoning behind Harold Wilson's decision to bring in legislation during those last years of his second Government was that if anyone was going to take action against the trades union movement, it should be a Labour Government; if anyone was to correct what was increasingly seen by many as an imbalance, it should be the Labour Party, owing as it did its very existence to the trades union movement.

In later years, it was assumed that Harold Wilson had rushed to legislation because he feared the situation had got out of control. This was not the case; what he did believe, though, was that if the country's confidence was eroded, industrial chaos would be a consequence, and the unions would regard themselves as a disproportionately strong section of the electorate. His firm conclusion was that the correction of an overly powerful element within itself would be healthy not only for the Labour Party – who would be seen as courageous and clear-sighted – but healthy for the country and parliamentary democracy.

Today, there are almost as many views on why 'In Place of Strife' was introduced as there were clauses in the Act. One thing only is certain: the whole argument about the Bill earned him a great deal of hostility. Its eventual proposed emasculation only succeeded in annoying the hard-liners without appeasing those who were against it altogether. The result was that when Harold Wilson lost in 1970, his position as Leader was extremely awkward, with a credibility gulf yawning between himself and the trades union movement – just when he most needed their support. Thus, when Edward Heath introduced his own more stringent Industrial Relations Act into Parliament, it was extremely difficult for Harold Wilson to appear sincere and wholehearted when he opposed it, both in Parliament and outside.

For James Callaghan there was no such dichotomy. He had been bitterly opposed to 'In Place of Strife' from the earliest moment, even breaking the rule of collective Cabinet responsibility by publicly

speaking out against it; in consequence, he was the trades union movement's hero. After 1970 Harold Wilson, in Opposition, was forced to
lean very heavily on Jim and his special relationship with the unions
over both the Common Market argument and industrial relations policy
on the floor of the House.

Meanwhile, in complete contrast to his stated policy at the beginning
of his Parliament, Edward Heath in his turn was producing the big stick
of legislation. At first he had told the trades unions that he believed in
a voluntary incomes and wages policy, and on this basis had secured
their agreement to co-operate. But when a hard-and-fast statutory
wages policy with which they did not agree was arbitrarily imposed on
them, it meant hard fighting every inch of the way – with the miners'
pay claim as Waterloo.

Edward Heath's dilemma was thus, in a curious way, almost the
mirror image of Harold Wilson's. He, too, had to change his position:
from the early Selsdon-Man monetarist policies, so like Margaret
Thatcher's were to be, with a general 'free-for-all' on both wages and
salaries, to interventionist government. This about-turn took place
against the fiscal background of the Barber boom, with its accompanying mushrooming of fringe banks and property companies, and speculation both here and overseas.

But at the beginning of the Barber boom there was no question of
treating the unions as any kind of partner in government. Instead, there
was the Industrial Relations Act; legislation that caused the most extraordinary scenes of chaos during its passage through the House. The
House was almost literally torn apart with shouts, jeers and cries of fury
evoked in an almost primitive response from both sides. The spectator
of one of these storms would have found it quite unbelievable that some
of the Tory members, red-faced and shouting with rage, would in two
or three years be sitting down with the trades union movement in
Downing Street and Whitehall offices to discuss the role of those unions
in the economy; and what is more, to plan it in a way that had never
before been taken so far, so formally designated or so clearly spelled out.
It is, perhaps, ironic to think that it was Edward Heath, the man
toppled by the unions, who did much to formalize the role the unions
had previously played on a less official basis.

The unions themselves never looked back from this greater recognition of their importance. They had beaten Harold Wilson over industrial relations, they would beat Edward Heath with their strategy on
wages policy; they had, all told, arrived at a point where they were

admitted partners in government, and important key members of the corporate state – all this with the full co-operation of that other powerful estate of the realm, the Civil Service.

The return to power of Harold Wilson in 1974 necessarily saw their role expanded even further: he had inherited from Edward Heath an economic situation which there was no hope of stabilizing without trades union co-operation. When James Callaghan, the acknowledged partisan of the unions, was elected Leader, their power was increased still further.

How deeply involved in government they should be is still a key question, subdued as they may now be in relative terms, and it is a question complicated by the fact that apart from economists (and they speak from a purely economic standpoint) no one has ever clearly defined what is meant in Britain by the corporate state and, more important, who should be the governors thereof? Should they be the political operators or those who put their policies into effect? The financiers? The producers? The managers? The union members or the big block votes? Or do we believe in a parliamentary democracy so structured that it represents the many and varied interests existing in this country – including the trades unions themselves?

The debate on where power should lie is never honestly conducted either within the main parties or outside them: in the Conservative Party business interests predominate; the Labour Party is not only wedded to the trades union movement historically, but in terms of hard cash – a bondage which now rules out impartial discussion on the merits of parliamentary democracy *vis-à-vis* the corporate state. There is, too, the added dimension that corporatism inevitably strengthens the administrative arm of government, putting much of the power into the hands of a greatly swollen Civil Service – a body which, whatever its merits, was not democratically elected to govern.

No discussion of the role of the trades unions would be complete without mention of two other points. First, although the trades unions claim to represent the workers, fewer workers belong to unions than do not belong. In addition, there are large minority groups with little or no political clout: the disabled or old, the sick, the widowed, the disadvantaged.

Whether or not the corporate state is likely again or desirable, attitudes towards the trades union movement have undergone a process of polarization that began over ten years ago. The idea of 'In Place of Strife' undermined the trades unions' confidence in Labour leaders by the very fact that there was such sharp division on its desirability, and that with any mention of this Bill unity flew out of the window. Once in Opposition, where a united front was essential, union power was advanced because of Labour's need to support the unions (and in turn to be supported by them) in any conflict with the Conservative Government – so much so that to the Labour Party the unions became almost sacrosanct.

What if in 1969 the Bill had been passed in its original form? Although most members of the present Labour hierarchy (and certainly Jim Callaghan) would disagree, I believe that many ordinary Labour voters, including staunch union members, would have liked to see some government action on the troubled state of industrial relations at that time, and would have continued to give the Labour Government their support.

Alternatively, what if there had been no such Bill presented at all? This, I am sure, would have served merely to delay argument and conflict rather than to remove it: a confrontation would have occurred during a Labour Government if it had been re-elected in 1970.

The real tragedy was that what was intended never reached the Statute Book and we were left with just a Declaration of Intent by the TUC on behalf of the trades union movement. It was a watershed in the political history of this country; with its deleterious effect on the credibility of the Leader of the Party, it was no less a watershed in the political life of Harold Wilson himself.

SIX

Pre-Campaign: February 1974

Those years in Opposition had affected the standing of Harold Wilson. The Parliamentary Labour Party was divided in its support for him, many of them saying openly that he should make way for someone new.

Who this should be was never overtly stated, although there was, in fact, only one possible candidate: Jim Callaghan. Neither Roy Jenkins nor Denis Healey would have been the PLP's choice. Michael Foot and Tony Crosland were not well enough placed at that time to compete effectively, but Jim said repeatedly that he had no ambitions towards the Leadership. Nevertheless, it was clear that if Harold Wilson had fallen under the proverbial bus, it would have been a walkover for Jim.

The attitude of the PLP was to some degree reflected in that of the group of advisers round Harold himself. At one of the first meetings – held to discuss tactics in the event of a snap election – Harold left the room and Joe Haines remarked, 'This horse won't run.'

Harold Wilson had the unenviable job of mobilizing an effective parliamentary and personal campaign team. He was worried, initially for example, about integrating Bernard Donoughue, a senior lecturer in politics at the London School of Economics, into the office team, in particular *vis-à-vis* Joe Haines. Bernard was a right-wing Gaitskellite and former member and organizer of the Campaign for Democratic Socialism. Joe had always expressed the most tremendous aversion to university graduates, and here was Bernard, not merely a graduate but worse, a lecturer – and in politics, to boot. In the event, all went smoothly; Bernard went out of his way to conciliate Joe, and Joe later conceded to Harold Wilson that as far as Bernard was concerned, he was prepared to take back all he had ever said about people who went to university.

Though they were at first wary of each other, by the time the campaign proper began they were getting on famously and were quickly recognized as a duo, though they were in every way as different as chalk and cheese. Physically, this was immediately apparent. Bernard was full of life and jokey stories, with mocking eyes and grin beneath curly brown hair, clad in his 'trendy-lecturer' long-haired white fur coat, giving the impression of half-dancing rather than walking, as he paced along beside his friend, over whom he leaned slightly (Bernard was a good bit taller than Joe). By contrast, Joe – if only he had possessed the felt hat to pull down low over the eyes – could have doubled as a secret agent, with his steel-rimmed glasses, raincoat, black lace-up shoes, neatly done hair, and occasional sardonic smile. In keeping with his more severe appearance, he was a master of the well-turned phrase and jokes that ranged from sharply witty to grim. I remember when, just before the 1970 election, we were shown a film of the Ronan Point disaster, Joe's comment on it was an adaptation of the American Republican campaign slogan from their 1968 election: 'The risks are too great for you to stay home.'

At the outset, the internal difficulties, coupled with bitter criticism and hostile moves against Harold Wilson within the Parliamentary Labour Party (which he attributed solely, and wrongly, to the right-wing Jenkins group), appeared to offer him an inauspicious start to any election campaign. I was constantly surprised that he was able to maintain a genuinely cheerful and determined outlook.

But his attitude was the logical one. Though within the PLP and the metropolis there were individuals and groups whose attitude towards him shaded from a vague disenchantment to outright hostility, outside these small circles it was different. Among Labour Party workers and the public generally, behind the usual grumbles and criticisms, there was warmth, affection and support. Emotionally, this was a tremendous boost; practically, it was here the votes lay.

The public's attitude towards him was shown by the reception they gave him from the moment the campaign was under way. This rallying round is something that most Leaders – unless they have committed some truly disastrous gaffe – can count on; it was certainly the case for Edward Heath during the 1974 campaign.

Morally, Harold Wilson had much to sustain him. He knew that by the time he was defeated in 1970 the country was in a far better state than when the Labour Government had inherited it in 1964; in addition he felt very strongly about the return to Downing Street. He wanted not only to ensure that the Labour Party was returned to power, but also personal vindication for his policies and the opportunity to prove that he, Harold Wilson, still had the confidence of the electorate.

His determination – if he were not so good-humoured and easy-going it could have been called implacability – was therefore fully understandable. But how well justified was the Leader's cheerfulness? Would he even have been Leader if Edward Heath had been able to stay until the last permissible moment, summer 1975?

As one of Harold Wilson's political advisers I did not envy my opposite numbers in Downing Street, involved in the unenviable task of advising when an election should – or should not – be called. On their shoulders was the burden of judging it correctly; our handicap was that we were, as a Party, linked in the public mind with the very issues that were bringing the election nearer.

Most obvious of these was our close association with the trades union movement. Our links with the unions put us theoretically into a defensive position. For us, 'Who Governs Britain?' was an uncomfortable slogan. If the Party in power chose this issue as the main battleground, then we were indeed in a difficult position, tied as we were to the 'union line' because of our retreat from the principles of 'In Place of Strife', and our subsequent defence of the trades union movement in Opposition and in long argument and debates on the Industrial Relations Act. It would be comical if it were not so distressing to see Joe Gormley now claim that Harold Wilson wished to use the miners' strike to force an election. His first and early reactions were quite the opposite. Only when the point of no return had been reached did he then seek to ensure that Labour did not suffer from its identification in the public mind with union power. Jim Callaghan, the man who had made the unions' cause his own, was the obvious spokesman here.

Harold Wilson, meanwhile, was attempting to widen the debate. Before Christmas 1973, in a major speech in Bolton, he had listed the ten points on which – should there be an early election – a victorious Labour Government would act. These were: an increase in pensions and food subsidies; stricter price control; tax reform; the EEC renegotiation; the repeal of the Industrial Relations Act; action to peg rents and mortgages; increase in public accountability for industry; plans to take into public ownership development and building land, and expansion of educational opportunity. To these he added further commitments on sex equality and superannuation.

He was convinced that the ground on which the Tories should be attacked and on which they were vulnerable was their handling of the economy, with special reference to the cost of living. On the delicate question of the unions, the inevitable confrontations with the Tories should be emphasized, thus throwing into relief Labour's ability to conciliate, rebuild and expand.

However, it is easier to choose the arena when you are in the seat of power. At first, Edward Heath, under pressure from his colleagues, allowed himself to be drawn into fighting on what seemed the obvious issue and the one that we had begun by fearing: the question of 'Who Governs Britain?' But perhaps sensing that he had got hold of not a grenade but a boomerang, and being essentially a man attuned to affairs on a world-wide scale, his main theme became the world economy and the effects of the oil crisis of 1973. In judging this as the dominating problem, he was surely correct: in world terms, as in its effect on Britain, we were seeing a major and irreversible change. That age of cheap energy was over. But the electorate saw the Tory campaign as essentially 'Who Governs Britain?' – confrontation and ungovernability – and, when this sank in completely, Labour was on its way to victory again.

SEVEN

Electioneering

25 December 1973 was the first Christmas Day we had spent without my father. The year before, two days after I had returned to London, I had been woken up in the middle of the night to learn that he had suffered a sudden heart attack and died in his sleep. The shock, as well as the sorrow, was still with us, making what should have been a happy family party a sad occasion. My brother, too, was absent, but for a happier reason: he had married in the summer and was spending Christmas Day with his in-laws in Yorkshire.

Celebrating Christmas 1973 together, then, were my mother – who was now living with me in London – my sister, myself and my two sons. We were a depleted party, and there was a further cloud: the severe but unspecified illness of Terry Lancaster, Political Editor of the *Daily Mirror* and long-standing friend of and adviser to Harold Wilson. Earlier that year, he had been taken into Bart's Hospital but, so far, the doctors had been unable to diagnose what was wrong with him.

I had promised to visit him over the holiday period, as most people were away. So on Christmas Day, leaving the turkey to cook under my mother's care, I drove over to Bart's. Despite his illness Terry was – as always – in great form. We joked and laughed, hardly mentioning politics. The idea that a general election was just round the corner certainly did not dominate the conversation; we had, of course, heard the rumours to this effect – but there were always rumours. At that time there was a curious lull politically, and we had all half-begun to believe that the Conservative Government might soldier on. They still had a further statutory eighteen months to run.

Despite the calm – deceptive, as it turned out – we were quite aware that we had reached that stage in the life of a Government when an election could be called at any moment. And once Christmas, with its artificially imposed calm, was past, it began to feel as though an election was, in fact, in the offing, though we still hoped that some dramatic turn of events might head it off: we did not want to fight on the 'Who Governs Britain?' ground.

Trades union power was already viewed with hostility by the electorate; ironically from our point of view, since we ourselves had illuminated its emergence with 'In Place of Strife' five years earlier. There was, we knew, a certain amount of public sympathy for the miners, thanks to their hard, difficult and dangerous work; how much, we did not at that time realize.

Though the battleground could not be of our choosing, the strategy and, above all, the tactics, could. The lessons learned in the campaign of 1970 still obsessed us; we were determined to achieve the same efficiency that the Conservative camp had shown then, both by putting right our mistakes and by improving our planning and organization.

Presentation was a key issue. Compared with the expert way in which Edward Heath had been 'put across', our efforts were a comparative failure. It was true that circumstances had caused difficulties, but it was equally true that professional advice might have overcome them.

Our main problem had been that the controversy over 'In Place of Strife' had resulted in the dwindling away of active support in the constituencies, and outright hostility from the disaffected. During the last two years of his second Government in the late 1960s, Harold Wilson had been experiencing an extremely poor reception when addressing public rallies – often he was completely drowned by the heckling coming from the very left-wing students who at that time seemed to be in control of most of the universities, or from members of the public who were fed up with the extremely high number of unofficial strikes that were causing such damage and disruption to their lives. Moreover, the endless jibes and cat-calls, the constant expression of hostility – all depicted in faithful detail on TV – were doing a lot of harm to the Government's image.

I therefore suggested that Harold Wilson should adopt a change of tactics in the 1970 election campaign, switching from the usual custom of addressing large public meetings to a more intimate approach: visiting committee rooms and small private meetings of Party members in an effort to put heart back into Party workers, and using the same technique, largely in the form of the 'walkabout', with the general public. I felt that speaking to people in shopping centres, in their own communities, even in their own homes, would produce more sympathetic TV coverage from the Party's point of view, and would result in Harold Wilson meeting, and being seen by, more people overall.

My idea had worked well in one sense, but in another had proved to be self-defeating. While the Prime Minister was always, on these impromptu trips, seen surrounded by people who were in the main friendly and smiling – in contrast to the anti-Government hostility expressed at large public meetings – the general effect, though amiable, was diffuse. No clear statement of intent emerged. Edward Heath, on the other hand, was addressing ticket rallies, attended by the Tory faithful, where he was able without interruption to put across a very clear theme indeed; these meetings were, naturally, also covered by the TV cameras, and their effectiveness was underlined by the very slick platform presentation of Heath himself.

Personally he appeared to great advantage, with his clean and shining silver hair, well-tended and sun-tanned face, immaculate blue suit and tie, all set off by a plain blue background broken only by the Conservative emblem and slogan. His surroundings were equally carefully chosen: on the platform with him were a few people only, to his left and right, and these had been clearly picked (we thought) for their ability to look attentive.

There were none of the bobbing heads, or people around the rostrum looking as if they had long since stopped listening to what anyone said – let alone the main speaker – that so often graced Labour rallies. Against this look of efficient simplicity, Heath himself put across a punchy, pared-down message to the electorate. The promise that both prices and taxation would be cut seemed to echo in our ears every night.

Labour's efforts in 1970 made a dismal contrast. Effective though the walkabouts were in terms of creating personal warmth for the Prime Minister, they were undoubtedly a messy way of putting him over on TV. When he appeared in committee rooms to speak, these were usually inadequately prepared. Often, he would be seen in front of a scanty audience (there were no empty seats at a Heath meeting) on a ricketylooking platform that had obviously been put up at the last minute. Sometimes, he was reduced to addressing a crowd from an open window, even, on one occasion, actually having to hold up the sash window with his shoulders (something impossible to imagine Heath doing). The impact of what he was saying was further vitiated by the people who were invariably moving about behind and around him in a way

distracting to the viewer. Altogether, there was a general image of
confusion and muddle.

All of us close to Harold Wilson were very conscious of the mistakes
of 1970 as we planned for the campaign of 1974. Much of my own time
was spent discussing with actor Stanley Baker, Michael Dealey and
Barry Spikings,* and their colleagues how we could improve Harold
Wilson's presentation this time. Stanley, like myself, believed that what
was needed was the professional touch. We would make use as Heath
did of everything from television and microphone control to make-up
man.

At Stanley's suggestion, David Wickes, a young man from the film
industry, who has since become a successful producer of films for cinema
and television including *The Sweeney*, was asked to help us, together with
Neil Vann, the athletic, energetic and efficient Youth Officer at Transport House. Their responsibility was to improve and restyle the public
presentation of the Leader of the Opposition.

Acquiring Neil, and with him the co-operation of Transport House,
had not been as easy as it sounds. Transport House were not keen on
political cosmetics, nor did they like outsiders working within their
organization. This was understandable up to a point: an election period
is analogous to a time of war, when the community spirit essential to
smooth functioning can only usually be guaranteed by forming teams
from those who have known each other for a long period of working
closely together. Our plans meant changes, hiccoughs in the accepted
regime – even the Regional Organizers objected to being asked to
rearrange their platforms to fit in with these new directives from the
Leader's Office. However, eventually the difficulties were ironed out
and, because the new arrangements worked well in the first, February,
election of 1974, everyone was quick to help further in the second one
in October.

David Wickes himself was not particularly politically-minded; his
own description of himself was 'Liberal-Left'. I first met him when he
came to Lord North Street to see the Leader of the Party.

This meeting had had a slightly inauspicious start. I had asked David
to pick up Neil Vann from Transport House first, so that – as they
would both be working together – they could meet Harold Wilson
together for a joint discussion of tactics; but when David, who had never

---

* Michael and Barry were Stanley's partners in film-making: Michael has subsequently produced a number of very successful films including *The Deerhunter* and *Blade Runner*, and Barry had
been in charge of film production for the EMI/Thorn Company.

visited Transport House before, arrived there to pick up Neil, he found the great grid gates closed uncompromisingly across the entrance. He was not to know that this happened on the dot of 5.30 every night. Eventually Jack Stoddard of the Labour Party Press Department came down, took charge of him and showed him the publicity material that was to be used in the campaign – including the rosettes that became such a major feature. When Neil Vann arrived, there was a quick introduction, and the two of them set off for 5 Lord North Street, where they found Harold Wilson, his usual approachable self, kindly and easy, working away in his shirt sleeves on a speech – in direct contrast to David's experience at Transport House's front door.

After a series of discussions, a 'battle plan' was worked out; it involved Neil and David travelling ahead of the Leader to each of his campaign meetings to ensure not only that the platform in each hall looked exactly as it should through the eye of the television camera, but also that the cameras themselves were placed where they would give a good image of the Leader. In 1970 some of the shots of Harold Wilson had been taken from strange and awkward angles, with unpleasing and unfortunate results. This time we were more successful in placing the TV crews where we, rather than they, wanted them to be, and the resultant shots were consequently more flattering – he looked decidedly less sinister and weary!

The back-drop against which the Leader appeared was of great importance. The visual impact of the 1970 platform presentation of Edward Heath had impressed us enormously because of the clarity of the images used, and the forceful simplicity of the message; we had learned an important lesson from this. The effective Heath back-drop, we knew, had been specially constructed by the Tories; Neil and David set out to do the same for Labour.

The first attempt (in Scotland) was of necessity makeshift, as virtually nothing was available. Neil and David begged eight 20-by-16 inch caption cards from Scottish Television, and from them cut a Union Jack and four arrows' motif with a knife they had bought from Woolworth's. The pieces of the Union Jack were coloured, the arrows fixed so that they pointed at the head of the Leader, and the whole motif pinned up at the back of the platform. Their ingenuity was rewarded, as it looked most effective; but they prudently prevented the television cameras from focusing on it, in case the crudeness of the workmanship showed in close-up.

This first experiment proved the importance of a professionally made back-drop. Convincing Transport House was another matter: once again, there was the familiar negative attitude, this time manifest in endless stalling and chronic financial queries over every item of expenditure from nails to card sheets.

Finally, though, David and Neil's idea went ahead. The basic structure was made in the carpentry department at Pinewood Studios and then taken back to Transport House to be covered in beige felt and have the campaign motif affixed. In the second, 1974 election, a large rosette was substituted. Both were brilliantly designed by Jack Stoddard under Percy Clark's guiding hand.

The lectern, too, was considered a suitable case for treatment. The one used during the first campaign was a collapsible wooden affair (when it was introduced, back in 1964, even using a lectern had been considered a revolutionary step). Alfred Richman of the Mirror Group, who had been over twelve years or more a devoted and invaluable helper and who attended every meeting, was in charge of it; he carried it about from place to place in a large holdall. The whole arrangement, though it had worked well, seemed a trifle primitive and old-fashioned, and eventually Neil and David managed to streamline this too.

But the main problems were with the Constituency Party officials around the country. It was Neil and David's job to organize the various meetings the Leader was addressing, and in most cases the various Party officials involved considered David, Neil and their vanful of equipment an unnecessary nuisance – in Wales, particularly, they hated the intervention of these two 'outsiders'. Luckily, David knew most of the television people on the tour very well, and this proved a great counterbalancing asset.

In the first campaign, all the equipment could be packed into the van: there was the portable lectern, the back-drop and dressing for the table at which the Leader sat. By the time the second campaign came round later in the year, the whole concept had been refined into a unified design, with the three pieces slotting together; and two of everything, including vans, had been acquired. The second set, built by a professional firm, was expensive, but this doubling-up was well worth it as it meant that one set could go ahead to the next venue, where preparation need not be quite such a frantically hurried and last-minute affair.

One essential part of this equipment was the public address system: usually, those in the various halls around the country were not good enough for the Leader's Rally. Supplementing them with extra microphones would have meant a collection of various shapes and sizes, taped

together in a very Heath-Robinson way that did not fit in with the
image of an efficient, forward-looking Party. Neil and David had managed to cut down the number of microphones needed in front of the
Leader to three, with a feed for up to thirty more in a box off-stage; by
the second election, the three had been cut down to one only, giving an
infinitely less cluttered appearance.

The Leader himself did not escape this streamlining process. Perhaps
the most startling departure for the People's Party was the addition of
a make-up man, film industry expert George Blackler, to the travelling
team (sometimes he travelled with the Leader, sometimes he would go
ahead with David and Neil so that he was ready waiting near the
platform when the Leader arrived). His job, as with the ordinary studio
TV broadcast, was to eliminate as far as possible the dark shadows and
shiny skin that produce a bad picture. In the main, this meant make-up
under the eyes, powder on nose and forehead. Harold Wilson disliked
this form of grooming intensely.

Another duty of the make-up man was to see that the Leader's hair
was cut and washed, and his appearance generally spick and span. He
was always extremely reluctant to be asked, immediately on arrival at
the venue where he was speaking, to change out of the now-crumpled
suit he had travelled in and to get into the clean and pressed one waiting
for him. (David and Neil would immediately whisk away the discarded
suit to the nearest fast dry cleaners, so that within two hours it was
ready to collect and take along to the next speaking engagement.)

For any speaker, the voice and throat is always a sensitive area. A
mixture of lemon and honey had been recommended by the doctor as
the best possible drink for hoarseness or throat trouble; in addition,
Harold Wilson drank large quantities of Lucozade to give him energy
– bottles of these were always clanking around in the back of David's
car. Again, the TV cameras had to be considered: in an ordinary white
glass, the lemon and honey would have looked like whisky; so green
glasses and a carafe, in which it looked like the harmless beverage it
was, were bought from Habitat. These glasses were always disappear-
ing, presumably taken as souvenirs.

The 'wrong' colour glass was at one time a problem with Mary
Wilson too. Because of the glare of the TV lights, she had taken to
wearing dark glasses on the platform. On TV these looked like enormous
black circles and completely hid both her expression and the fact that
she was listening attentively to her husband speaking.

One problem that no amount of careful valeting could counteract was Harold Wilson's propensity for falling over things. 'The Gerald Ford of the Labour Party' was how Neil and David thought of him retrospectively. To them, again, fell the job of making everything 'Harold-proof': mainly by removing everything movable that could be knocked over, and sticky-taping down all the loose wires and leads from the TV cameras and lights that lay in coiled heaps across the floor and snaked up the stairways.

The TV cameras themselves were treated like VIP guests: that is, they were given the best seats – at the cost of grumbling from those who were displaced to make room for them – and everything on stage or platform was considered from the point of view of how it would appear to *them*, rather than to the audience as a whole.

Because much the most successful and flattering footage was obtained when the cameras were put in the centre of the hall rather than tucked into some corner where they would be 'out of everyone's way', this meant that they displaced forty to fifty seats – seats which the Regional or Constituency officials quite understandably wanted for the Party faithful, and which they were reluctant to give up. Today, when the presence of TV cameras is not merely accepted but welcomed, lessening the view of forty people in order to improve that of millions is taken for granted; but in 1974 cameras had never before been put in the heart of one of our meetings. Again, this was David and Neil's responsibility; Neil always carried a large tape measure with him to measure where each camera should go (they had to be no less than 40 feet and no more than 100 feet from the platform).

Television meant another change from earlier days: altering the technique of arrival. It is seldom possible for a Leader to be present at the beginning of every meeting in an election campaign. Usually he arrives when either the candidate, or another speaker, is in full flood. Previously, this had meant that the Leader quietly mounted the plat-form, seated himself beside the candidate without the meeting being interrupted in any way, and then listened patiently while the candidate – anxious both to get over as many electoral points as possible and to impress his Leader – wound himself up to his peroration. After the applause had died down, the Leader then rose to give the speech for which the Press and TV were waiting.

David and Neil both felt that the Leader's arrival should be more dramatic. Their solution was to bring him down the centre of the hall, with the cameras focused on him as he walked towards the platform. This meant first of all seeing that his car pulled up at the right door and that there were no needless obstructions beside it, and then co-ordinating with the TV crews so that lights and cameras swung round to focus on the Leader at the right moment. David himself carried a hand microphone that could cut out the platform speaker at will; this he used to announce the Leader's arrival. In order to complete the picture the principal Party workers were given aisle seats down the centre gangway so that they could be closest to the Leader as he walked towards the platform.

By the end of the two 1974 campaigns everything was running smoothly. David and Neil had two crews of four working with them, whom they referred to as their 'roadies'; they themselves were looked after by Albert Murray, who always made sure that they got decent meals and something to drink before they had to rush on to the next job.

Whenever Harold Wilson himself arrived at a hall, either David or Neil – or both – was there to help him change, see if he wanted to wash and brush up, check that he had seen the make-up man, take care of Mary Wilson, and organize the platform appearance.

Apart from Neil's salary from Transport House, he was not paid for his services, and nor was David; for the three weeks in both campaigns they were on the go from early morning until late at night, keeping to a gruelling schedule, and performing all their duties with great efficiency and, something which was at that time just as important, tact. Thanks to this lubricating quality, their clever and skilful innovations slid smoothly down the Party throat.

EIGHT

Election Jitters

'Will you? won't you?' could have been the theme song of those few weeks before and after Christmas 1973. Was Edward Heath about to invite us to the dance? – a dance that would end, we hoped, with a change of partners. Or had he decided to sit it out until the following year?

Before Christmas, Harold Wilson had felt confident that an election was in the offing. But as those days of early January passed, and there was still no announcement from Downing Street, he began to think that perhaps the danger was over.

I say 'danger' deliberately. The atmosphere was faintly like that of a war: with unlit streets, the three-day week, the electricity cuts, truncated television services (all stations shut down at 10.30 p.m.), and other emergency measures introduced by Heath following the miners' industrial action. As in a time of war, even the difficulties and shortages engendered loyalty among the faithful to the Tory cause; whereas for us (as I have already said) 'Who Governs Britain?' was not a question we wished to answer just then.

But as time passed, loyalty gave way to irritation, and the country became fed up not only with the measures that caused such public disruption, but also with the Party that imposed them. We realized that any delay could only favour us.

It proved exactly thus. Businessmen whose profits slumped, workers whose pockets were affected by being laid off, housewives who found their homes less comfortable – all wanted normality to return. Very early on, it became apparent that the Tories had misjudged the public response to the 'confrontation cuts'.

Although we wanted to put across the idea that Labour alone could break the industrial deadlock, we were also terrified that the miners would announce that they would co-operate only with a Labour Government and never with a Conservative one; we were convinced this would damage our standing and credibility in the eyes of the country. But the Tories were equally fearful of such a declaration: *they* felt that such a development would persuade even more people to vote for Labour to secure peace and harmony and to get Britain working again.

Every Party believes that its opponents are better organized, more efficient and their morale generally higher. Only later did we learn that the Tories were suffering as much from being the Party in Government now as we had in 1970. The links between their Party and Government had weakened; Ministers were more than ever involved in the crisis; Heath and members of the Cabinet were listening increasingly to the advice of senior civil servants – with an election close at hand, this was a destructive form of dependence if political advisers were not also consulted, especially as the officials themselves, as in most times of crisis, were more and more reluctant to advise.

All of us knew how important it was to win this election. The glittering prospect of North Sea oil was ahead; there was a powerful, almost mythical, belief that anyone who could get into power and hang on until this liquid gold flowed limitlessly into the country's coffers would remain in office for at least twenty years. 'And after that', ran the argument, 'they would be the natural Party of Government, to whom the people were accustomed and who, in turn, attracted to themselves the brightest, best, and most ambitious.'

On 7 February 1974 the answer to the question 'Who Governs Britain?' lay just three weeks ahead. We learned it on Polling Day, 28 February.

For Harold Wilson, the five-week pre-campaign period ended with a clear indication as to what he could expect from his own side. Party backing was lukewarm, and the officials at Transport House displayed no confidence in the outcome of the struggle ahead; they gave the impression that this was not just because of the odds against us, but because the Leader himself was not the big attraction he had previously been.

Accordingly, fighting the campaign that followed became a team affair, with Harold determined to avoid overplaying his role of Leader among his colleagues; although he was at the same time always conscious of the need to present a compelling and convincing focal image to the general public – an image that was above all reassuring. For as we quickly realized, people throughout the country were anxious and frightened about the future. They did not want a political punch-up between Edward Heath and Harold Wilson; they wanted to hear the real issues debated from every side.

The first days after the announcement of an election do not really count in a campaign: not until the House has been dissolved does battle begin. Even then it takes a couple of days to get the pre-arranged programme rolling smoothly, and we had, in any case, first to install ourselves in Transport House. In fact the office was divided into two parts: key workers moved across to Transport House, and the rest remained in our rooms in the Palace of Westminster doing routine and servicing work there. (The removal from the House of Commons was a business in itself: we had to take with us a large part of our office, from paper clips to personal files, although a photocopier was provided for us by Transport House.)

In those preliminary days it was difficult to feel enthusiasm. Even if we had, the entry into Transport House would have dampened it. I had never been able to sympathize with the Party belief that drab tones and utility were more politically virtuous than bright colours and a bit of style, which need not necessarily cost more. Creating attractive and efficient working conditions, especially for those at the heart of an organization, engenders an enthusiastic attitude that spreads out to colleagues and subordinates like ripples on a pond. Alas, within the Party there was always antagonism and resentment towards those who had – or seemed to have – better, brighter and more luxurious working surroundings (the hostility of the Party workers at Transport House and around the country towards those in the 'glamour' jobs at Westminster stems from this same attitude).

Working environment, however, is a detail; and with the new headquarters at Walworth Road, no doubt this feeling has disappeared. More serious, because less easily definable or overcome, is the lack of a good working atmosphere.

Harold Wilson was now fighting his fourth election for the Party as Leader. Despite this, he was still greeted by Transport House as a 'comer-in', to use that telling Yorkshire expression. In some eyes, his chief fault was that he had captured the Party in 1963 from the Transport House establishment (they were supporting other candidates from the Right), without having even the compensating factor of the backing of one or more of the great trades unions. By contrast Hugh Gaitskell had been a union-backed leader and the darling of Transport House; as was James Callaghan later. Harold Wilson was an outsider – except where, perhaps, it counted most: the Transport House Publicity Department. This was run by Percy Clark, a veteran campaigner of great experience whose wife, Doreen Stainforth, was our Broadcasting Officer.

Just before the campaign announcement in 1974 we had one bitter personal blow. Peter Davis (now Lord Lovell-Davis), who, with Dennis Lyons, ran a small Party publicity group covering TV and radio broadcasts as well as general publicity, suffered a sudden heart attack. I was stunned when his wife Jean, who made me promise not to disclose the seriousness of his illness, rang to tell me the news: Peter was a fit-looking man in his early forties. Although he was temporarily out of action, he wrote to Harold Wilson that Bob Worcester and Bernard Donoughue would continue some of his work on a private poll for the Party during the campaign.

Before Harold Wilson definitely accepted Bernard into his personal team, he had asked for a report on him by Peter Davis. It was extraordinarily accurate, as I could testify: Bernard and I came from the same part of the world, he had been at school with my brother, his best friend was Gerry Fowler (later a Labour Minister), whose parents knew mine well. It was pleasant to be working with someone who came from the same part of Northamptonshire.

The main outline of the Leader's campaign tour had already been agreed, via a series of meetings I had had with the National Agent and the Meetings Officer of the Party. We had started planning back in the days before Christmas when the first rumours of a possible election had been heard.

Now, only the details remained, which were dealt with on a daily basis during the campaign itself. On one point superstition was allowed to dictate: the venue of the opening rally. We had always been successful if this was in the North – for us, Scotland had been the luckiest of all – whereas Wales was to be avoided. In 1970, with everything seemingly going for us, we had started in Cardiff. . . .

In this period before the campaign started, our own working days were spent in the Leader's Room at the House of Commons. In contrast to our opponents, who (according to Douglas Hurd, Edward Heath's Political Secretary and now a Foreign Office Minister) enjoyed enlivening glasses of champagne in the morning during drawing-room meetings and dinner at Pruniers in the evening, for us it was coffee, sandwiches and the occasional whisky in our Westminster rooms. Personally, I agree with Douglas Hurd that champagne, in the evening at least, is better for you, and less expensive, than the more commonly consumed hard liquor.

Once the campaign proper started, the reality for us became sending out for paper cups of coffee and tea from a local café near Transport House, the only bottle of whisky or brandy being kept on one side to provide the Leader with a much-needed drink after a gruelling television or press session. After several days of this, I brought vacuum flasks of real coffee, sandwiches and bars of chocolate from my home, which we munched during the late hours.

As soon as dissolution was out of the way, we were off on Day One of the real campaign. It was to be the shortest we had ever experienced: a mere twenty-one days (the longest campaign had been that of 1970, strung out over five weeks that included a Bank Holiday).

The daily campaign routine was quickly established. Harold Wilson was up early to attend a meeting of the campaign committee and briefing at Transport House before returning to Lord North Street to meet his personal staff – a group consisting usually of Joe Haines, Bernard Donoughue, Peter Lovell-Davis, Dennis Lyons, myself, and occasionally Albert Murray, as well as Thomas Balogh and Gerald Kaufman (who both kept in close touch with daily telephone calls).

For Harold Wilson, his home could not have been more fortunately sited. The house in Lord North Street was five minutes from the House of Commons in one direction, two minutes from Transport House and his other office in the other. Later on in the campaign, this accessibility was to prove crucial.

Picture us, then, gathered each morning that February in the Wilsons' elegant first-floor drawing room, with its tall, narrow sash windows that looked out on one of the loveliest streets in London at the front and over a small paved garden at the back. This beautiful period room still had its original wood-block floor, which the Wilsons had covered with Persian and Romanian carpets presented to them on various official visits. It was filled with other mementoes of their years at Number 10, most of the more precious and unusual gifts, from presidents and princes, being housed in a sizeable display cabinet. Against the light oak-panelled walls Mary Wilson's china looked particularly good; she collects Staffordshire figures and commemorative ware depicting Victorian Prime Ministers, as well as pretty individual pieces that catch her eye.

Built into the bookcase was, rather incongruously, a drinks cupboard, whose door was disguised by simulated book spines and shelves designed to seem a continuation of the genuine article it was part of. All this ingenuity was to little purpose: this curious and literary-looking cocktail cabinet seldom contained more than a solitary bottle of beer. The drinks were kept on a sofa table by the wall opposite.

To reach the narrow stairs leading to the drawing room, you walked through a dining-hall into which the front door opened. From the beginning of the campaign, its long dining table was covered with election documents, briefing material, leaflets and letters. This great mass of paper was usually left untouched, unless something urgent happened to catch our eye as we walked past, our own arms full of paper.

Off the dining-hall was a tiny room used by Harold Wilson as a private study. Another narrow flight of stairs led to the basement, with its cheerful modern kitchen and the bedroom where Mrs Pollard, the Wilsons' housekeeper, slept. Above the drawing room were one large and two small bedrooms; the large one was used by Harold Wilson, the other two by Mary Wilson and Giles, their younger son.

Each of the houses in Lord North Street has a special history, and Number 5 is no exception. It was owned by Lord North himself, and one of his mistresses lived in it. Amatory echoes of the past were, however, the last thing on our minds as we gathered on those cold February mornings – although the coffee that invariably appeared shortly after our arrival was a truly welcome sight.

Harold Wilson, who likes what I would describe as 'space, scatter, and shirtsleeves' while he is working, sat in his favourite chair with its back to the three long windows looking out on the distractions of Lord North Street. Here, with his papers strewn around him on the occasional table at his right hand, on the long coffee table in front of the fireplace, on and around the chair, and on the floor, he would first sit, then rise to his feet and walk about, pacing the length of the room, behind the sofa, round the chairs while talking, discussing, or turning some thought over in his head, watched by Joe, Bernard and myself. My own seat was an armchair in the L-shaped alcove at the back of the room overlooking the garden; it was beside the table that held the telephone, so that I could answer this immediately.

Straightaway we plunged into the first two main problems of the day: what subjects the Leader would deal with at the press conference immediately following our meeting, and what would be the main topic of his speech that evening. These were dealt with in fairly fine detail, and then we moved on to the next day's themes, so that we could prepare handouts for the following morning's press conference and evening speech. Later in the day, once Harold Wilson had left for his campaign meetings, Joe, Bernard and I could get down to working out the speeches for the following day, first dealing with the previous night's prepared work, which often had to be substantially altered to include new points that had appeared overnight.

The first three days of that campaign were frantic and muddled, largely because there was no prepared speech. After the first two mornings, when Harold Wilson had desperately attempted to dictate a new, separate and full speech each day, we all realized that this would not work, because there was neither the time, nor the staff, to achieve this.

Our answer was the Master Speech. In one exhausting and lengthy session, Harold Wilson dictated an enormously long and comprehensive speech, covering every major issue. This was then divided up into sections, under separate headings including 'Prices', 'Energy', 'Unions'. After this, depending on where he was speaking and to whom, or what had been said by the Government or featured in that day's news, we could pull out the relevant section, supplement it with up-to-date material and whatever press handout had been drafted the previous night – and there was that day's speech. It was Joe's job to put the words together for radio interviews; for television, Harold Wilson preferred to prepare his own material.

After the meeting in the civilized surroundings of Lord North Street came to an end, it was over to Transport House for the 11.30 a.m. press conference.

Here, too, we had learned a lesson from the 1970 fiasco. Then, our conference had taken place before that of the Tories, and consequently for the rest of the day we had been on the defensive over questions that Edward Heath had raised at the end of his press conference. This time, Harold Wilson had insisted that we go last, and also that the press conference was held at Transport House and not – as it had been in 1970 – at a school near Lord North Street, where the platform was so constructed that the Leader was barely visible over the top of the platform table.

Each day, as we left Lord North Street to troop off in a crocodile to Transport House, the number of photographers outside Number 5 increased; as we emerged, they would follow us across the square, clicking all the way to Transport House, where more were waiting.

It was a strange feeling to be part of this curious procession. A glance sideways at Central Office showed the same thing there; cables and wires tumbled from both buildings to the outside broadcast units parked in the square. There seemed to be camera crews, lights and vans everywhere. The traditional Labour Party entrance to Transport House is the one opposite the Marquis of Granby pub, but we used the door nearest our first-floor rooms: the door hallowed by the Transport and General Workers' Union as their main entrance, opposite the beautiful church of St John in the middle of Smith Square.

Only a few moments were spent in the Leader's room, to check on anything urgent and for make-up man George Blackler to see that the Leader's coat and hair were brushed and to erase any shine on his face. Then it was down to the General Secretary's room on the ground floor.

Here there was a brief meeting before the press conference, culminating in the breathless appearance of the staff member who had been attending the Tory press conference across the square. Quickly she read out the main points made by Ted Heath and the line taken by the press; her efficiency often pointed us in an unexpected direction, or provided valuable anticipation.

Then it was into Transport Hall, where the Leader joined Ron Hayward and others on the platform, while Percy Clark, Joe, Bernard and myself found places in the body of the Hall. These were all at different spots, so that we could see how the platform party looked from different angles, and each assess the reactions of different members of the press.

When the press conference was over and the Leader rejoined us, he was given the speech for that evening with its accompanying press handout, after which the drivers – if there was a train or plane to be caught – would arrive to take the whole entourage to station or airport.

These drivers, whom we made part of our campaign 'family', lent a touch of individuality to the routine business of chauffeuring. One had been a stock-car racer: he went round Hyde Park Corner with more speed, flair and dash than anyone I have ever met. The second driver had been a steward on a yacht. His former occupation showed itself not only in his infallible memory for detail, but in the way he helped you out of your coat, hung it up, cast a professional eye over your appearance and, if necessary, brushed you down too. The third one was more in the traditional mould, older and extremely experienced; he never put a foot wrong except for one occasion when he insisted on driving Mary Wilson down a one-way system in the wrong direction – all of them accompanied by a police escort.

If the evening's meeting was in London or the Home Counties, then Harold Wilson would return home to Lord North Street for lunch with Mary. Sometimes he would return to Transport House afterwards, sometimes we would go to him in Lord North Street.

It was during these 'London days' that radio and TV broadcasts were slotted in. I usually accompanied him to Lime Grove or Broadcasting House, and occasionally Joe Haines came too. Joe was more interested in radio (for which he prepared the speeches), whereas I felt television was more important: that is, I felt that although a good TV appearance might not necessarily swing many votes, a bad one could be damaging.

Once again, even the smallest detail of presentation proved to be important. One of my first chores at the beginning of February was a sortie to the shops to find the sort of tie that our experts, David Wickes and Neil Vann, recommended: a blue one with a small motif including a little red or white.

Lunch for me was sandwiches, devoured – I was always hungry as my day started at 7.00 a.m. – at my desk. At around 3.30 I took about an hour off, then got back to Transport House at about a quarter to five for the evening's work.

Those evenings were the best part of the day. The three of us, myself, Joe and Bernard, laughed a lot – I certainly enjoyed myself more than in previous election campaigns in which I had been involved. At about 5.00 p.m. we would have a preliminary discussion about the lines of the following day's press handout. Joe would seat himself at the typewriter at the desk in the window, on the opposite side of the room from Harold Wilson's desk, Bernard and I on the armless easy chairs in another corner. I would start by giving the themes Harold Wilson had suggested, then we would all three expand on them. Suddenly, Joe would say 'I think I have the words!', and start pounding away on the typewriter. Once he had finished, the three of us read it through to see how it sounded, made any amendments or changes we felt were necessary, and slotted Joe's paragraphs into that section of the Master Speech that was to be used the next day.

Sometimes the whole process went so easily that we were finished by dinner time. On other days, it took far longer to get right, and we had to slip out for a meal break in the middle. But always Joe was very good about it. After the initial sparking-off that he seemed to need, he quickly and skilfully produced passages that dovetailed smoothly into the main speech, yet had attention-getting content and headline-grabbing phrases.

Intermittently, we watched television to see how the morning press conference had come over and, if the evening meeting had been early enough for the BBC and ITV deadlines, how successful that had been.

The TV set, a tiny (9 in) black-and-white portable, was also used to watch Edward Heath and leading members of both sides, so that we could compare, contrast and, if necessary, slightly change the presentation of the Leader and his message. This bit of our work was particularly enjoyable. We all loved watching: this was politics in action, a panoramic view of the hustings that would have been impossible in an earlier age. While we watched, we discussed, chatted, gossiped. There were always journalists, MPs and minor characters on the fringe of politics at the Marquis of Granby, all full of stories or information that ranged from the believable – like gossip from the industrial correspondents on the miners' dispute – to the bizarre. Sometimes these titbits would be heard in the pub, sometimes they would be brought over to the office. In any case, they made for a lively evening's conversation.

We were in excellent fighting spirits in those first days. Although we believed that the outcome would go against us, we were determined to do everything we could to ensure that the margin of victory for the other side was as narrow as possible. Nor were we being defeatist: all the polls showed that at the end of that first week, things were going badly for us.

By the time we entered the second week of the campaign, it was clear that one of our major problems was to counter the impression that the battle was being fought between the Leaders of the two Parties rather than on the merits of two differing policies. The public had long since picked up the personal hostility that existed between Heath and Wilson and – as it is always easier to think of issues in terms of personalities rather than abstracts – had decided that this was a 'single-combat' affair on presidential lines.

This impression was encouraged by Heath's fighting the election from Smith Square rather than from the more impersonal surroundings of Downing Street; and also because he totally dominated the team around him, so that the Tory Party appeared to the electorate at large as a one-man band (an impression they still give).

Harold Wilson, by contrast, tried hard to push forward those around him. With so many experienced colleagues, this was no hard task (as it had been in 1964 and 1966). Indeed, with Jim Callaghan no push was needed: he had made everything to do with the unions virtually his own, and the Conservatives (still fighting on the 'Who Governs Britain?' question) not unnaturally felt that he was a far more effective performer than his chief.

But by the second week (as Harold Wilson had predicted), other issues that sprang from the Tories' record in government, coupled with the clear need for new policies, came to the fore. Their emergence was helped by the need of the press for a question other than 'Who Governs Britain?' to write about.

Foremost was the country's overwhelming desire (shown by both public and private opinion polls) for tough government action on prices and incomes. At first this and the need for industrial peace and harmony gave an illusory hope to the Tories; but Harold Wilson, knowing that the whole country wanted peace and an end to roaring inflation, and remembering the lessons of 1970, knew that the electorate would vote for the Party whose policy on bringing down both the cost of living and inflation was the more credible. For this, Labour offered the best prospectus: they promised to end confrontation, get Britain working again, and cut inflation through co-operation with the unions.

The publication of the Retail Price Index figures at the start of the second week (on 15 February 1974) focused interest on this issue; it was the first of the turning points in the campaign.

Hand in hand with this went the selling of what was later to be known as the Social Contract. This was the result of a somewhat desperate bid by the Party while in Opposition to remedy what – they felt – had been lacking in previous governments: the full co-operation of the trades union movement on wages and prices. Accordingly, an agreement had been reached on the social and economic policies that should be pursued by a Labour Government when returned to office, and it was assumed that this would secure co-operation on the wages front. But this was never spelled out clearly, with the correspondingly unfortunate effect that during the campaign union leaders often refused to confirm that any such agreement existed – the most damaging occasion being when Hugh Scanlon denied it outright on television. Even Len Murray was lukewarm in his support.

Other issues that arose were North Sea oil (and energy generally), and Europe.

In Scotland, the minority parties – from the Liberals on the one hand to the ScotNats on the other – were gaining ground at the expense of

Labour. Focusing attention on North Sea oil, and Labour's promise to nationalize it, was one way of holding the Labour vote: Harold Wilson's argument that oil should not be 'abstracted from the pockets of the British people for the benefit of overpaid multinational corporations owing no loyalty to this or any other Government' holds as true now as it did then. Indeed, if the oil crisis which occurred just after the 1979 election had happened either just before or during the run-up, Mrs Thatcher's majority might have been a narrow one; the British consumer might have preferred to keep his own oil rather than have it denationalized by the Conservative Party.

Most of the expert advice on this vital fuel as well as on other sources of energy came from Thomas Balogh (who later became Deputy Chairman of the British National Oil Corporation). Invaluable though it was, his frequent telephone cells irritated my colleagues, who did not hesitate to show it. Usually, therefore, it fell to me to speak to him when Harold Wilson was busy, and I had the task of simplifying his messages for transmission to the Leader and bringing the call to an end as quickly as possible when urgent matters demanded attention elsewhere. Later I could reassure him of what was always the fact, namely of his high place in the Leader's estimation and affection which remains to this day, and of the invaluable contribution he was making to the campaign on the energy issue in particular.

Unlike energy and the other main planks of our platform, Europe was an issue apart. True, it had dominated the Parliament prior to the February election; but it was not something that would swing a large number of votes one way or the other.

It was, however, extremely important, though almost more in a negative than a positive sense. Europe could be blamed for many of our economic ills, Europe gave us something to compare our own inflationary difficulties with, Europe was a scapegoat. Labour, therefore, promised a new look at Europe: a renegotiation of Edward Heath's terms of entry into the Common Market so that Britain got a fairer deal.

It was here that an almost farcical element of cloak and dagger crept into the campaign. It had started – rather like a game of Consequences – when Harold Wilson met Enoch Powell in the Gentlemen's lavatory in the Palace of Westminster, just before the beginning of the election campaign. To continue the metaphor, what they talked about (briefly) was the forthcoming campaign, Powell imparting the confidential information that he would be making only two or three big speeches, *and that it was likely these would deal with Europe.*

This was enough for Harold Wilson. He knew that Powell was a man with a large following, especially in key regions like the West Midlands where elections can be won or lost; he knew also that Powell almost invariably received excellent press coverage. If Powell was making Europe his major topic, therefore, Europe would figure largely in the press – and Labour could certainly not afford to ignore it. The problem was that he did not want to appear to follow Powell.

Joe Haines and myself were both privy (if I may use the word in this context) to the Wilson–Powell encounter; and it was through Joe that the eventual 'consequence' came about. A few days into the campaign, Joe told us that Andrew Alexander of the *Daily Mail* had informed him that he would act as the 'go-between', tipping Joe off about the time and place of the Powell speeches. Thanks to these arrangements, Harold Wilson was forewarned about each of the major speeches. Somehow, it felt extraordinary at that time to be acting if not in concert then in reasonably close harmony with the representative of a newspaper that could be called the trumpet of Toryism.

The last week of the campaign opened with two memorable episodes: one of which gave Labour the opportunity of putting across its message to the electorate in no uncertain way, the other being by contrast almost ludicrous. The latter occurred when the film star Gina Lollo- brigida suddenly appeared in the Wilsons' Lord North Street home. Exotically dressed in clothes that focused attention on her well-known figure, wearing what was an attractive and life-like but recognizable wig on her head, and with the beautiful young man who was her assistant in tow, she erupted into the Lord North Street drawing room. Here, in furtherance of the photographic career on which she had just embarked, she placed the Wilsons in various attitudes around the room. The result was a slightly absurd photograph of Harold and Mary. She had apparently been to the Heath office earlier, but I never heard how she (or they) fared.

More important from the political point of view was the Relativities Board Report giving its decision on the miners' dispute, followed almost immediately by the publication of the disastrous trade figures for the previous quarter-year. We could remember what the publication of trade figures showing a deficit so tiny as to be almost comic had done to us in 1970; that day's – thanks mainly to the energy crisis and its effect on world prices – was enormous. We seized the opportunity of saying that as Labour had been successful in clearing up the mess last time, we were the Party who could do it again now. To put this message across required not only the right emphasis but the right timing, all of which was to be settled in the course of one memorable evening.

Joe and I were alone in the Leader's Room when the news came through on the evening of 21 February (via a leak from the Pay Board). It was, clearly, a bombshell of the first order: the nation was to be told in so many words that the Government had been wrong on the stand it had taken against the miners. Equally clearly, as we were obviously among the first to know about this, it was important that we made the most of this tremendous opportunity. The first priority was to get a speedy message through to Harold Wilson; and also, straightaway, to tell Ron Hayward, the General Secretary, in case he had to field any queries before the Leader could be got hold of. We went straight down to his room to tell him, and then began to try and track down the Leader. While I sat at the telephone, Joe worked out a brief statement, which we felt would give Harold Wilson the initiative that night; it was to be followed up by weightier, more considered remarks the next day. It all went according to plan; we were very satisfied with that evening's work.

Other occasions also stand out clearly in my memory, especially the 'gossip sessions' that Bernard, Joe and I used to have together on the days when there were no planned meetings or conferences. One unusual evening saw a burst of high spirits from Bernard at the re-emergence of the Liberal Party as a force to be reckoned with.

'It's just like 1924,' he said delightedly, adding that, yes, of course, we would like to win outright – but how exciting would be another 1924 situation with all that it might mean for politics in the future. Should the Liberals succeed in holding the middle ground between the two Parties and the balance, he forecast 'a colourful and exciting' period ahead.

He was right in that the real menace to both Parties during those closing days of the campaign came from the strength of the Liberals.

At both Parties' morning press conferences, questions flew thick and fast as to what would happen if there was a stalemate caused by a high Liberal vote on Polling Day. As it was, the Liberal vote was to prove the key to the election. Labour had taken the decision not to refer to it, as it was felt that a blanket of silence might minimize this danger, whereas any reference – however derogatory – would only serve to build it up. The Tories felt the same, perhaps with more reason, as when the Tories are in office the Liberal protest vote inevitably rises.

That February, it was surging ahead, giving Jeremy Thorpe and the Liberal Party momentary delusions of power – and causing the Tories more than the usual number of headaches. Thorpe himself stated clearly to them that he would only co-operate 'outside' a government; the Labour Party in its turn later could only get Liberal co-operation in a pact without Jeremy Thorpe.

From then on, it became a major objective of both the far Left and the far Right to get rid of Jeremy Thorpe, the man who symbolized the Liberal resurgence and had managed to mobilize the large Liberal vote.

I single out one other occasion because, retrospectively, it was amusing, and because it showed how completely both sides in that February election were misled by the opinion polls. These polls had been so bad, with even the private ones spelling gloom and doom, that Joe – a great worrier at times – spent most of one evening asking, rhetorically of course, what was the best way for Harold Wilson to announce his resignation. 'Should it be after he is defeated on Polling Day, or should he stay on for the Party Conference?' he demanded.

Edward Heath, too, was mistakenly thinking that he would win with a clear majority. Our most optimistic forecast was that we were in with a chance – but only just. The only person cheerful about the outcome was Albert Murray; but then, he was travelling with the Leader and actually seeing how large was his following in the country and the size and enthusiasm of the crowds who gathered to hear him speak. Albert, who had lost his own seat in 1970, was extremely sensitive to election atmospheres. I felt I could rely on his reaction; moreover, I was determined to believe that we were going to win.

There was also another 'happening', a personal one that was to cause me great unhappiness. One afternoon at the beginning of the third week, the *Guardian* rang and asked to speak to me. I was out of the office, and fortunately Joe Haines took the call. It was about the land my brother owned at Wigan. (As the whole issue is dealt with later in Chapter 16 of this book, I shall merely say here how it affected my campaign work.)

Joe, who had got to know my brother quite well when Tony had been coming to the office prior to 1973, knew most of the background. He knew also that, as nationalization had figured largely in our campaign, those who sold land at a profit, even if it was land worked on previously, were by definition 'land speculators'. He therefore felt that any story about this must be kept out of the press until after Polling Day – especially when he and Bernard discovered that the *Daily Mail* were also making enquiries and had posted a photographer and a reporter in Smith Square, where they were sitting in a parked car.

Joe therefore rang me to tell me not to come back to the office, so for the rest of that day I worked at home. A bright note was a telephone call from Bernard, saying he would be along with the bottle of champagne given to us earlier by Harold Lever as a morale-booster; we had been going to drink this in the office, but he thought this would be a good moment and would cheer me up. So he came to my house, and we drank champagne and talked about what the future might hold, in more ways than one. As neither paper pursued the story next day I thought, mistakenly, that one potential storm cloud had drifted away, and that there was nothing to deflect me from total concentration on political rather than personal affairs.

NINE

The February 1974 Election

With hindsight, it is clear that until the last moment – and almost beyond it – Edward Heath thought he would win the February 1974 election with a clear majority. As it was, many Tories believed that if the campaign had taken place three weeks earlier (as had been mooted) the Government would have won. I myself doubt this: they had been unpopular before the confrontation with the miners and the long hard winter that followed – far more unpopular than the miners, as it turned out.

But, their Leader apart, most of the Tories were less than positive that they would win. We were in the same frame of mind. Not one of us had ever before known a situation where coalition was such a strong possibility; although Harold Wilson remained confident that if he could obtain even a small majority on Polling Day, he could build upon this for the next election. What few of us realized was that we were entering a very volatile period in politics.

All in all, though, we felt pleased with the way we had fought the campaign; we had been far more professional than in any previous ones I had had experience of. The other 'magic ingredient' was excitement: 1974 echoed the high drama of that election ten years earlier when Labour had snatched power from the Tories after thirteen years of Conservative government. Admittedly, there had only been three and a half years of Edward Heath to argue over this time, but the State of Emergency added fuel to the fire of argument; and the electorate itself was far more sophisticated than it had been in those earlier days, when even the basic premises had seemed simpler.

Today, there were the creation of images as well as the debates on policies, the personality clashes, the increased role played by the media, the argument about u-turns and broken promises, and, what is perhaps a twentieth-century phenomenon, the credibility gap.

So this exhilarating campaign drew to a close. With the last press conference came the summing-up of the main lines of argument deployed throughout; for Labour, these had been based on the ten points Harold Wilson had set out in his Bolton speech.

Repeatedly, he had said during the campaign that Labour expected to be judged on how they delivered these promises – a pledge that was greeted at every meeting by a roar of applause from an audience cynically aware of the fragility of politicians' vows. By 1976, when Harold Wilson left office, he was able to claim that most of the ten points and the Manifesto commitments had already been honoured by government or legislative action.

During the last few days of the campaign there was one notable meeting. Early one evening Ron Hayward rang to ask whether the Leader could look in, if only for a few minutes, to shake hands with someone he described as 'a special friend' of the Party's. Together Harold Wilson and I went down to meet this special visitor. 'May I introduce you', said Ron Hayward, 'to Eric Miller.'

I had seen him briefly only once before, at the London Labour Mayors' Association annual dinner in December 1973. We shook hands, exchanged a few words, and returned upstairs to prepare for the Leader's evening meeting.

A few days later there came a second call; this time, Harold Wilson was not in the office, so I went down to the General Secretary's room on my own to exchange, again briefly, the cordialities I felt were due to someone who had always been a great supporter of the Party, and who was close to Ron Hayward. Ron, who was moving house, needed a London base during these vital three weeks, and Eric Miller gave him one in Park West, a block of flats in the Edgware Road that he owned – a kindly and helpful gesture from the Treasurer of the Socialist International, a colleague and a supporter.

Finally there came the moment when everything we could do towards victory had been done. All that remained was to wait and work. Harold Wilson, as always, went to his constituency for the Eve of Poll and Polling Day itself. He took with him to Liverpool a large entourage, the senior members of which travelled with the Wilsons on the small executive jet hired by Transport House, the others by car and train.

With the feeling that everything was now out of our hands, the tension lessened, and the atmosphere was rather like an end-of-term party, with everyone making jokes, talking and enjoying the relaxation of the journey north.

In Liverpool, we were met by our drivers, who had gone ahead from London, and taken to our first-floor headquarters in the Edwardian elegance of the Adelphi Hotel. All five of Harold Wilson's election campaigns had ended there, four of them successfully, and the hotel was quite used to the whole campaign circus, with its swarms of journalists, cameras, lights, cables, food and drink at odd hours, and constant telephoning.

For his staff, there was now little to do except cope with press enquiries and keep in touch with London; for the Leader, it was much more hectic – a whirlwind tour of as many meetings and committee rooms as possible in his own constituency, under the auspices of his devoted and capable Huyton agent Arthur Smith.

Like all good agents, Arthur Smith was slightly contemptuous of the sizeable entourage that surrounded the Leader. He believed in small numbers, and as the allocation of tickets for the Polling Day count (as well as the size of the band allowed to accompany the Leader on his constituency visits) was entirely in his hands, it should have been no surprise that only two were marked 'Staff'. I got one, doubtless because I had been present at all Harold Wilson's counts since 1959; the other went to Joe Haines. In fact, except from the point of view of comfort these tickets made very little difference: everyone else sat in the large room next door, where there were armchairs, television sets, coffee, and a general atmosphere of relaxation. The Huyton with Roby Local Authority (now expanded and renamed Knowsley), under Donald Willgoose, were efficient and generous hosts.

That Leap Year, Polling Day dawned cold and rainy. Mary and Harold Wilson went off early on their committee room tours; we – in contrast to the frenzy of the past few weeks – were left momentarily in limbo while we waited for the last act of the drama to be played.

Bernard, always lively and a 'mover', decided that we ought to go out for 'a brisk walk'. We set off, a disparate but closely welded group: Bernard in his big white shaggy fur coat; Terry Boston – the former Labour MP for Faversham who lost his seat in 1970, and is now Lord Boston of Faversham and chairman of Television South – living up to his image as a City lawyer in a formal suit; Harry Mitchell – the Assistant General Secretary of the Parliamentary Labour Party and senior campaign aide – with his trilby hat and warm woolly scarf; and myself

in raincoat and headscarf. Our verbal contributions were as characteristic as our sartorial ones: Bernard was funny, jokey and entertaining,
Terry polite and deferential, Harry as non-committal as a Party official
can be. All of us, however, were equally refreshed and invigorated by
that hour spent walking on the Liverpool waterfront.

The day drew on. By late afternoon, we had organized a meal for the
staff in the Leader's room; it was served on small trolley tables. By this
time, the earlier slow-motion effect had passed, and the atmosphere was
more like that of a speeded-up film as waiters darted around with dishes
and plates serving everyone, while between them people rushed in and
out with reports on last-minute crises, rumours, or exciting new developments. In the background, there was the non-stop, stomach-turning
pontificating by the various well-known pundits with which television
fills in the long hours before the first results come in. We made up our
minds that once a clear trend one way or the other was perceptible, we
would leave the Adelphi and move over to a small hotel called The
Golden Eagle, in Kirkby, in Harold Wilson's constituency.

The timing of this had to be exact. Harold Wilson wanted to arrive
in his constituency neither too early, before we knew what was happening, nor too late, so that everybody else did. He did not relish the idea
of having to return all the way to Liverpool after his count to face the
press, whichever way the result went.

Accordingly, rooms were booked for senior staff members at The
Golden Eagle, an hotel that had been built in the 1960s to take the new
trade from Merseyside, but which by now had become rather down-
at-heel. Other members of the staff were left behind at the Adelphi; and
this helped to disguise our 'flight'.

By now, rested and fed and prepared as well as we could be for the
long night ahead, we were all gathered in Harold Wilson's suite,
crowded closely against each other on sofas and chairs ranged in a
semi-circle round the television set. Harold Wilson, as usual, had an
armchair by the door near his bedroom, but he hardly sat in it, preferring to walk up and down. Occasionally, when he wanted to think
carefully about a particular result and discuss its implications with us,
he would sit down. As always, results were coming slowly during this
early part of the night, but it was clear straightaway that there was a
swing, and that it was in our favour.

What also soon became obvious was that the Liberals were polling
very heavily indeed. Harold Wilson had already calculated how seriously this would affect the overall vote; when the results began to come

in from the regions, we were to see that the minority parties also were polling in a similarly forceful way. It soon became clear that, although the figures showed a Labour lead, any victory was going to be a narrow one.

But before victory was anything but a wild and joyful surmise, there was a telephone summons for the Leader to come to his constituency for his own count. As we left the hotel, after hearing only the first few results, we walked through a great crowd of Liverpudlians, cheering and clapping, who had gathered to see Harold Wilson leave for Huyton. I had not seen this sight since 1966, and it seemed like a good omen.

The journey to Huyton seemed endless. Our car radios were turned up full to catch the results that were now coming faster. At one point, the Leader stopped our motorcade and came back to the car in which Joe, Bernard and myself were travelling, and we held a quick *ad hoc* discussion on the implications of the Liberal vote, now emerging more clearly than ever as a threat to any form of decisive majority.

By the time we arrived at Huyton, one thing was clear to me at any rate. The Lancashire police thought that the Leader of the Opposition was about to become Prime Minister for the third time. I remembered how great in 1970, when all the expectations were that we would win, their numbers had been on our arrival at Huyton – and how dramatically those numbers had dropped by the time, disaster staring us in the face, we had left. Today, a large contingent of the Merseyside Force was mingling with the local Huyton police who had performed so excellently this protective function for Harold Wilson at intervals over the last seventeen years.

We settled ourselves in the room next to the large hall where the count was taking place. Bernard and Joe sat making calculations in their notebooks as the results came in. Harold Wilson increased his own majority substantially and – after making as always some kind and friendly remarks to his defeated Conservative opponent – emerged from the count looking happy. After a brief assessment of the results so far with his staff, he was whisked away to the Huyton Labour Club to thank his supporters. They had not only held the vote for him during four campaigns, but increased it.

Here, in the small hours, euphoria ruled: loud music, bright lights, full glasses, excited people all greeting Harold and Mary with warmth and celebration. For Joe and Bernard, it was their first sight of an election night party with the Leader – a victorious Leader – present. By the time the speeches were made, we were all a little tearful. We left the

Huyton Club with laughter and cheers ringing in our ears.

Our hearing was restored to normal pretty smartly on arrival at The Golden Eagle. The lady on the desk greeted us with a welcome that was less than rapturous: indeed, her disapproval suggested that, if it had been left to her, all the rooms we needed would have been boarded up before our arrival. But it was election night and we could not be put off – let alone by a few frowns. We went first to the large private dining room set aside for us, to confer over the results and discuss the implications for the morning. We could see that we were unlikely to have a majority, but also that we would be the largest Party. Bernard was the only one really fascinated by this. Here was the 1924 situation he had anticipated. For Harold Wilson, the main victory was the moral one. By the time we went to bed, I was feeling cold, a little bleak and overwhelmingly tired.

A few hours later, we were up again. First there was a press conference at the Adelphi, then we were whisked off to Liverpool Airport to catch the plane back to London, surrounded by the same considerable police strength. We spent the flight comparing the present situation with past events in Labour's history, and trying to calculate Edward Heath's reasoning. By this time, Heath himself was back in London, unwilling to admit defeat but unable to claim victory.

From London Airport, we were driven to Transport House. The election scene here will be familiar to anyone who has ever accompanied a victorious Leader to his headquarters: a swarming cluster of photographers round both entrances to Transport House, lights slung across the square, milling reporters, TV cameras everywhere with their usual accompaniment of a quantity of large parked vans; down the road at the Wilsons' home, 5 Lord North Street, it was the same. Ahead of us lay a curious three days.

We went straight to the Wilsons' house in Lord North Street, for a quick preliminary meeting before facing everyone at Transport House. It was almost impossible to reach the door of Number 5: pressmen, cameras and photographers were crammed into the narrow street, all jostling and shouting as they jockeyed for a better view.

The police came to the rescue, and with their help the crowd parted to let Harold and Mary Wilson through and into their home. Alas, it closed after them like the Red Sea, leaving the staff to fight their way through as best they could. Once again, the police moved forward, and with their help we fell across the threshold clutching bags, papers, briefcases and, in some cases, each other. Once inside, the rooms were lit up by the brilliant TV lights outside, and we had to speak in hushed voices because the press on the narrow pavement were so close to the windows.

The respite was only momentary. Once Harold Wilson had deposited his personal baggage, it was out through the *mêlée* and over to Transport House. This time we were followed by a throng of pressmen and preceded by photographers, running backwards on the pavements in front of us as they clicked away furiously during the five-minute walk.

In Transport House there was no sign of the previous night's euphoria. No one doubted that if a Labour Government was formed, there would be a bumpy ride ahead. In 1964 we had had a majority, albeit a tiny one; now we were simply the largest Party. Once again, the name of Ramsay MacDonald hung in the air. We tried to raise our spirits by thinking of Heath sitting it out at Number 10, refusing to concede though the victory was really ours. 'Rather as if the referee had blown the whistle and one side had refused to leave the field,' commented Harold Wilson.

No one knew exactly what was happening. I remember leaning out of the window of our rooms above Ron Hayward's office to see if there were any signs of jubilation, or sudden surge of pressmen, on the other side of Smith Square, which could have meant that Edward Heath had by some miracle put a government together with the Liberals or some other grouping. Later we learned that their mood of uncertainty was rather similar to our own.

Indecision is enervating. It was agreed that Harold Wilson should call a meeting of as many members of the Shadow Cabinet as possible for later that day; meanwhile, we would all go back to Lord North Street to await events – events which might include a telephone call from Number 10 or the Palace. In any case, we were all hungry, and at the Wilsons' home we could get sandwiches and hot coffee. Once again, there was the trek through photographers and pressmen; once again, the hushed voices in the brilliantly lit rooms.

The long day wore on. By the time it was dark, Robin and Joy Wilson had arrived from Oxford; Harold's sister Marjorie Wilson, Mrs Pollard the housekeeper, the Wilsons themselves and their son Giles, Gerald Kaufman, Joe, Bernard, Albert Murray and myself were all there, glued to the television and radio sets in the drawing room to try and find out what was happening at Number 10.

Gradually it became clear that Edward Heath was going to consult at some length, and that nothing would happen before the weekend was out. When my advice was asked, I said I thought that the Wilsons should go off to Grange Farm, partly to try and spend a restful weekend, partly because staying in London looked over-anxious. Jim Callaghan said exactly the same thing later. Before I left that evening, the Wilsons had settled on doing this; they had also decided that if Harold did become Prime Minister they would continue to live in Lord North Street and use Number 10 only for official work (there were plenty of precedents for this, including Clem Attlee).

That evening I was glad to go home, dazed as I still was by the turn of events and completely exhausted. Next morning, after a good night's sleep, I also went down to Buckinghamshire, to my own home near Grange Farm.

All that weekend the telephone did not stop. Some calls were congratulatory, some sycophantic, some from people who were worried by the long wait. I spoke to most of my colleagues and, in particular, had several long conversations with Bernard, who reaffirmed his belief in the need for a Policy Unit at Number 10 and for his own appointment. He also wanted to find out about salary and what his title would be. All of this I passed on to Harold Wilson, who that weekend definitely decided to take Bernard in with him.

The weekend was made particularly vivid by Jeremy Thorpe's domination of the media. He seemed to be always on television, making visits to Number 10 in a blaze of publicity – the natural outcome of his enormous success in the election campaign, which had resulted in him becoming a powerful national figure with a large personal following. At this moment, he had the centre of the stage, and he played the part for all it was worth. All the same, we did not feel seriously worried that he would link up with Heath in a Conservative–Liberal coalition: his natural political inclinations were to the Left, and an accommodation with us would have been more to his liking.

While Edward Heath attempted to put something together to save his Government, Harold Wilson was relaxing. It was a genuine relaxation: even at the most stressful times he has always had the ability to 'unwind' completely given a few hours' break. In the bright, clear, cold weather, he went out for walks, was photographed kicking a ball for the approval of his dog Paddy and the assembled photographers, and strolled round the garden.

By Sunday evening, we were all back at a meeting in Lord North Street. We expected Edward Heath's efforts to run out of steam within the next twenty-four hours. Joe, Bernard, Albert Murray, the Wilson family and myself met again in the drawing room, this time to make arrangements for the following day. It was a momentous occasion, this feeling that we were on the eve of confirmation of a victory so little expected. Harold Wilson, as always at moments of great importance, was calm. Knowing that we would be almost too tense to think the next day, we seized the opportunity of making a final decision on the Wilson family's living arrangements, and sorting out the technicalities of the return to Downing Street.

As for the major business, that of the nation, Harold Wilson had already discussed with senior colleagues the need for immediate meet- ings with both the CBI and the TUC to achieve the ending of the miners' strike, the State of Emergency and a return to normal work.

Everyone was making plans. Bernard was especially effervescent: it was a heady atmosphere for right-wingers. He was convinced that the Liberals would keep a Labour Government in office to prevent a Tory return, and told me that John Pardoe – Liberal MP for Cornwall North and a friend of his – had already intimated as much.

That evening when we broke up, Bernard took me home in a taxi, which drove us past the rear of Downing Street. We saw the lights burning in the Prime Minister's study and knew there was no escap- ing the events of the morrow. Bernard's expression was one of fascina- tion: for him, the scene was a glittering one, hitherto unobtainable for someone like him with his ultra-right-wing friends and contacts in the Party and with his former secretaryship of the Campaign for Democratic Socialism – the forerunner of today's Social Democrats.

Next day we were back early at Lord North Street. Everything was the same: the pressmen, photographers, TV cameras, the walk across to Transport House accompanied by hurrying members of the media, some trailing behind seemingly like the tail of a comet, the paper cups of coffee, the discussions about the future. Without the stimulus of certainty and action, we all experienced the feeling of unreality, of tension, almost of a curious lethargy, that overhangs any period of waiting.

Suddenly, during the afternoon, events started to move. It became clear that we could expect a message from Number 10 by the late afternoon. And sure enough, around 4.00 p.m. Robert Armstrong, the Principal Private Secretary, rang to say that the Prime Minister was going to the Palace at 6.30.

Everything began to move fast. My next call was from Sir Martin

Charteris, the Queen's Private Secretary (and now Lord Charteris), at the Palace. I remember his exact words, because they were far less formal than I had imagined. 'Would it be convenient, Marcia, for Harold Wilson to be at the Palace at 7.00 p.m.?'

We set off in three cars – Harold Wilson wanted all his family with him, as well as his senior staff – and, while he went into the Palace, we waited outside. Inside the Palace, Robert Armstrong was awaiting Harold Wilson, having seen Heath leave after tendering his resignation; a perfect example of the public servant's role: 'The King is dead, long live the King.'

Before leaving for the Palace, Harold Wilson had time to tour Transport House, thank the staff and have a drink with the General Secretary. As he proceeded to repair to the Palace, I told him that, with his permission, after the Palace visit I would go home; as I had explained to him, as well as to the others, I did not want to be involved in the return to Number 10. I really did not feel that I could face for a second time what was likely to be a struggle for power similar to that of 1964.

But Bernard, Joe and Gerald Kaufman, who was also with us, insisted that I should go with them to Downing Street. It was unthinkable for me to go home, they said, when we ought all to be arriving in force at Number 10, to show from the outset our intention of a strong political presence. While we waited in the car, parked in the Palace courtyard, as the Leader of the Opposition kissed hands and became Prime Minister, I repeated my view and again came their reassurances that we would be united and strong enough to do any necessary fighting together, but my bones told me that it would not work out like that. Nor did it.

The doors of Buckingham Palace opened and the Prime Minister appeared at the top of the red-carpeted steps. Accompanied by Sir Martin Charteris, he walked quickly towards us. Sir Martin, who had spotted me sitting in the second car, came over to exchange a brief and pleasant word or two while the Prime Minister was getting into his own car; then the police waved us forward – and on to Downing Street.

It was a journey heavy with precedent and authority from the moment we drove through the great archway and into the wide expanse of the forecourt of Buckingham Palace. Out through those high Palace gates we went, past the waiting press, the flashing cameras, the excited and enthusiastic crowd, and down the Mall towards Horseguards Parade. Here we turned right. As the Prime Minister's car swung across

Horseguards Parade, the sentries posted under Horseguards Arch saluted – apart from royalty, only the Prime Minister and his Cabinet Ministers may drive this way into Whitehall. Slowly we passed under the Arch, and into the street of government on the other side. In Downing Street, the crowds were already waiting to cheer the Prime Minister back into office; he was out of his car as soon as it stopped and, with Mary at his side, paused only to wave and say a few words about a job to be done and the need for getting on with it right away before hurrying into Number 10.

Behind the Wilsons, Bernard, Joe, Gerald and myself got out of our car a little farther down the street. Bernard put his arm firmly through mine and propelled me through the cheerful crowd into the silent hallway that I knew so well.

In another few minutes Big Ben had struck 8.00 p.m. The staff fulfilled the Downing Street tradition of clapping and cheering the newly elected Prime Minister into Number 10. As I saw among them the familiar faces of some of the policemen, custodians and messengers, as well as senior staff, it was as though the past three and a half years had melted away.

As we were greeted by the staff of Edward Heath's Private Office, I was struck again by the absurd but curious strength of the British system: here were the same people who only a few minutes ago had been saying goodbye to a Tory Prime Minister after nearly four years of implementing his wishes and who now had to perform of an instant mental switchround in order to give the best possible advice to Harold Wilson, whose own orders they would then have to carry out. Instead of uttering these thoughts, however, we introduced Bernard to them. A measure of our self-conscious wariness was that we were most careful to call him 'Dr' Donoughue to make the introduction more effective.

First, we were given a celebratory drink in the Cabinet Room – unthinkable back in 1964 when the personal staff of that day were all confined to different rooms, separated not only from the Prime Minister but from each other. And then to work.

I went back to my old room, newly vacated by Douglas Hurd, who as Political Secretary had worked there during the Heath years. How familiar it looked, with its beautiful deep Georgian sash windows overlooking that part of the back garden of Number 10 that was shared with Number 11, its Suffolk School oils of seascapes and the small portraits on the cream half-panelled walls. There were even the same almond green carpet and deep green curtains and, above all, the same massive double-fronted desk with its cupboards on one side and drawers on the other.

It was a room with two doors. The one opening into the main corridor that leads to the massive front door of Number 10 is faintly unusual: it had originally been a double door, and opens out of the room instead of into it. The other one opens into the Cabinet Room – as did the Private Secretary's room – so that we both had access if the Prime Minister was working in the Cabinet Room, as Harold Wilson used to in the main in the 1960s. This time, however, it would happen that he mainly worked from his upstairs study.

While I was absorbing all this familiar detail, Joe Haines had gone directly to the Press Office (at the other end of the corridor) to study what was needed and to prepare for press statements, such as the announcement of Government appointments that would obviously be made that evening. Bernard was taken round to George Wigg's old offices and, within hours, looked very much at home.

A whole working week lay ahead. This time I was not exhausted, as I had been in 1964, having had precious sleep and rest over the weekend to revive me after the hard work and tensions of the election campaign. This time, our whole team was more experienced, our vision was sharper, clearer, our aims were more definite. In terms of office structure and behaviour, we knew exactly what we did *not* want – something almost more important than a more positive approach when dealing with the Civil Service.

I looked round my room. It was a little more worn, a little more faded and could, I decided, do with a larger bookcase and a television set. Essentially, though, it was the same, with the same atmosphere as when I had last stood there four years ago. As I snapped out the light on that Monday evening of 4 March 1974, I did not know how different everything else was going to be for me.

TEN

Return to Number 10

Going back into Number 10 was both daunting and, in many ways, depressing. First, of course, we *knew* that we were going back into crisis – into crisis on a scale that had been made familiar by the very circumstances of life that spring in 1974. It is true that 1964 had also been a time of crisis, but Labour had been unaware of its extent until the arrival in Downing Street, when 'the books' were opened.

On a personal level, excitement and the thrill of novelty had been replaced by the knowledge of the limitations (especially on personal freedom) that being in office entailed.

Number 10 has to be able to contact senior staff at all times, rather as a doctor is 'on call' even when off duty; this means that every time you so much as go to the dentist, let alone on holiday, out to dinner, or to any less formal engagement, your address and telephone number have to be known to quite a few other people within the building. There is also the intangible but no less pressing consideration that you are, to however small a degree, in the public eye rather than being a purely private person.

This rule of immediate accessibility was obviously necessary for myself, as Political Secretary and personal aide to the Prime Minister; but it applied equally to everyone else employed along with me, or whom I employed in the Political Office. Most of the staff there were those who had been working in the Opposition Political Office – girls like Doreen Andrew, who had been with us since 1965 (with a brief spell away working for the Deputy Leader of the Party) and who still works at the House of Commons. Two others were Clare Dent, recruited from the Civil Service in 1966, who worked in the Political Office from then on both in office and Opposition until she finally left in 1976; and

Susan Utting, a slightly more recent arrival – she joined in 1973 – who worked first on the general side of the Political Office for me and then as a secretary to Harold Wilson from 1976 until the present day.

One of the nicest aspects of working in the Political Office was undoubtedly the ties of friendship it formed: I am still in touch with a great number of those who worked there from the first two governments on. Some I see or write to; Christmas, birthdays and weddings are occasions for being in touch with others, and then there is always the small party that we try to give every year for some former and present staff and friends.

In 1964 the Political Office had not existed. At its inception, it had consisted of one woman and two assistants; now in 1974 it was a team of people used to working together who moved back into Number 10 as a political presence.

Nevertheless, despite these years of precedent, there was a certain amount of confrontation with the Civil Service of the type so familiar of old. New colleagues and situations were 'sussed out' in the way that, I suppose, normally heralds an arrival at any office.

For my part, as I said earlier, I had no wish to go back. At all costs, I wanted to avoid the situation in which I had found myself in 1964; then, I had been engaged in a daily struggle. In that context, I had to attempt the construction of something that would be a beneficial influence politically.

It had been a nightmarish existence. I did not want to go through the difficulties that I had then endured all over again. Everything had seemed to be cause for debate of some kind, from the serious matter of how much time a Prime Minister should devote to political work to the most trivial details – whether or not I was qualified for tea on a tray in china teacups or coffee in a silver pot served in my room, or just a mug of tea made upstairs.

One particularly long-running dispute in the 1960s had been over the Downing Street writing paper. Was the Political Office, situated as it physically was in Number 10, allowed to use writing paper with the distinctive black Number 10 heading?

We understood the Civil Service's point of view. Number 10 notepaper (redesigned while we were there from the old Gothic typeface in use since notepaper was first printed for Number 10 to a plain modern heading) has an immediate impact in Whitehall. The moment this famous address, printed in black on a white ground, appears in front of a civil servant's eyes, he knows he is receiving a communication either direct from the Prime Minister or from someone extremely close to the seat of power. He regards the contents of such a letter with especial interest.

Naturally, the Civil Service wished to establish that anyone using this distinctive notepaper would use it with responsibility. But the argument was not so much about *how* we in the Political Office used it, but whether we were allowed to use it at all. As our address was Number 10, Downing Street, it seemed to us absurd that we were not allowed to say so. Eventually, we wound up with a compromise: our notepaper was headed in red instead of black so that, in Whitehall, we were recognized as the political arm of the Prime Minister. When Edward Heath came to power there was no such dispute: his Political Office immediately used the normal Number 10 paper – as we finally managed to. This kind of storm-within-an-inkwell was not merely boring, it was time-consuming. I had no wish to undergo those experiences again.

Even my title had caused difficulty in the 1960s. In Opposition, I had been the Private Secretary to the Leader of the Party and, as such, in charge of his Private Office. But in the Number 10 of 1964 this was impossible: the words 'Private Office' referred to a completely different department run by the Civil Service, so to call me 'Private Secretary' there, it was argued, would have been misleading. Nor could I be called 'Personal Secretary', because all the Garden Room girls, the Civil Service shorthand typists at Number 10, were each, individually, known as the Prime Minister's Personal Secretary. Political Secretary on its own was a far from adequate description: although essentially political, my work spread into many other areas (including that covered by any good personal aide).

Eventually, and after an amount of argument that seemed to have become almost routine where Downing Street and the Political Office were concerned, I wound up as Political and Personal Secretary to the Prime Minister, an ungainly title that singled me out.

My own preference would have been simply to have been added to the list of Private Secretaries. If John Wyndham could be Harold Macmillan's Private Secretary without being on the Civil Service pay list, why could Marcia Williams not be Harold Wilson's Private Secretary on the same basis? The fact that John Wyndham volunteered his services to Harold Macmillan, while I was paid by Harold Wilson, was in this context irrelevant.

When we went back in 1974 the whole atmosphere in Downing Street was much more relaxed and flexible. The Political Office had continued throughout Edward Heath's tenure and survived as an established fact; certain posts – such as that of Political Press Officer, which had caused so much argument with the Civil Service in the earlier Government – were now accepted and integrated into the machinery of Number 10. Many of the staff were familiar and friendly.

So back I went into the room that I had first been given in 1964.

At first, Joe Haines and Bernard Donoughue took a severe view of the Private Secretaries already in Downing Street when Harold Wilson arrived in March 1974, among them Robert Armstrong, a personable, likeable man with a high reputation.

They asked me to put to the Prime Minister the suggestion that Robert Armstrong, and most of the other Private Secretaries, should be moved on as quickly as it was possible to arrange their promotions. I told them that I would put to the Prime Minister what they had said – namely that he should let the Principal Private Secretary go, and possibly one or two other senior people in the Private Office, replacing them with his own selections – and make it clear that they both regarded this as a priority. I acted as promised, and he turned down the suggestion at once.

For myself, I found Robert Armstrong extremely courteous, easy to get on with, and apparently anxious to make sure that those who came in with the Prime Minister were made happy and welcome. The other Private Secretaries were certainly talented people: particularly Robin Butler (now Principal Private Secretary to Margaret Thatcher at Number 10), whom I would describe as a high flyer; Nick Stuart, now in the Department of Education and Science; and Lord Bridges, the Foreign Office Private Secretary. Indeed, I cannot recall any time in Number 10 when the staff was not of top quality, though those there during the 1960s have been particularly successful. That was never the problem.

In those early days of March 1974, however, the question was: how long would we be in Downing Street? Although the largest single Party, Labour had no overall majority to give it a reasonable parliamentary base. Instead, we had to rely on minority Parties to support and act on legislation introduced.

Even more to the point, we had returned to Downing Street surrounded by the outward evidence of crisis: the three-day week, limitations on lighting and heating, and the early shutting-down of television programmes. Political commentators were asking: 'Is Britain ungovernable?' As for the economic situation, there was an astronomically large

balance of payments deficit (incurred in part by the oil imports bill) –
in 1964 a 'mere' £800 million deficit had left everybody speechless.

In 1974, the whole country knew that we were in a state of national
emergency – something unheard of in peacetime since the General
Strike of 1926. The election itself had been fought in terms of crisis, with
Edward Heath emphasizing the dire effect the increase in oil prices had
had on the international scene and the domestic emergency due to the
challenge to the authority of government by the trades union movement
in general and the miners in particular.

In the Labour movement we found it difficult to understand why a
Conservative Government had, in view of their own historic past, picked
what so clearly seemed the wrong field of battle. Rights and wrongs
apart, mining is a very emotive industry: the miners themselves have
strong ties and loyalties, and rightly feel that no one who does not lead
half their life underground knows what it is like; the general public has
a picture of a dark, dirty and dangerous industry (although it is true
that many pits have now with modernization been transformed). With
sympathy for the miners existing almost as part of the national sub-
conscious, with the memory of Baldwin's mistake over the last miners'
strike, Edward Heath's choice of opponent seemed surprising then –
and in retrospect even more so.

These were pressing problems indeed (and their weightiness was
aggravated by the knowledge that, with no overall majority, one shrewd
blow by the Opposition might force Labour out of office). Central to
them all was the need to establish co-operation between the Government and the trades union movement without resort to a statutory
prices and incomes policy. A counter-inflationary policy was to prove
crucial to Labour's survival as inflation rates soared until, by July 1975,
there was a record level of 26.3 per cent over the previous year.

Much work also had to be done during those early months to establish
what terms would be on offer from Europe to a Labour Government in
the renegotiations we had promised before the case for staying in the
Market could be put to the country.

So major, interdependent and complex were these two problems that
the Prime Minister quickly decided that no real progress could be made
on inflation until the whole question of the Common Market had been
resolved. It was not, therefore, until after the Referendum in 1975 that
he was able to turn his full attention to the second essential: curbing the
inflationary spiral.

Running through this whole period was the separate, unrelated, but constantly weeping sore that was the Irish situation. The Heath Government's Sunningdale proposals for power-sharing between all the parties in Northern Ireland had recently come into effect; but by the time Labour took over, power-sharing in Stormont had begun to break down – thanks largely to the ultra-Protestant Right. Murders and other acts of violence dominated those early months of the Labour Government, followed by a sudden, outright challenge to the Stormont Government by workers on the Right in the form of a general strike. This in turn resulted in whole sections of the community being cut off from food and energy supplies, the calling-in of the army, with more soldiers brought over from the mainland; finally, in the summer the breakdown of the Stormont Parliament and the return to direct rule.

Looking back, 'breakdown' seems the operative word for that whole period. It was evident in whatever area you looked at: from the relationship of government to the miners and the smooth running of industry in general in the United Kingdom, to Europe with the uncertainty over the Market; and in Ireland, with its breakdown and withdrawal of democratic government – as well as the constant 'incidents' that were merely a polite term for murder.

For Harold Wilson, the exhaustion and difficulties of this period were aggravated by the continuing disagreement within the Party on Europe. On the other two issues there was a consensus view, but even in Government there were the same two bitterly opposed factions on Europe within the Party as there had been during the years of Opposition.

Domestically, the outcome was happier. The closer relationship that had been forged with the trades union movement during the years of Opposition helped secure a speedy end to the miners' strike and the State of Emergency. The promise of co-operation on the unions' side was given in return for government legislation on certain aspects of economic and social policy they regarded as essential to a favourable working climate.

The speed and smoothness with which this first, essential priority was put into action was noticeable (especially to those close to the Prime Minister) when contrasted with the initial climate of the 1964 Government. Then, although Harold Wilson knew how government worked because he had previously been in a Cabinet, his Cabinet colleagues had in the main been newcomers to government; whilst in 1974 most of the Cabinet had already held office in previous Governments and were thus experienced administrators familiar with the procedural methods of the Civil Service.

ELEVEN

The Political Office

Such is the prestige, the aura of power and political glamour that emanates from Number 10 Downing Street, that it is easy to forget that its occupant holds not only the highest office in the land, but another position as well. In addition to being Prime Minister, he or she is also Leader of the Party. And just as the Prime Minister is serviced by the Private Office at Number 10, backed up by its highly efficient Civil Service machinery, so the Leader of the Party needs the same sort of servicing, but in a political sense. Hence the creation of the Political Office.

The Political Office is of comparatively recent origin in the history of Downing Street. Until 1924, new Prime Ministers entering Number 10 brought their personal staff with them and incorporated them into the Private Office. Sometimes they made a clean sweep of everyone already there in order to substitute their own people. It was only when Ramsay MacDonald, who had no previous knowledge of the Civil Service or how the machinery of government worked, became Prime Minister in 1924 that the decision was made to keep on the experienced staff of the previous Prime Minister. They became career civil servants – and the format of permanent staff was set, to be followed by subsequent Prime Ministers, until I made an alteration to the system in 1964 by initiating a Political Office at Number 10. Indeed, I can fairly claim that, while the first post-war political aide (in the person of John Wyndham) was introduced by Harold Macmillan, a Political Office proper was established for the first time in the 1964 Wilson Government. Both, however, follow the tradition of political aide and confidant laid down by, for example, Disraeli with Montague Corrie, Lloyd George with Lord Davidson.

Harold Macmillan, as I have said elsewhere, changed the face that politics presented to the people. A consummate politician himself, he understood the importance not only of the Prime Ministerial 'image', but also that the Prime Minister – any Prime Minister – has to play two roles . . . and succeed in both. As Leader of his Party, he must maintain his political support not just at election times but throughout his tenure of office. Nor is it the job of the Civil Service to help him keep the goodwill of Party workers, voters for his Party and his own MPs. Hence the importance of a political presence within Number 10.

Macmillan's method of ensuring Conservative Party representation in Number 10 could be likened to the placing of a Trojan horse within the citadel. Cast in the role of equine invader was John Wyndham, a man of great intelligence, charm, ability and wit. Above all, he was not motivated by any personal ambition; with Harold MacMillan's interests at heart, all he wanted was to see his friend succeed.

John Wyndham operated from within the machine itself rather than as a separate unit. He became an honorary civil servant – as a rich man, he did not need a salary – working as number two in the Private Office. The Principal Private Secretary was then Tim Bligh (later Sir Timothy Bligh in Macmillan's Resignation Honours list, when Wyndham himself was given a life peerage and became Lord Egremont).

My own position, if I too had gone into the Private Office instead of setting up a larger unit, would have been similar in almost every way (even down – or up – to the peerage!). I remember confirming to Sir Timothy in 1964 that Harold Wilson too would want a political presence in Number 10, and explaining that I was his choice for this, but that I would not be going to the Private Office. There had been a debate as to whether I should follow in John Wyndham's footsteps in this way, but we had decided against it largely because of the hostility – sometimes instinctive, sometimes conscious – that the Civil Service as a whole at that time showed towards Labour, with a few shining exceptions, not least in the Treasury. Certainly it was Peter Jay's impression that there was a goodly number of 'young bloods' who were looking forward to a change of Government and presumably some action.

This attitude was partly the result of thirteen years of Conservative power: a whole generation, including those entering Downing Street, had grown up in the tradition of the Conservative way of doing things. Partly it was due to something even more basic: the very methods of recruitment and selection for the Civil Service ensured that –

particularly in the higher echelons – people were chosen who by their background alone were more likely to be Conservative than Labour. And lastly, there was and still is something even more subtle: a barely acknowledged desire to have the Prime Minister to themselves. By clearly defining the role and function of the Political Office from the start it would, we hoped, come to be accepted as a viable entity rather than as a constant stone-in-the-toe irritation.

So, although for Conservatives at that time John Wyndham's presence in the Private Office proved invaluable as a watch-post, for us a separate Political Office had much more to recommend it. And so it turned out; the greatest proof of its effectiveness was, perhaps, the fact that when Edward Heath won the 1970 election, he continued with a very similar arrangement run by Douglas Hurd.

The *raison d'être* behind the establishment of a Political Office in 1964 (and presumably behind Heath's retention of it) was that the Prime Minister must be seen as the Leader of his Party as well as the Head of Government; and these two functions have to be catered for, separately, within the same building. As I have said, Ramsay MacDonald brought with him none of his own people, with the exception of one personal secretary. In this age of instant, electronic communication the importance of being under the same roof may not be immediately apparent. But as anyone who has worked in the government machine knows, Whitehall is much more immediately responsive to an approach from Number 10 than to one from any other government building. Civil servants are quick to recognize that, even if you are supposed to be one of the Prime Minister's principal advisers, if you are located elsewhere you are out on a limb. I had seen an example of this in Thomas Balogh's experience in the 1964 Government: when he was first appointed as Economic Adviser to the Prime Minister, working in the Cabinet Office, he had found life extremely difficult. Every time he wanted to get into Number 10 to see the Prime Minister, he had to go through the performance of getting the doors between the buildings unlocked – a process that the necessary security precautions made somewhat long drawn-out. It was not until after 1966, when he was given rooms in Number 10, that he was able to function at maximum efficiency – fortunately, because his last year at Number 10 was made critical for Labour with the introduction of the Statutory Wages and Prices Policy. (By that time he had already decided, partly because of his wife's wishes, to go to the House of Lords. It is sad, in retrospect, that he was not persuaded to stay on as an adviser at Number 10, but he wanted to play a more active Party role.)

The setting up of the first Political Office in 1964 was fraught with difficulties and complexities. But its function, as I saw it then and still see it, can be expressed in one sentence: to service the Prime Minister as Leader of his Party, in a political sense.

But simple as these words sound, they cover a multitude of different activities.

There is the paperwork – the unending paperwork! – that flows back and forth between the Prime Minister and the representatives of his Party at national, headquarters, regional and purely local levels.

There are the letters that flood in from the constituencies, well-wishers, people with a grievance, the genuinely distraught, or those who claim they are supporters but who merely want to receive a letter on Downing Street writing paper.

There is the preparation for meetings, rallies, Party conferences and election campaigns – when a by-election is impending, it is the Political Office that processes all the details that the Leader of the Party needs to know, and supplies him with reports and information. Sometimes, through its day-to-day contact with members of the Party organization, the Political Office serves as a transmitter of unofficial but nevertheless useful information: that an allegiance is shifting, a new alliance is being formed, a seeming sudden inefficiency is due to family troubles, some local government question is about to become national.

It is essential that the Prime Minister be kept in touch not only with Party opinion on matters of high policy – an issue like Northern Ireland, for example – but with the feelings and attitudes of the general public; as Party Leader, maintenance of these close links is vital for future electoral success – but electoral success is *not* the business of the Civil Service. Thus, the impression that the public receives of the Prime Minister in a political sense is the business of the Political Office; and, just as in Opposition, the Political Office has the responsibility of projecting him as Party Leader.

Fundamental to the success of the Political Office – or any personal adviser or aide – is an understanding of the overriding importance of the Cabinet. Nothing can rival the quality of the advice given by a man or woman who has reached Cabinet level, with all the experience and knowledge that this implies, who has a position within not only the Government but his or her political party.

Nevertheless, by its very nature, advice from someone of Cabinet rank implies certain limitations. No one, quite naturally, is in the

Cabinet who is not ambitious, who does not see him or herself as a potential – even a possible – Prime Minister. Inevitably, the advice given to a Prime Minister by an individual member of his Cabinet thus reflects some self-interest: it may be affected by the political circumstances of the moment, by the Minister's own standing within the Party or his long-term plans, by the advice of his own Department (even up to a mild case of brainwashing by strong-minded civil servants!). On the other hand, the Prime Minister's personal appointee (for that is what a Political Secretary is) is not motivated by the pursuit of his or her political good or advancement; in a word, where a Cabinet Minister is by the nature of the job an interested party, the personal appointee who is head of the Political Office should have only the good of the Leader of the Party at heart.

This aspect of the role is vital: because of their contacts at every level of the Party and feedback of opinion via the Leader's constituency, as well as his postbag, the Prime Minister will also use them as a sounding board. In this sense, they advise, describing what they know of the current political climate and of the likely reaction among their network of contacts to any Prime Ministerial decision. In turn, the Prime Minister can bounce ideas off a dedicated and disinterested man or woman who has an obvious strong interest in public affairs.

In this latter role, incidentally, the political aide can take much of the weight of 'shop' talk off the Prime Minister's wife or husband. It is all too easy to 'take the office home' in any demanding and fascinating job, and there to discuss it endlessly; but not every partner wants, to use Clarissa Eden's remark, either the Suez Canal flowing through their drawing room, or the presence of the Falkland Islands.

To speak for a moment of my own personal experience as a political aide, I had the overwhelming advantage of having known Harold Wilson for a long time. When we returned to Downing Street in 1974, I had then worked for him for eighteen years. And when you have worked with someone for as long as that, you literally do begin to know how their minds work (astrologers might claim a mental affinity because Harold Wilson's and my birthdays are on adjacent days: 11 and 10 March respectively!). This working rapport sprang from the reasons why he originally offered me a job: a university background and an active role in Labour politics there, a trained mind, and two years spent at Transport House, Party headquarters, which had given me an invaluable and solid grounding in Labour politics nationally and the workings of the Labour Party.

I therefore had long experience of knowing what the Prime Minister was likely to consider important, and vice versa. This meant that I was able to shield him from the distractions of endless petty queries or trivial decisions; it also followed that I was often used as a channel of communication by those who wanted an unofficial sounding of his state of mind, or probable reaction. It also meant that I was asked to act as a go-between by those who were, quite simply, too frightened to tackle him about something themselves: Harold Wilson is a curious mixture of being extremely formidable and very easy to get on with. He has an extraordinarily powerful intellect and a sharp wit. When I first began to work for him I was often terrified – I used to draft and redraft my letters and advice notes until they were so perfect they could have been framed. It is not surprising that I was often enlisted to put something to him on behalf of another; it is not always easy to tell the Prime Minister of Great Britain something you know he will not wish to hear.

Thus the Private Office and the Political Office have two separate and distinct parts to play in the machinery of Number 10. Because of this clear division of function, co-operation and co-ordination between the two is much easier than if the lines between are fudged, with the inevitable friction and hostility that is thus aroused. The Political and the Private Offices are not Siamese twins: though the Civil Service serves different political masters, it must at no time feel that it is being asked to take on a Party political role. This was the attitude and the reality during the years between 1964 and 1970.

However, when Labour regained power in 1974, the position changed, although the original intention had been to continue a Political Office exactly along those earlier lines. That this concept altered was due to the 'politicizing' of certain roles within Number 10.

During the February election campaign, as the possibility of Labour being returned to power became a probability, one subject became more and more a part of our conversation. This was the need for a strong political presence in Number 10. Many of the semi-serious, semi-gossiping discussions between Bernard Donoughue, Joe Haines and myself centred on this. Joe and Bernard were anxious to continue and increase the reality of a political presence at Number 10, Joe, naturally, concentrating on his role as Press Secretary.

Originally, when the Political Office had been initiated, the incumbent Downing Street Press Officer was a civil servant, Sir Trevor Lloyd-Hughes. His interest, naturally, was in putting across the Government's message as the *Government's* rather than as that of the ruling political Party; in fact, he had received clear instructions to the effect that the political side of the work must be kept separate. The result was that for a year (1964–5) this adherence to the principle of impartiality meant that there was no one to answer any media queries on the Party political aspect of the Prime Minister's work.

To remedy this, Gerald Kaufman had been appointed Press Officer on the political side. This tandem system worked extremely well; both were able men who got on well together. In order to keep it going, when Sir Trevor retired in 1969, Joe Haines came in as the Downing Street Press Officer, working with Gerald; again, this worked, and it also helped Joe to learn the ropes, particularly as he came under Gerald's sponsorship.

In 1970, when we lost office, Gerald left to become an MP, and Joe was taken on to Harold Wilson's personal staff. This was the turning point: when we returned to office in 1974 Joe decided that we did not need a separate Political Press Officer – he believed that a Labour Government should speak to the country from a Labour Party point of view – and thus the two roles became merged.

For Joe, the building up of an efficient and loyal Press Office meant, quite rightly, having a staff who were loyal to him personally, and who thought and felt the way he did. In sum, he wanted a Labour-orientated organization. This meant, obviously, that while some of the present staff passed his test, some people already there would have to be moved on, and still others brought in from outside the government network. Joe had obviously given his approach to his job and overall role a great deal of thought, much of which was based on his one year's experience during the previous Labour Government; the result was a determined, clear-cut approach.

By contrast Bernard, who was brought in without any such experience to head the new Policy Unit, regarded the historic, shadowy interior of Number 10 as a fascinating and mysterious world, of which he longed to become part. Bernard was a highly political animal who viewed his job as policy adviser, on Party political grounds, on every aspect of policy that came before the Prime Minister. A first priority was given to political interpretation and advice on policy, with the result that the Unit was more short-term in its working than the earlier smaller, but higher-powered team which Thomas Balogh had headed in the 1960s. Thomas Balogh's unit had been more academic, more long-term in its thinking. While Bernard's team were excellent on presentation and did a first-class job, they were not necessarily as expert on original thinking.

Like Joe, Bernard had a hawkish approach to the official staff. Both of them felt that any who were obviously obstructive should be got rid of with scant ceremony. This was how I had felt in the 1960s in those earlier governments. Experience had taught me then that anything really constructive would only be possible if there was a strong, clearly organized, independent political presence whose role was well defined and needed no defence or protection.

Bernard meant business. Both he and Joe agreed that a very tough line indeed should be taken with the civil servants, Joe in particular being critical of the influence they had upon Ministers. Both felt that Labour should be more ready to import outsiders to ensure the necessary aggressiveness for dealing with the negative and conservative influence of the vast Civil Service network. My own view had been set out in my book *Inside Number 10*, which covered the years 1964–70. Bernard carried his further than any of us.

His most revolutionary suggestion, half in jest, was to operate the Donoughue Card-Index System in Number 10. As he had explained it to his enthralled audience of two at the end of the election campaign, it would be an improved version of one he had used at the London School of Economics. There, every lecturer had a card detailing not only his subject and where and when he had lectured on it, but his political views, background, attitude to various questions of the day, and so forth; as the index grew, it was confined not only to lecturers. Bernard told us how this had helped him in crises – he knew whom he could count on – as well as making for efficiency in everyday situations. He thought that this system should be used in extended form in Number 10. It would show at a glance who to nominate for jobs and offices or – sometimes more important – who to keep out. It would be a formidable operation, but in time would have transformed our institutions and made Labour hard to defeat in future elections.

Impressive as these ideas sounded during our late-night, pre-election discussions, I assumed he was speaking half in jest at the time and wondered how the Civil Service machine would react to such efficiency. But then, Bernard's personality is both complex and contradictory, combining as it does the hard-hitting and the charming, the dedicated and the jokey. The notes he wrote were normally business-like, but some were a pure delight with quotations from W. B. Yeats (a poet we both love). Indeed, of Bernard's card-index I might have said with Yeats:

> When I was young,
> I had not given a penny for a song
> Did not the poet sing it with such airs
> That one believed he had a sword upstairs.

The end result of the reorganization of Number 10 in 1974 was that there were three separate political areas in the one building; areas that were separate physically as well as in function. There was, inevitably, a blurring of the lines, not only between the political side and the Private Office, but also between the three political sections themselves. It could be – and indeed often was – argued that for one or other section to work hand in glove with the Civil Service, or to combine two roles, made for closer co-operation, but I do not think this is necessarily so. When jobs are ill-defined there is endless scope for duplication, lack of co-ordination and sometimes frustration, whereas a clear-cut but more aloof presence – and by then the fact that the Prime Minister has to operate politically as well as governmentally was no longer in question – makes, in my view, for smoother and more efficient operation.

Roughly the system then designed continued when Jim Callaghan took over in 1976: Bernard Donoughue remained, Sir Tom McCaffrey took over from Joe Haines in the Press Office, and the Political Office that I had run continued with fewer staff under Tom McNally (now an SDP MP). The idea of the Political Office as a single entity, managing the political side of the Prime Minister's life, diminished. I believe that it is time this concept be re-introduced in strong and definite form.

The present Prime Minister relies to a much greater extent than her predecessors on the Civil Service. She has however moved towards the appointment of a number of outsiders, who, while not politicians as such, are obviously there to advise politically and on presentation.

A strong, well-established and staffed Political Office might well have caused her to rethink certain actions, or to omit or strengthen others, on the basis of its knowledge of Party and public feeling. Perhaps, too, it might have diverted her from those external affairs, the Falklands apart, for which all Prime Ministers have a predilection – the overseas visits, summits, conferences, peace plans and initiatives of one kind or another – that distract the country's First Minister from his or her primary function of serving their own people. She might also have benefited from more reliable and trustworthy ears at times when the Party knives were out.

TWELVE

Working Lunches

Although the Political Office had become an established fact since those first difficult, distant days of the 1960s, one small facet of its existence was not yet acknowledged. Those of us who worked there had nowhere in the building where we could eat – although there are several kitchens in Downing Street.

On the ground floor, there is the very large kitchen used by the caterers from Government Hospitality to produce the food for State luncheons, dinners, receptions and other functions. On the first floor, there is another sizeable kitchen that can, again, be used by Government Hospitality or privately – that is, by civil servants who want to cook themselves an omelette or beans on toast, though this is usually carried out in the Garden Rooms, where facilities do exist for preparing the odd snack. Senior civil servants also have the use of the Cabinet Office Mess; although this is not in the building, it is a fairly simple procedure to have the door between Number 10 and the Cabinet Office unlocked. For senior staff, lunching in the Cabinet Office Mess has the additional advantage that they meet all their opposite numbers from the various departments round about; this custom is undoubtedly partly responsible for the highly efficient Civil Service grapevine as well as helping general communication. As for the Prime Minister's own family, they of course have the use of the kitchen in the private flat on the second floor.

But for those who do not fall within the definition of either government staff or family members, there is nowhere within the building to eat: the choice is either a restaurant, sandwiches at the desk, or the House of Commons cafeteria or Staff Canteen.

Although eating out cannot possibly be described as a hardship (although it can sometimes be an interruption), being able to have your cup of coffee, snack, or whatever in the company of the colleagues with whom you have just been discussing some important problem – or arguing some hotly-disputed point – gives all of you the chance of viewing whatever-it-is in a more relaxed way. Because you aren't in a work situation, the pressure is off, and very often some new angle, some fresh consideration, even a satisfactory solution, appears almost by chance in the conversation. A break like this is also a good way of catching up with 'semi-shop' – the news and views of colleagues, relevant personal factors, and so on.

Tony Benn was always very conscious of this: he used to say that there ought to be a 'Number 10 cafeteria', where after a Cabinet Meeting Ministers could discuss items of Cabinet business in complete security with colleagues whom they might, otherwise, see only across the Cabinet Table.

Personally, I feel sure that if his idea were put into practice, and accommodation within Number 10 freed to create something on the lines of a College Common Room, with perhaps a small dining room to one side, a certain level of communication and understanding between very senior Ministers would improve – which would surely help in consequence towards co-ordination between their Departments.

From the Political Office standpoint, it was clearly important that senior staff on the political side and those from outside – like trades union leaders, the National Agent, or the General Secretary of the Party – who were concerned with a particular piece of policy could see the Prime Minister in a setting slightly more relaxed than that of a formal interview.

Mrs Pollard, the Prime Minister's housekeeper, obviously could not take this on: her hands were full looking after the house in Lord North Street (where the family were still living), as well as working when necessary in the private flat at Number 10. So I suggested that she be asked to find, and subsequently supervise, a girl who would be prepared to come in on an *ad hoc* basis to cook a simple meal on the days when these working lunches were envisaged.

As it happened, it was Bernard Donoughue who found someone, with help from the Private Office – a girl who had done just this sort of job before. Her fee was paid partly by the Prime Minister and partly by the Government, as many of the people invited were those who had claim to official hospitality. The new girl's theatre of operations was the kitchen on the first floor by the large State Dining Room, and the meal was served in the small State Dining Room.

Over the months lunches began to change character. Eventually, all the Private Office staff were invited, along with the senior members of the Press Office. Occasionally a senior Party official would be invited, but this practice fell away.

As a method of keeping the staff of Downing Street in touch with one another it was a great success; as a facility for ensuring that the Prime Minister met those from outside Downing Street, whose unofficial views or information could be useful to him, it failed.

The Downing Street working lunch staggered on for a while – rather like a headless chicken – until we were told that the cook had once worked for Edward Heath, as crew cook on his yacht. One guest who recognized her actually whispered the question as to whether it was all right to talk in front of her; and, risk or not, even the idea that someone might be listening with undue interest to your conversation interfered with the necessary atmosphere of relaxation.

She was extremely efficient and bought only the best. But as the bills from Robert Jackson had to be paid for by Harold Wilson, he found this rather expensive. Otherwise, her excellent cooking was much appreciated.

Altogether, the working lunch proved an abortive exercise for everyone. It has subsequently, I understand, been revived by Mrs Thatcher, particularly on Prime Minister's Questions' days to enable all the staff to gather together before going to the House. It was worth trying: I believe very strongly that something half-way between the Tony Benn idea of a Cabinet cafeteria and a fully-fledged dining service would serve an extremely useful purpose for the Prime Minister, his or her Cabinet colleagues, and important outside personalities who visit Number 10.

THIRTEEN

Changes at Number 10

After the extraordinary sensation of walking once more through the great black front door of Number 10, Downing Street, the first thing that struck me on returning in February 1974 was the number of changes that had been made inside the house.

In the previous Wilson regime, little had been altered. The interior of the building had been rebuilt, reorganized and redecorated during Harold and Dorothy Macmillan's time, and when the Wilsons arrived in 1964, for the most part they 'left well alone'. There were one or two changes of note: Mary Wilson turned the first-floor corridor between the offices and the State Rooms into a small gallery of modern British painters; display cabinets were installed next to the State Rooms where the priceless gifts presented to the Wilsons were set out for visitors to see; the heavy mahogany furniture in Mary Wilson's bedroom was replaced by lighter, more modern chests and cupboards; and there was a general lightening of the furnishings in the Prime Minister's study. In all, not many changes in five and a half years.

But on our return in 1974, it was evident that Edward Heath had not been idle, decoratively speaking, in his three and a half years. Every part of the building seemed to have been redecorated, with the exception only of my own room – in Heath's day Douglas Hurd's room – on the ground floor, which did not appear to have been touched.

The Cabinet Room was completely changed. Gone was the dark red carpet on the hall and corridor floors leading to the Cabinet Room; this was replaced by a rich gold. Gone were the dark greens and reds of the room itself – the green felt on the long, coffin-shaped Cabinet table, the old, dark green leather blotters, the even more worn leather of the chair seats. Now there was a symphony of muted browns ranging from palest to deep tobacco: the table top was covered with fawn baize, even the blotters were new light brown leather. It all looked elegant and co-ordinated, but I felt a touch of nostalgia for those dark and serious colours, shabby though the room had become, that seemed to underline the weightiness of office.

As for the main reception rooms, though the colours of each remained basically the same – the Middle Drawing Room, for instance, was still the same blue – everything had been repainted, recovered, and the walls hung in silk. The dry rot had been tackled (necessitating consider-able structural alteration), but alas not completely eradicated: there was still some dry rot in one of the State Rooms, in a corner of the Pillared Drawing Room and a little elsewhere.

Many of the heavier portraits of English statesmen had been removed, especially from the large State Dining Room (designed by Sir John Soane), and replaced with a collection of French pastoral paintings – perhaps this was another facet of Edward Heath's pro-French, pro-Common Market policy. Whatever the reason, the pastoral scenes did not last long: Harold Wilson took one look at them and asked the Department of the Environment to bring back the absent portraits; these were, in fact, excellent copies of the original, major portraits of Wellington, Charles James Fox, and the like.

Most stunning – in the sense of dismaying – of all the picture changes was the removal of the portrait of Winston Churchill, depicted wearing his boiler suit, from where it had hung on the wall of the annexe outside the Cabinet Room. Here Harold Wilson, who revered and respected Sir Winston almost more than any other man, had passed it every day for five and a half years; here, it had looked down on Ministers, officials or visitors, as they waited outside the Cabinet Room. It was discovered in one of the second-floor political offices – the room used by Edward Heath's Parliamentary Private Secretary, to be precise – and was im-mediately brought down for reinstatement.

Although the State Rooms had remained virtually the same (apart from redecoration), it was clear that, like the Douglas-Homes, Edward Heath had used them far more extensively than the Wilsons. Both Heath and the Homes had treated the White Drawing Room as their own, in contrast to the Wilsons, who preferred to stay upstairs in the private flat with its smaller sitting room.

Edward Heath's choice of the White Drawing Room for his grand piano may have been dictated in part by the room's superb views (it is a corner room). From one set of windows you look across the L-shaped garden of Number 10 to St James's Park; from the other, on to Horse Guards Parade across the other leg of the 'L', an aspect that comes into its own on the occasion of the Queen's Birthday Parade. Grown-up guests are seated in the forty to fifty seats allocated to the Prime Minister in the stand next to the garden gate onto Horse Guards Parade (for which seats the Prime Minister personally has to reimburse the Ministry of Defence); his guests' children have a much more agreeable view of the ceremony from the window seats of the White Drawing Room. The words of command are clearly audible; only the trees, in full leaf, make the view a little less than comprehensive – but the orange juice and cakes that are served throughout seem to compensate the small audience adequately.

Near these first-floor State Rooms can be found the most practical and comfort-making of the alterations made by Edward Heath. This is the division into two of the washroom leading off the Prime Minister's study.

The study that Harold Wilson inherited from Alec Douglas-Home in 1964 was a nice square, medium-sized room with a door at one end leading into a very long, narrow corridor of a room: the PM's private cloakroom. At one end was a washbasin, and twenty feet away along a blank wall was the lavatory in solitary splendour. Sensibly, Edward Heath divided this weirdly-shaped washroom into two, partitioning it so that the door from the study led into its own cloakroom with basin and w.c., and the other half became a second cloakroom with access from the corridor outside, for the benefit of visiting VIPs. The concept was admirable; but, alas, the decor chosen was not up to the design: in contrast with the heavy mahogany and the rather old-fashioned air of the whole building, the new cloakrooms, with their mirrors, chrome and laminated surfaces, looked as though they came out of a modern chain hotel.

On the second floor, there were also quite a number of changes, ranging from the laying of new and different carpets to turning the sitting room into the bedroom and vice versa. Here Edward Heath had a precedent: this was the way the rooms had originally been arranged, and only the Wilsons and the Douglas-Homes had preferred them the other way round.

All in all, there had been a general modernization, an improvement of the building's facilities, and considerable refurbishment. To some, Edward Heath's ideas and, in particular, his choice of colours, were objectionable: Barbara Castle, for example, says in her *Diaries* that she found the changes 'vulgar' and 'brash', those in the Cabinet Room being the most objectionable of all.

One change, however, was welcomed by all: flowers had now become part of the official budget. Prior to the Heath regime, any flowers had to be personally organized and paid for by the Prime Minister; on our return, we discovered that the strategically placed bowls of blooms were arranged weekly by a florist and paid for by the Government – a truly sweet smell of success.

The big change in the entertaining at Number 10 took place before the years covered by this book. (By 'entertaining', I am here talking about the official dinners, luncheons and receptions, as opposed to any purely private parties given by the incumbent of Number 10.)

Before Harold Wilson became Prime Minister in 1964, the names of those to whom invitations would be sent was pretty predictable. If, say, the Prime Minister of Czechoslovakia was in Britain on a State Visit, the guest list for the big dinner to which he would be invited would automatically include the Head of the Foreign Office, ex-Ambassadors to Czechoslovakia, those Members of Parliament who were especially interested in Czechoslovakia, perhaps the head of the CBI and, to balance him, the head of the TUC, top industrialists with contracts or connections in Czechoslovakia, and various people from within Number 10 itself – the Private Office and Principal Private Secretary, the Foreign Office Secretary, sometimes the Press Secretary, and perhaps one or two more.

But Harold Wilson believed that most visiting Prime Ministers would prefer to see a bit more of Britain than the Establishment and that they might, indeed, find a purely official dinner party a trifle boring. He felt that if the mixture were leavened by one or two outside guests, the whole evening would be more entertaining for the visiting dignitary.

Accordingly, in the 1960s visitors were asked whom they would like to meet. This had one curious result: it was the time of the outstandingly successful TV series *The Forsyte Saga*, and Susan Hampshire, Nyree Dawn Porter and Eric Porter were asked for with almost monotonous regularity – so much so that at one reception Eric Porter remarked to me, 'You know, I think I ought to bring my bed and sleep here!'

It was not, of course, always actors and actresses who were invited to these parties. There were sportsmen, dress designers, musicians, writers – anyone who represented British talent – and, on occasion, those who were unknown but who related to the visitor's world.

When the Mayor of Berlin came, soldiers who had been in the British garrison in Berlin were also invited; when a party was held at Downing Street for the first men to go to the moon (Armstrong, Collins and Aldrin), the Prime Minister felt that they were so much a part of the future that British youth should be involved, and so disabled youngsters (whose names were suggested through the relevant organizations) were given the opportunity of meeting the astronauts. One of them, a blind boy called Kevin Geary who later graduated from Cambridge and then Harvard to become successful in his chosen career of radio and TV, still keeps in touch with Harold Wilson.

Naturally enough, these evening receptions gradually expanded; but there was one limiting factor that could not be altered. The foundations of Number 10, a building once described by Sir Winston Churchill as 'jerry built', have always been insecure and, according to most expert calculations, a maximum of around 120 people is all the floors will support with safety.

During the Opposition years of 1970-4, Edward Heath continued these changes in the format of Prime Ministerial entertaining, but in a slightly different direction. As is well known, Mr Heath is extremely fond of music; his innovation was the singing of madrigals in the Pillared Room before or after evening functions like dinners or receptions. He also introduced music to the entertaining at Chequers, where the Great Hall makes a perfect setting for a musical evening.

When Labour returned in 1974, it was not unexpected, therefore, that Harold Wilson would wish to continue in similar vein. But just as a cultivated flower reverts to its wild progenitor, so the Civil Service tends to return to type if left alone. Once again, lists that were purely 'Establishment' were produced, and suggestions for other visitors were of the previous, predictable, head-of-ICI kind. But this time, a more streamlined routine was established whereby the political staff – including new additions like Bernard Donoughue and Joe Haines in the Press Office – should see the various lists and add their own suggestions for names. Now, both Virginia Wade and Diana Rigg figured among the 'constant visitors'. My own particular contribution was to follow up a suggestion that where a woman was invited, she was allowed to bring an escort (hitherto this had not been the custom) in the same way that men were always invited to bring partners. This idea arose after a request from Shirley Williams, a Cabinet Minister, that she be allowed to bring an escort to a Government dinner. Male members of the

Cabinet were automatically accompanied, female members only if they were married, which seemed to me to be an unnecessary piece of discrimination.

'Getting on the list' was a major preoccupation among some members of the Downing Street staff. Those who qualified to attend official dinners and luncheons were greatly envied by the ones who did not. In my position as aide to Harold Wilson I was often asked to intervene on behalf of some member of staff who wanted to be added to the famous list.

Difficult as it was to say 'No', those who organized the functions had to remember that too many staff members present meant an unbalanced table. Not only would there be far more men than women, but the staff had to be seated in a cluster at the end of the table, so that they could leave the room with as little disturbance as possible if wanted in the middle of dinner. They used to do this in a sort of half-crouch, which I can best describe as 'Don't look at me, I'm being unobtrusive' expressed in body language. For a woman in a long evening dress this kind of posture is even more difficult. In my case, a further complication was that I was often seated higher up the table, and consequently had more ground to cover before I reached the door.

The room in which these manœuvres took place is one of the most dramatic in Downing Street. It was designed by Sir John Soane and is panelled in light oak. The long dining table seats thirty-two, which is a smallish number for an official State function; for a large dinner party of, say, sixty people, a horseshoe table would be brought in and set up with the curve of the 'shoe' at the far, Whitehall end adjoining the Cabinet Office. The Prime Minister and his guest of honour sit on the outside of this curve with empty seats opposite so that everyone can see them clearly.

For a 'horseshoe' dinner party, the usual heavy dining chairs are replaced by small gold chairs from Government Hospitality which are so light that a full-skirted dress can send them flying as its wearer rises for the Loyal Toast. Food is served on white and gold china with the Crown in the middle (again, supplied by Government Hospitality). In Harold Wilson's day the menu for one of these parties would have been simple, as his preference is for very good, plain, English cooking; a typical dinner menu might consist of smoked salmon or whitebait, followed by roast beef and Yorkshire pudding or roast lamb or duck, and occasionally a *tournedos Rossini*. He was not particularly fond of puddings, although often a superb *soufflé* would be produced. It had, I was once told half in jest but half in earnest, a loaf of bread in the base so that it kept its perfect outline until the last person had been served!

After the pudding, cheese and liqueurs came the Loyal Toast, which was also the signal that smoking was permitted. After the Loyal Toast, there was a pause of ten minutes or so before the other toasts, which entailed speeches of welcome and reply.

Finally, everyone retired to the Pillared Rooms as major functions were in two parts: a dinner at 8.00 for 8.15 followed by a reception timed for 10.00. Often, if the dinner went on late, the guests for the reception would start arriving, their presence outside signalled by a gradual crescendo of noise that, on occasions, almost drowned the speeches within.

In Harold Wilson's time, receptions tended to go on until very late, whereas when Jim Callaghan took over they never lasted beyond 10.30. This was the hour by which Jim insisted upon being in bed – and the time by which Harold Wilson would be just about getting into his swing, ready and intrigued to meet any new guests or have a glass of whisky with an old friend.

Late night was also a time when Harold Wilson liked a good gossip, going over the day's events in his study with some member of the staff – a Private Secretary, the Assistant Press Secretary or sometimes a driver – occasionally to the slight irritation of the Number 10 maintenance staff, who were unable to lock up the building and complete the routine of safeguarding it for the night until these conversations had finished.

If Harold Wilson is an owl by nature, Mary Wilson is a lark. She would be sleepy and ready for bed at 10.30 in the evening, but up and dressed and ready for action by 7.30 a.m., whereas Harold, although woken at that hour, rose much more slowly, breakfasting and reading the papers in bed before appearing for his first appointment at around 9.15 a.m.

There are certain special days in the Downing Street entertainment calendar. The Queen's Birthday Parade and Beating the Retreat provide the occasion for two summer festivities. The Prime Minister's guests watch these ceremonies take place from their reserved seats in the stand directly in front of the Number 10 garden, and afterwards there is a party.

Of the two, the day that most Prime Ministers would, I think, remember with the greatest pleasure – though Margaret Thatcher's party in 1982 was marred by the Falklands Crisis – is the Queen's

Birthday Parade (or Trooping the Colour): it is almost always good weather – a pleasant summer day if not actually hot – and the party, which starts at about 12.30, ran in those days on that delicious drink, Pimms No. 1, whose enlivening effect is well known.

If the weather was good enough, the party was held in the garden; usually, too, the Prime Minister would take guests over the building and show them the Cabinet Room and the State Rooms, which he loved doing, before everyone left at around 2.00. For those who stayed on until the end, food – in the form of light, party-type snacks – was provided.

Beating the Retreat was the same sort of occasion, but this, of course, was in the early evening with a later reception.

Another memorable, but purely political, party was the Eve-of-Parliament reception, when the whole of the Government, including Junior Ministers down to PPSS, were invited to Number 10. Once there, the doors of the Pillared Room were locked on the assembled party and everyone not in the Government excluded (except for those close advisers of the Prime Minister who already knew the contents of the Queen's Speech). The Chief Whip then read the Speech, the Prime Minister gave a talk of amplification and encouragement, and then there were drinks and conversation.

As well as the regular, grand parties, there are those the Prime Minister will give on behalf of his own special interests. In Harold Wilson's time, these included the Open University, in which he had been much involved during his earlier Premiership, his own old university Oxford, Bradford University, of which he is Chancellor, Toynbee Hall, the Round House and the D'Oyly Carte Opera Company. Downing Street is also used as a kind of entertainment centre for august, non-political (in a Party sense) national, international or commonwealth bodies, like NATO, the Commonwealth Parliamentary Association, the Inter-Parliamentary Union and the United Nations Association.

At Christmas, the main celebrations took place at Chequers. I do not recall even having a Christmas tree at Number 10 in those early years in the 1960s, although by the time the Wilsons returned in 1974 it had become the custom for a tree to be brought up from the Chequers estate. Because it was so tall, it was always placed in the Pillared Room (the largest of the State Rooms); as for the decoration, this was originally done by the personal staff, but later even that was taken over and done officially.

Christmas, however, had always meant a party of a different sort. In earlier years, Harold and Mary Wilson had invited the staff and patients (mainly paraplegic) from the nearby Stoke Mandeville Hospital to spend Christmas Day or Boxing Day with them. Now, in 1974, we wondered what could be done in Downing Street along these lines. I must confess to feeling extremely proud and happy that a suggestion of mine has become a Downing Street tradition: that of the Christmas party given for disabled children, the first being in 1974.

It was one of the most moving occasions at which I have ever been present. The atmosphere of love, sacrifice, caring and tenderness which filled those august and splendid State Rooms was almost palpable. The children – whose names had been put forward by local authorities or the charities concerned – had handicaps ranging from spina bifida to spasticity, so special arrangements had to be made, up to and including the alteration of doorways and the provision of ramps for invalid chairs and, in a few cases, for stretchers. One little boy called Freddie, a spina bifida case, a very bright and intelligent child, was unable to stand or sit up and was provided with a little glass mirror in which he could see those talking to him. He recognized Harold Wilson by his pipe and clung on to it.

Preparing for this party was a major operation, but to all concerned – including those entertainers who gave their services free – a labour of love. Presents had to be chosen with special care, as the child's disability had to be taken into consideration; they also had to be wrapped and labelled clearly so that the right child received them.

Bill Housden, the Prime Minister's driver, dressed as Father Christmas and did the actual handing-over of presents to the child, the parents (or other relatives) or nurse; one of the musical members of the staff played the piano; stars like Morecambe and Wise, Vera Lynn and Mike Yarwood (who that first year pretended he was Edward Heath returning to claim his residence) came to the party and stayed to entertain.

The following year, by way of a change, we got hold of those perennial childhood favourites, Walt Disney's characters. As it happened, the 1975 party coincided with a major economic meeting with the TUC, whose chiefs emerged from the Cabinet Room to meet Mickey Mouse and Donald Duck going in. There were even cartoons of this at the time, and it provided much-needed light relief to what was in essence a period of monetary crisis. It is very pleasant to know that these parties were continued after Harold Wilson resigned.

Another entertainment given by the Prime Minister during 1975 was special in a different kind of way. This was a large dinner given for the representatives of the British film industry in order that they could put forward their views on what was needed to rebuild and strengthen the industry.

For the Prime Minister, this dinner also had a personal side: since his Presidency of the Board of Trade in the Attlee Government (when he had helped create the prosperous industry of the 1940s and 1950s), he had continued to take a close interest in the film industry.

From the film-makers' point of view, that dinner gave rise to a number of initiatives not just on film-making but on points relating to exhibition and distribution – including the suggestion of a British Film Authority to represent every sector of the industry from feature films to the new video and satellite outlets. Harold Wilson was particularly pleased that, as one of his last acts as Prime Minister, he was able to do something to help an industry so full of artistic merit, and so potential a money-spinner for Britain.

Quite separate from all the foregoing is the entertaining a Prime Minister does on behalf of his Party, such as the Socialist International Conferences, which were attended by leaders like Willy Brandt, Helmut Schmidt and François Mitterrand. Whether or not they happened to be Heads of State at the time, at these convocations they were present as Socialist leaders; in consequence, these events were funded by the Labour Party or the Prime Minister personally, rather than by Government Hospitality.

The traditional English meal of tea is very much a part of Downing Street entertaining; but it is entirely separate from the mainstream, being the province of the Prime Minister's wife. Her guests are the wives and family members of visiting VIPs. When Mr Gromyko came over, Mrs Gromyko would take tea with Mary Wilson; so did the wives of ambassadors, so did Pat and Tricia Nixon and so did their security men.

These were an eye-opener to us. Until the Nixon visit, security had been spelt with a small 's'. President Sadat – later to be so tragically assassinated while surrounded by protective weaponry – and the Saudi Arabian king both dined at Number 10 with minimum difficulty over their protection. But with Nixon, there were problems from start to finish, because the Americans guard their Head of Government in a far more elaborate, detailed way than the comparatively casual European methods.

Arguments started even at the airport. Nixon was bringing over a bullet-proof car, but the Prime Minister – who was to greet Nixon at

Northolt and drive with him in the same vehicle to Chequers – felt that he really could not be seen, in his own country, jumping into an American bullet-proof car. Moreover, for reasons both of protocol and patriotism, he felt that Nixon ought to ride in a British car. In the event, a compromise was reached: they went one journey in one car and returned in another. Nixon's guards amounted to a small army of T-men (as they are called). Although it is commonly believed that those who guard the President are CIA or FBI agents, they are in fact employed by the Treasury, who recruit them on a strange basis: to seek out those who are breaking currency laws and forging, and to protect the President.

In pursuit of this latter aim, hordes of these men invaded Number 10 and almost took it apart before they agreed that it was safe for their President to pass through the front door. No item was too small for them to overlook: I remember that later we spent much time searching fruitlessly for one of the ornamental pokers that had disappeared from in front of the drawing-room fireplace. The ever-watchful T-men had removed this as being a dangerous and potentially offensive weapon with which, presumably, the Prime Minister might have bludgeoned the President if their after-dinner conversation happened to take an unhappy turn.

FOURTEEN

Home Life

When it became clear that Labour were likely to win the February 1974 election, the problem of the Wilsons' accommodation recurred. Neither of them wanted to move back into Number 10; Mary in particular was reluctant to live there again. She had found it uncomfortable before, chiefly because of the lack of privacy: many of the staff have access to the private flat. The narrowness of Labour's victory gave even more weight to their decision to keep on the house in Lord North Street.

A similar situation obtained over Chequers. Mary had never been really happy and relaxed there, and did not relish the idea of spending every weekend there for the next five years. She preferred Grange Farm, their home six miles away at Great Missenden – accordingly, it was here she spent most weekends for the next two years.

Living at Number 10 – or, for that matter, Chequers – is far less relaxing for the Prime Minister's family than the normal atmosphere of a home. Previous Conservative Prime Ministers had had their 'bolt-holes' – usually a large and substantial country house or estate like Sir Alex Douglas-Home's Hirsel, Harold Macmillan's Birch Grove, or Sir Winston Churchill's Chartwell – but it was, I think, assumed that a Socialist Prime Minister would spend his time between Number 10 and Chequers.

Clement Attlee only lived in Downing Street for a brief period, although it was Harold Wilson who created a precedent for those who followed: Jim Callaghan kept on his flat in Kennington as well as his farm in Sussex; and Margaret Thatcher retained both her homes in Flood Street and in Kent.

Where there are children, keeping on the home base obviously helps to give a sense of continuity and security (coincidentally, Margaret Thatcher's children were roughly the same age when she became Prime Minister as the Wilsons' were in the election in 1974). For Mary Wilson, with her instinctive desire for privacy, her dislike of large functions and formal entertaining, home is a place that is exclusively for the family – unlike either Downing Street or Chequers. She had what could be called almost a fixation that the Wilsons should keep both their homes (as well, of course, as her own bungalow in the Scilly Isles).

The only real problem that arose out of living at Lord North Street was that the Prime Minister often got to bed at night much later than if he had been sleeping in Downing Street. The fact that he had a car to take him from Number 10 to Lord North Street often meant that he would stay working late in his study, perhaps doing his boxes, perhaps having a little gossip if there were staff still around. More often than not it would be after 11.00 when he got back to Lord North Street; whereas in his earlier years in Downing Street he would go straight upstairs to the flat after his last appointment. As the years passed, he seemed to go to bed later and later. Mornings, too, had a slightly later start, as he had to be brought from Lord North Street.

Otherwise, the main headache was that suffered by the security people. Two homes are more difficult to look after than one; especially when they have to be not only burglar-proof, but telephonically secure (special scrambler telephones have to be installed) and protected by the local or Metropolitan police. This security, including the various communications devices, continues to surround the Prime Minister in exactly the same way when he goes on holiday; a sizeable burden assumed by the Cabinet Office.

At the weekends, the Wilsons set off for the country together. First they would go to Grange Farm, where Mary preferred to sleep – she used to say that she liked her own bed and her own things round her, a feeling with which many can easily sympathize. Then, if there were meetings at Chequers the next day, the Prime Minister would drive on there for the night. The aim was to leave Number 10 at around 4.00 on Friday afternoon to beat the traffic, but this was not always possible. If the Prime Minister knew that he would be delayed, Mary Wilson would sometimes go down by train and be picked up by their housekeeper, who by now was based at Grange Farm but who came up to London to look after them for four days a week at Lord North Street.

The bungalow in the Scilly Isles belongs to Mary. Although it was actually bought by Harold in 1958 (when it was built), Mary took over and paid off the mortgage with the earnings from her first book of poems, upon which its ownership was transferred to her.

All the same, going even to this small house was more like a military operation than a visit to a secluded holiday retreat. When Harold Wilson went there, he would be flown down to Culdrose by the RAF, then taken over from Culdrose to the Scilly Isles by Sea King helicopter, in order to ensure the security of the red boxes, the Prime Ministerial papers, and all the other paraphernalia – including his baggage!

Once on the island, the business of both communications and security continued but on somewhat different lines. The bungalow is so minute, with its three bedrooms (two of which are very small), tiny sitting room and kitchen, that no one except the Wilson family could possibly fit in. The communications centre had perforce to be sited in the Customs House, which was taken over by the Cabinet Office during Harold Wilson's tenure of office. One of the compensations for the customs officials was that the house was kept in a perfect state of repair and redecoration, which has since been allowed to lapse somewhat from time to time.

On a seaside holiday the impedimenta of security are more obvious than anywhere else – what with the security police and the men fitted out with walkie-talkies so that the link with Number 10 is permanently maintained. It is impossible to be unaware of the importance of the visitor in your midst – so much so that the driver of the bus which toured the Scilly Isles always used to say as it went past the Wilsons' bungalow, 'We are now going past Number Ten and a Half, Downing Street.'

FIFTEEN

Chequers

You come to Chequers unexpectedly: as you round a sudden bend in the road, there are the main gates ahead, with the long drive over open parkland to the slight eminence on which stands the weekend retreat of the Prime Ministers of England.

Chequers is a Tudor house, built in the beautiful small Elizabethan brick of mellow red, tawny and golden shades. Yet despite this warmth of colouring, Chequers has always seemed to me faintly cold and threatening rather than welcoming. Perhaps it is the site, 630 feet up on a grassy plateau in the Chiltern Hills, that gives it a vaguely ominous air – it seems to brood over, rather than nestle into, the hilly countryside. Always, as I approached it down the drive, it gave me the feeling that something – a not-very-nice something – was about to happen.

Once inside the front door, this sensation for me was enhanced in the 1960s by the darkness of the panelling that covered most of the walls of the house. With the passage of the centuries, and the application of coat after coat of varnish, this had darkened until the original oak was almost black in places. The Elizabethan windows, with their small panes, did nothing to lighten those dark rooms. Only the White Parlour, a very pretty room with its wood-panelled walls painted white, escaped the general gloom which – for me – contained another element: the lack of that atmosphere possessed by houses where families have lived, loved, grown up, married and brought up children. It is a place of transients: not only the Prime Ministers and their families, but the thousands of visiting dignitaries and VIPs who have passed through briefly for conferences, visits or official business.

Outside, Chequers is deceptively large. Inside, the Great Hall –

originally the Elizabethan courtyard and the focal point of the whole building – takes up much of the space. It rises two storeys, with a balustraded gallery running along one side on to which the main bedrooms open.

In the 1960s this gallery was the scene of one of George Brown's more effervescent moments. Late – very late – one night, when Chequers was packed with Chiefs of Staff and senior officials down for a defence conference, the unmistakable high-pitched and carrying voice of George was heard, loudly rending the silent night air. Door after bedroom door nearby opened, and the inmates tumbled out, sleepily pulling on their silk dressing-gowns. The only word clearly distinguishable in George's cries was 'Oliver!' As the guests had heard that evening not only that the house was supposed to be haunted but that the Cromwell family had once lived at Chequers, and as many of them had in addition seen his death-mask in the Long Gallery, for one terrible moment everyone thought that the Great Protector himself had come back to confront George. But to the relief of most, there had been no such visitation; it turned out merely that the Secretary of State for Foreign Affairs, in exuberant mood and struck by a late-flowering idea, had been bellowing at the top of his voice for Oliver Wright (later Sir Oliver Wright and our Ambassador in Bonn and now Washington), then one of Harold Wilson's Private Secretaries seconded from the Foreign Office to Number 10.

There are seven main bedrooms opening on to the scene of George's night alarm. Here the Prime Minister, his family, and guests all sleep. These bedrooms were named after the various Prime Ministers who used them. We were first told this by the housekeeper, Mrs Kathleen Hill (who had been Sir Winston Churchill's personal secretary during the war years), when she met us at the door and showed us round the first time we visited Chequers after the 1964 election. But only the principal bedroom – named, naturally, after Sir Winston – then had its own exclusive bathroom *en suite*. This room became the one used by Harold Wilson during family weekends; Mary slept in a smaller room next door, with Giles on the other side with a shared bathroom. In all the bedrooms, with the exception of that used by the Douglas-Homes, which had twin beds, there were large and beautiful four-posters.

On the second floor, up a rather narrow flight of stairs, is the Prison Room – the chamber in which Lady Mary Grey, the sister of Lady Jane Grey, was imprisoned. Poor Lady Mary, the Queen's cousin, had committed the cardinal sin of the Elizabethan court: she had married without the Queen's permission. Not only was the man she married well below her in social class (he was a sergeant porter in the royal household), but their appearance together was extraordinary. She was tiny, almost a dwarf, and he was over six feet tall. The Queen, who did not like royalty or its connections laughed at, thought their marriage so disgraceful and the physical contrast between them so obscene that she had Lady Mary locked up in this room and kept a virtual prisoner. Her ghost is supposed to haunt the Prison Room. I don't know anyone who has actually seen it, although one of the Service girls on duty at Chequers is said to have gone into the room and seen the impression left by a female form on the bed at a time when no one was staying in the house.

I myself, though, never found it 'spooky' on the occasions I slept in it (the bedroom usually allotted to me was a small room called the Prince's Room, on the first floor next to the Long Gallery).

The atmosphere of the Prison Room is added to by the secret staircase, hidden in the panelled walls, that leads down to the lower floors – to the first-floor Conference Room, and the Hawtrey Room on the ground floor.

Beside the Prison Room are two other little bedrooms, divided by a curtain; the Garden Room girls used to sleep here. Unless you came up the stairs from the kitchen, leaving the main part of the house, the only way you could reach the Prison Room was through these two bedrooms, with their low wooden-beamed ceilings. Nearby were the staff bedrooms, and the long connecting corridors with their linoleum floors; the shoes of the staff as they went down to work at 5.00 a.m. made a dawn chorus on the hard floors.

Until Edward Heath modernized Chequers during his Premiership, its superb comfort was marred by one unlikely flaw: there were very few bathrooms. The Heads of State who were lucky would find that they had a bathroom with intercommunicating doors between their bedrooms; the rest had to cross a corridor and hope that their shared one was unoccupied when they got there. You would find François Mitterrand (then Socialist leader in France) sharing with Willy Brandt, or Lee Kuan Yew of Hong Kong with Kenneth Kaunda.

Much of the sanitary ware in these large, old bathrooms was equally imposing; it dated, I suppose, from the turn of the century, with its plunger lavatory handles set in dark polished wooden 'thrones'.

The Long Gallery opposite the main bedroom corridor is, to me, the most fascinating room in Chequers, so redolent of history that you can almost smell it along with the *pot-pourri* that the housekeeper places in bowls in every room. It has more of the collections – both historical and appertaining to the house's history – that are found in every room of Chequers than anywhere else. Here is kept Nelson's watch, and the ring that was taken from Queen Elizabeth's finger when she lay dying and sent to James VI in Scotland as the signal that it was now time for him to come and claim the throne. The messenger who took the ring was a Douglas-Home; by one of those neat historical twists his descendant came to Chequers many years later in his own right as Prime Minister.

In the Long Gallery, too, is Oliver Cromwell's death-mask, and his coat of arms is now immortalized in stained glass in the fine window of the Long Gallery.

The Long Gallery itself is not actually a gallery but a narrow room running the whole length of the south side of the building, overlooking the Chiltern Hills and the Bledlow Ridge. The floor is covered with rush matting overlaid with Persian rugs; the large central fireplace with its stone surround is remarkable for the Cromwellian duelling swords that surround it. The walls are lined with a magnificent collection of books, many of them very old and of great value.

But for politicians, the special feature of the Long Gallery is the Prime Ministerial windows. The Gallery has a great number of windows – two have bays in which you can sit – and each of the many smaller, upper windows, Gothic in shape, is divided into three. The upper third is taken up by the coat of arms or armorial design (for those Prime Ministers who do not have a coat of arms) in stained glass. Beneath this motif is the name of the Prime Minister, and his dates of office.

An ex-Prime Minister's 'window' is usually only installed when he has decided that he has retired for good and will never come back. After Harold Wilson resigned in 1976, Jim Callaghan was always jokingly enquiring when his window was going up; one got the impression that he could not sleep peacefully in bed at night until its installation. The persistent questioning paid off: Harold Wilson had his window put up within months of his resignation. Jim Callaghan's took considerably longer. The only ex-Prime Minister who has not yet had a window put up is Edward Heath.

Next to the Long Gallery and opening into it is a large conference room used for Cabinet meetings. Below it, on the ground floor, is the Hawtrey Room, a square, imposing room with a large alcove into which opens the secret staircase from the Prison Room two floors above. It was in this room, on the immediate right of the front door, that the alterations made by Edward Heath were most dramatically apparent.

The most obvious difference was that Chequers was now far, far lighter. Edward Heath had instituted major alterations and refurbishments. When we returned in 1974, we found that all the old panelling, dark with the varnish of years, had been stripped to its original light colour; it now looked warm and glowing rather than dark and forbidding. Experts had been called in to refurbish carpets, curtains and covers generally; the pictures throughout the house had been cleaned and restored; the books had been catalogued; and the number of bathrooms had been increased (mainly by dividing large ones into smaller units).

Thanks to Edward Heath, the Hawtrey Room is now a very impressive drawing room, with comfortable seating and showcases filled with beautiful glass; and the large alcove turned into a small separate TV annexe. The result was that the Hawtrey Room was used more than ever before as a main reception room. After its transformation, coffee and after-dinner drinks were usually taken there rather than in the Great Hall – as had been the custom in the 1960s.

Most important of all, Edward Heath had also had the contents of the house catalogued. Some of the treasures there had been stored away in attics and more or less forgotten; Heath had them all looked at, repaired where necessary, and brought out and put on display or where possible used. He had everything inventoried, from the collections of porcelain and glass to the rare books on the shelves, whose cataloguing was a long and difficult task. By instituting these changes, Edward Heath has made a great and lasting contribution to the history of Chequers. This overdue labour turned up some horrors: notably the discovery that all the old glass from some beautiful medieval mirrors had been removed by some previous housekeeper because it was spotted or clouded, and replaced by bright modern glass.

In the dining room, however, the panelling was left untouched, its dark tones making a splendid foil for the spectacular candelabra and gleaming silver. With the addition of an extra table, thirty-six people can be seated. The china, too, is beautiful, with a superb special service, covered in gold leaf, for State entertaining. When the Wilsons first went to Chequers, this was never used, simply because no one told them of its existence; but it made its reappearance during the Heath years, so the Wilsons were able to use it on their return in 1974.

One of the sad facts of that earlier time at Chequers was the early in-built resistance, amounting at times almost to hostility, that faced any request from a Socialist Prime Minister in an establishment that had been Conservative-dominated for the previous thirteen years. Thus the Wilsons ended up asking for very little, simply in order to avoid the appearance of causing change or trouble.

All the same, those dinner parties were often great fun. There were certain distinguished foreign visitors to whose arrival I always looked forward. Willy Brandt was always very good company; he had a much more impact-making personality than Helmut Schmidt, whose approach was, I suppose, more serious. Willy liked to live as well as to work. After the Socialist International meetings at Chequers, to which all the international Socialist leaders came, the more conservative ones would disappear to bed fairly early. But people like Willy Brandt, Tage Erlander (Prime Minister of Sweden) and Otto Kraag (Prime Minister of Denmark and married to a very beautiful actress) would make a night of it. These three personable-looking men would sit drinking schnapps, getting jollier and jollier, and always very friendly.

They were a great contrast to some early conference delegates and visitors. Sir Seewoosagur Ramgoolam in particular invariably fell asleep, and always woke up at the end of a conference saying, 'Oh yes, very good, very good!' Len Williams, General Secretary of the Party, always used to sleep a lot at meetings too. I remember one Socialist International conference which both of them attended, and at which both had enjoyed the usual long, refreshing slumber, at the end of which Sir Seewoosagur Ramgoolam asked to see the Prime Minister. 'I have the task of making recommendations as to who should be the next Governor-General of Mauritius,' he began, going on to say, to Harold Wilson's astonishment, 'I would like to suggest Len Williams. I am terrifically impressed by him.' As both of them had spent most of their time together unconscious, Harold could only suppose that they had shared the same dream.

Like everyone else, they enjoyed the Chequers food. It was always excellent, whether it happened to be a simple family weekend or a grand dinner party during an important conference. The house style could be called 'traditional English': everything was home-made, and most of the raw materials came from the Chequers estate – fruit and vegetables from the garden, most other produce from the Chequers farm.

A dinner party usually started with home-made soup, melon or grapefruit (one of the Chequers specialities was grapefruit with liqueur baked in the oven), followed by a fish course. The main dish was almost always a roast of some kind or – in season – pheasant, partridge, salmon or trout. Harold Wilson's own passion was for roast duck, so duckling from the farm figured prominently on the menu. At formal dinners, puddings were often sweet *soufflés*, which the kitchen staff did to perfection, or another Chequers speciality: baked Alaska. At a simple family meal, the pudding was more likely to be apple or gooseberry pie, or junket.

Simple as this food sounds, because it was all so fresh and home-grown it was far more delicious than most *haute cuisine*. This insistence on quality runs right through to the smallest detail: not only the tea-time scones but the jam to put on them is home-made, as is the chutney that accompanies cold meat. (During the week while the house is empty, the staff cook, bottle and pickle to great effect.) Even breakfast in bed – at Chequers, breakfast is always served in the bedrooms – is a luxury, with anything you want to order from scrambled eggs to every available newspaper.

At Christmas-time, the staff excelled themselves. Christmas at Chequers was truly an experience, of the old-fashioned English kind that is nowadays only found within the pages of novels. Dinner on Christmas evening meant paper hats and crackers as well as turkey, plum pudding, mince pies and the best brandy butter I have ever tasted, and presents from the large Christmas tree that stood in the Great Hall – this, with its enormous open fireplace that ran almost the whole length of one wall, made the perfect background. All the rooms in Chequers had their original open fireplaces; usually, though, fires were only lit in the Great Hall, the Long Gallery, the White Parlour and the Hawtrey Room.

The Great Hall is the grandest and most imposing part of the house with its gallery above, where Edward Heath, we were told, had madrigal singers placed during evening entertainments. There, too, is the grand piano, which was used then more than it had ever been before, no doubt.

The Great Hall, with its polished wood floor and Persian rugs over the central carpet, is also the setting for some of the most beautiful pictures at Chequers: some wonderful Van Dycks, a Rembrandt (about which I believe there is now some doubt), and the famous painting of Androcles and the Lion by Snyders that Winston Churchill is supposed to have touched up. The story – no one knows whether it is truth or myth – goes that Winston decreed that the painting was inaccurate because it did not contain the mouse of the original story. Allegedly, the great Prime Minister called for his step-ladder, paint brush and palette, and, mounting the former, used the last two to paint in the missing mouse.

In all old English country houses the most interesting book is usually the Visitors' Book. Chequers is no exception. The Visitors' Book there has a fascination all its own, casting new and revealing light on times and events recorded freely in the newspapers of the day, but clearly only half-seen and partially interpreted. What a delight it would be to sit with all the old Visitors' Books looking back through them and seeing the curious gatherings of unlikely names at luncheons and dinners over the past sixty years.

One of our rare finds, which Harold Wilson was to record in his book, *The Chariot of Israel*, relates to the time of Suez, when the air had been filled with stories of collusion and secret diplomacy. He wrote:

> ... I had occasion to look at the Visitors' Book at Chequers. For the Sunday in question the guests were listed, but strangely a civil servant's name was included, contrary to the usual practice. It seemed to me that a name had been scratched out by a sharp instrument, such as a razor blade, and the official's name written over it. At Chequers there is a powerful hand magnifying glass, used to illumine the locket of Queen Elizabeth I, and showing her own picture and that of her mother, Anne Boleyn. This confirmed that the rough surface had in fact been caused by a razor-like instrument. I concluded that the name excised had been that of an Israeli general. I was wrong. It was that of General Challe.

For family weekends, the Wilsons, in common with most other Prime Ministers and their families, used the White Parlour. This beautiful room, with its white-painted panelling, which looks out over the rose gardens, is sunny and light, with plenty of comfortable chintz-covered armchairs and three-seater sofas, a lovely conversation painting on one wall, the priceless Constables, and more of those collections of objects that are a feature of Chequers.

To the visitor, one architectural surprise is the comparative smallness of the staircase. In most old houses, the staircase is a dominating and imposing feature; at Chequers, it is small and tucked away. Exactly as at Downing Street, there are photographs of all the Prime Ministerial occupants down the wall at the side, above the red-rope banister. The carpet, too, is red. Apart from the bedrooms, the White Parlour is the only room with wall-to-wall carpeting; others have Persian rugs over rush matting or wood floors, on which the beautiful old bow-fronted chests of drawers and Regency sofa tables look their best. As the former owner Lord Lee said, it is not a museum but a representation of what 'an old English house may contain which has been owned and cherished for many hundreds of years by people of taste and moderate means, who loved it as their home and who adorned it for their own gratification and comfort'.

As a machine for living (and working) in, Chequers is superb. It is staffed entirely by service personnel. Usually the chef is a man, from the nearby RAF base Halton Camp. The woman in charge of the staff (who is not the custodian) is called Chief; if she is a Wren, the girls under her are from the WRAF, if she is WRAF, then they are Wrens. Sometimes the team is mixed, as in part of the Wilson years. They run Chequers with the highest degree of organizational efficiency, and see that it is kept looking impeccable – with a freshness assisted by the vases of garden flowers and porcelain bowls of lavender on the side tables. This lavender is also made into lavender bags by the present custodian, who gives them to those visitors she particularly likes.

Miss Thomas, the present custodian (a Group Captain (retired) WRAF), is a highly efficient, attractive, humorous and remarkable woman to whom we all became very attached. A great deal of the credit for the superb way in which the house is run must go to her.

The garden itself is mainly lawn, though there are still the remains of a formal Elizabethan garden, now in the shape of a paved rose garden with gazebos at either end. Two of its most beautiful and ancient trees were blown down in the gales of 1977.

From the garden, too, can be seen Edward Heath's most noticeable innovation: the swimming pool – or, strictly speaking, the building that houses it.

A swim in this beautiful new pool was most proudly offered by the Prime Minister to Lord Weidenfeld, when the latter came to stay at Chequers. Once they were in the water, the Prime Minister, not noted as a strong swimmer, surfaced by the side of the pool about two-thirds of the way down where the bottom began to slope sharply, and for the weak swimmer dangerously, towards the deep end. The spot was marked by a commemorative plaque put there in honour of the American Ambassador who had donated the funds for the pool's construction. It read: 'Donated by the Honourable Walter Annenberg on the occasion of the visit to Chequers of Richard Milhous Nixon.' Pointing to this plaque, Harold Wilson remarked to George Weidenfeld: 'I always swim only as far as the last letter in Annenberg's name. After that it's not safe to swim: I'm out of my depth.'

This pool is twenty-five yards long and enclosed in a modern structure that is well tuned to the old house, along the sides of which are large windows that, when open, turn it into a semi-outdoor pool. It has every possible facility, from changing rooms and showers to a pantry for drinks and tea-making. The pool is in almost constant use, either by the visitors who come for a conference or – during the week – by the families of staff. Douglas Hurd's two sons learned to swim at Chequers, as did mine.

Harold Wilson loved Chequers (Mary Wilson's feelings towards it were cooler); one of its main attractions was the Ellesborough golf course, of which all Prime Ministers are made honorary members. In the 1960s, he usually managed to play golf at least once during a weekend; but by the 1970s the workload was so heavy that, although the course was only a mile away, he had no time for golf – nor even for a swim or a turn around the garden.

Even during a 'quiet' weekend, the work of a Prime Minister has to go on. At Chequers, most of it takes place in the large room to the left of the front door. Here, the Private Secretaries and the Garden Room staff work; this room also contains all the electronic equipment and general impedimenta of modern government that connect Downing Street with the rest of the world.

Here I must say that no Prime Ministerial line could be called truly 'hot' without the girls from the Downing Street switchboard. Quite simply, they are the best telephone girls in the world. They can find anyone, anywhere, at any time; and they perform their duties with a charm that is equal to their efficiency. Three of these girls go down to operate the switchboard, on the second floor, every time the Prime Minister spends a weekend at Chequers. Usually, their arrival is only minutes ahead of the Prime Ministerial car, but traditionally they use a different entrance.

For everyone except the Prime Minister and certain distinguished visitors, for whom the main gate is opened, the side entrance is the rule. This is manned by the police, with a barrier at which you stop to identify yourself (no matter how easily recognizable you are, or how many times you have been there before). At night-time, as you halt, you find yourself beneath the glare of an enormous arc light and, necessary and right though this security procedure is, it never failed to remind me of all those films about the war. Once inside the house though, all such feelings are banished by the peculiar atmosphere of Chequers, at once powerful but strangely characterless.

Chequers was handed over to the nation at the beginning of 1921 by its owner, Lord Lee of Fareham, then Lloyd George's Minister of Agriculture (the deed of settlement transferring the property was actually executed in November 1917, but the Lees did not move out of the house until nearly four years later). Lord Lee's intention was that Chequers should become the country home of the Prime Minister of the day, where he could rest, relax and return to work refreshed. In his deed of settlement he wrote:

> ... the better the health of our rulers the more sanely will they rule, and the inducement to spend two days a week in the high and pure air of the Chiltern hills and woods will, it is hoped, benefit the nation as well as its chosen leaders. The main features of this scheme are therefore designed not merely to make Chequers available as the official country residence of the Prime Minister of the day, but to tempt him to visit it regularly and to make it possible for him to live there, even though his income should be limited to his salary.

The inscription in the stained glass window of the corridor above the porch reads:

> This house of Peace and Ancient Memories
> Was given to England as a thank-offering
> For her deliverance in the Great War, 1914–1918
> And as a place of peace and recreation
> For her Prime Ministers for ever.

Since then, every Prime Minister of England, with the exception only of Bonar Law, has enjoyed Lord Lee's magnificent gift. The first to use it was, of course, Lloyd George, and so much did he and his family enjoy it that when his daughter Megan heard that he was going to resign (in October 1922), her immediate comment, we are told, was: 'Damn! There goes Chequers!'

SIXTEEN

The Land Deals Affair

In any account about 'the Land Deals affair' it is, I think, necessary to set the scene again. The timing, too, is crucial: it was a storm that blew up between two elections (those of February and October 1974), both of which were won by Labour. But it had already made a first appearance during the last week of the February campaign.

As I have said, the weeks immediately after the February campaign were taken up with action to end the miners' strike, to return Britain to a full working week, to achieve the transformation of industrial relations from a mood of confrontation to one of hope, co-operation and determination, and to end the State of Emergency under which Britain had lived since November 1973.

The practical measures to back up the new Government's approach were put into force immediately: they included a freeze on rents (both council and private), the announcement of substantial help for ratepayers in inner city areas and of an increase in pensions and other social benefits, and the introduction of food subsidies to relieve the main burden on the family budget. The Government even intervened directly to halt the increase in bread prices. (Today, with bread prices so much higher, it seems strange to remember how astronomical they seemed then.)

There was no doubt that the Government's first changes were warmly welcomed; less, I think, for their political content than for the sheer fact that something was at last *happening* again. Most people realized we were in the middle of a grave economic crisis – brought about not just by the recent internal political confrontation and miners' dispute, but much more by the world-wide oil crisis and the consequent financial difficulties. They were anxious for, and in sympathy with, measures designed to unite the country. Most, too, agreed with Labour policy that in a situation of such severity the first priority was the protection of the weakest in the community.

Confidence flowed back dramatically. Nor did the City react negatively, as it had done ten years before, to the arrival of a Labour Government in the middle of an economic crisis; ironically, Edward Heath had succeeded in destroying the one inbuilt advantage enjoyed by a Tory Government – the City's belief that the Tories were the party of good managers with a special ability to handle financial and monetary policy. (Under the Thatcher Government, the City's natural affinity with the Tories has often been strained for different reasons: Conservative policies that lean towards monetarism and away from their earlier semi-interventionist attitude, together with the fact that the City itself has changed and become much more internationally educated.)

Once back in Opposition, the Conservatives found themselves in something of a dilemma. They had to make a judgement on whether to attack the new Labour Government or whether to 'play it cool' and not indulge in controversial opposition for its own sake. After all, their calculation had to be on whether or not, by being too forceful in Opposition, they might force Harold Wilson to seek a better mandate. Was this what they wanted when they were themselves vulnerable and weakened by the events of the previous six months? Some Tories, however, believed that if the Prime Minister approached the Queen on this, she would have to refuse and send for Edward Heath again. It was a situation Harold Wilson enjoyed. He knew that the one weapon a Prime Minister possesses in these circumstances – namely, asking the Queen for a dissolution and another election – would act as a powerful deterrent. In recent years there has been considerable debate over whether or not he would have had the right to ask for another election so quickly within weeks of an earlier appeal. In any similar situation at any future time, should there again be a 'hung' election result, this question may well have to be resolved.

It is arguable whether the Queen on the advice of her constitutional experts would have granted Harold Wilson his request if it had come within weeks of the February result. Looking back on the atmosphere in the country, I am certain the Queen's advisers would have felt called upon to advise that she grant a dissolution. An election forced so quickly by a Conservative Opposition, without the Government having an opportunity to show what it could do, would have been badly received in the country. An alternative scenario – and one widely discussed now as a future hypothetical case – that the Queen might have been advised to refuse and send for the Leader of the Opposition to ask him to attempt once again to form a Government seems to be unlikely in the extreme.

Such an act was constitutionally possible, but the situation would have been too sensitive for such a response and I have no doubt that the Palace was well aware of this. However, to make doubly sure, Harold Wilson decided to put a shot across the Tories' bows: to warn them that a defeat in Parliament might result not in a call to Edward Heath but a second early and unwanted election. He was determined to warn them off. It was decided that at a political rally he was to address in High Wycombe on 15 March, he would make the position absolutely plain. This he did:

> I believe that the British public want to see the Labour Government given a fair chance to get the country back on the road to recovery and strength. I believe they would be impatient of any further manœuvring designed to put back into office the administration which almost had to be dragged from office ten days ago. As a realist, I recognize that if the Opposition Parties are determined to play around with the future of this nation, they are in a position to do so. I want to give this warning. If they are realists, they will recognize that they do so at their electoral peril. The Labour Government will not emulate the Conservatives in a desperate attempt to hold on to office for we believe the electorate will know how to respond.
>
> The British public will not lightly forgive politicians and parties who, having been rejected by the voters, seek to prevent the Labour Government from taking the measures necessary for the nation's survival. Their motives are dictated more by internal Party tensions than by the national interest, for which, unitedly, we are working.

The Government was still feeling the elatory effects of having fought a good election and won. It felt, too, I think, as never before, that as a government Labour offered the nation policies that really were national policies, designed to meet the needs of the majority of people at that time. It also had an experienced team with an adept and experienced Cabinet chairman in Harold Wilson. Both political and policy advisers within Number 10 also felt confident and competent in their ability to advise the Prime Minister in this critical period.

However, the PM's confidence in himself and his Government, and pleasure at having been returned to Number 10, were diminished to a very considerable degree by a separate and peculiar dimension which was to develop in the political atmosphere over the immediate weeks after that High Wycombe speech.

Suddenly, in a way that not one of us at Number 10 could have foreseen, the political climate was to alter. It is difficult to write about these few months without inviting a charge of paranoia – an accusation directed from time to time against Harold Wilson. Nevertheless, as they are an integral part of the inter-election period, I shall set them down as I saw them.

The inter-Party situation was not as straightforward as is usual after an election. In such a 'hung' situation there was no political honeymoon for the Government. On the one hand, Labour was the Government, dictating the pattern of affairs to which the Conservatives as Opposition had to respond. On a more intimate and internal level, however, the Government was responding to a situation and series of events instigated, not by the Conservative Party as such, but by its more powerful, broadly based and overenthusiastic supporters, who wished to see it back in power. Increasing this state of general formlessness was the continuing cause of apprehension for the Conservatives about the timing of the next election. What worried them was that Labour would go for a snap election in June (something indeed discussed at length among ourselves) that would result in a greatly increased Labour majority and consequently a more decisive mandate for the Government's policies.

As I have said, even before the first election of 1974 there had been certain potentially disquieting signs. Information of a purely personal kind about various Labour personalities was being brought to the attention of the Tory leadership, and presumably also their headquarters. Although there is, of course, always the argument that the public has 'a right to know' details of the private lives of those in the public eye, there comes a point beyond which it is no longer in the public interest. In those early post-February election weeks, the Conservative leaders were rightly contemptuous of these tittle-tattle stories and dismissed them as counter-productive.

But their attitude started to shift. In his book, *Inside Story*, Chapman Pincher, a distinguished journalist, claims that 'while the leadership still disliked the whole idea of using personal denigration', some of them felt that the times were desperate for them, and they should therefore consider using any means to prevent Harold Wilson going to the country in June and consequently confronting them with a major electoral defeat rather than the close-run thing it had been in February. It is clear that Edward Heath resisted suggestions that certain of these stories should be used by the Conservatives – but it is equally true that he must have known of the proposed campaign, to which presumably he gave the go-ahead. Leaders of Parties are always aware, since it is essential that Party Headquarters and the Leader's own office should keep in step at every point, particularly when an election appears to be in the offing.

One characteristic of the press, as opposed to radio and TV, is the snowball effect. Once a story starts, not only does every rival paper rush for a piece of the action, but a cuttings file quickly builds up. This file, checked by every journalist worth his salt before he adds his two-penn'orth, has the advantage that it is more easily accessible than its radio or TV equivalent; at a certain point, a story or personality with a big enough cuttings file achieves a momentum of its or their own. We all know the people who are news simply because they are news. Hence, once the spiteful stories fed into Tory Party headquarters filtered out into the newspapers that supported the Conservative cause, they began to gather speed.

Among leading Labour politicians grew the fear that they would be next to receive 'the treatment'. Some had already been victims: Ted Short had already been unfairly treated, and was subsequently to be given another 'dose'. I was told later by the Prime Minister that James Callaghan had warned him that he, Callaghan, might be next in line for gossip stories about his business connections, in particular with the Italian Bank and his friend Julian Hodge, the South Wales financier and industrialist. Jim felt, I believe, at that time that there would be a final decision between stories about him and about me. I was in very good company, but I'm sorry I won the contest.

Some of the stories circulating were so highly coloured as to be absurd: tales of drugs, orgies and nameless vices in mysterious blocks of flats off Baker Street – not, I assume, Sherlock Holmes's old quarters. Most of these eventually found their way to the Prime Minister's Office during the course of their circulation. But the main story, that grew ever more elaborate and detailed, was the one that affected me: the Land Deals affair.

It really began during the second half of March – though, earlier, as I have said, during the election campaign itself the *Guardian* and the *Daily Mail* had questioned Harold Wilson about it. No story was published during the campaign and, after the weekend of 15 March when Harold Wilson warned in his High Wycombe speech that the Conservatives' behaviour might force him back to the country, there was another lull.

The first inkling was a story run by the *Daily Mail* (on an inside page) entitled 'The case of Ronald Milhench and his £950,000 land deal'. At that time, I did not take the daily papers at home, so it was not until I went into Downing Street to work that I heard about it. Even this was almost by chance: I ran into Bernard Donoughue on the main staircase as I was going to see the Prime Minister in his study, and his first words to me, smiling broadly, were, 'What has your brother been up to?' I read the story with foreboding because I could see at once that it was something that could be picked up for comment, but I had no idea how monumental this would prove to be. Curiously enough, it was still not immediately picked up, and during the next few days seemed to have died away.

As a story, it was sufficiently newsworthy to rate attention and explanation. What it did not warrant was a campaign of innuendo and overall denigration. The facts are these.

In 1967 my brother, Tony Field, decided to go into business for himself. He was a trained geologist, starting his career (after graduating from Nottingham University) with the Iraq Petroleum Company. For them, he had worked as a senior exploratory geologist in Iraq, the Persian Gulf, in the Emirates, Kuwait and Bahrein. After eight years overseas he had decided to come home. After a short period with the Bath and Portland Group he decided to 'go it alone', and to this end he bought some land near Wigan, on which there was a great deal of slag; shortly afterwards, he purchased a stone quarry nearby.

At the point when he bought the land with its slag and the quarry, the Labour Government was in office and socialist policies were being applied – with, of course, the necessary legislation to back them up. My brother was well aware of this. When he bought the land with the slag, and later the quarry, he had no idea in mind of what would happen once both slag and quarry had been worked out. But certainly if he had given it thought, he would have done so against the background of socialist legislation. His intention was to sell slag (which could be used for building and in industry) and stone (which could also be used in road-building), and from this he expected a fairly healthy return. From the moment of his purchases, for the next six years he worked much of the business himself (even once breaking a leg while operating some machinery that was used).

Along with conducting his own business, my brother dovetailed in a certain amount of voluntary work for Harold Wilson. He started by acting as his driver for personal and political engagements: Harold Wilson no longer drove a car; my brother knew Great Britain well through his work; and, in addition, he enjoyed Harold Wilson's company and was glad to be of help to him. As for Harold Wilson, he could not possibly have afforded a private chauffeur at weekends for all his engagements, so he, too, was pleased with the arrangement. After some years of driving, acting as a weekend driver, my brother agreed to take on some part-time work in Harold Wilson's office.

I was involved with my brother's business from the beginning; in 1967, when my brother's company was first set up, I was invited to become part of it. My brother and the rest of my family felt that this would offer me some protection for the future. No pension was attached to my work for Harold Wilson, so that I had only the State retirement pension to look forward to. The same reasoning held good for the inclusion in the company of my sister and, in particular, my father, who had been forced to retire from his own work because of a series of coronary thrombosis attacks. Both he and my mother were already of pension age, and my brother wished to give them additional protection.

Then came Edward Heath and the boom years. As land values rose, so the piles of slag diminished until, in 1973 when prices were near their peak, the land was completely worked out. My brother had the choice of developing the land industrially or selling it off. What he could not afford to do was keep it without developing it, leaving it to stand neglected and unused. Indeed, in those circumstances it might well have been compulsorily purchased, in which case he would still have made a profit, a profit officially sanctioned by local government and presumably less newsworthy. It is a pity this is not what happened. The first option was the one that attracted him, and he had a series of discussions with various industrial companies in the North of England to try and reach agreement on some form of co-operative venture in which he himself could be involved. This would have been ideal, and I know he regrets bitterly now not going ahead with one of them. While these talks dragged out, he was approached by a number of land dealers, including a man called Ronald Milhench.

Milhench, it transpired later, was clearly an extraordinary and unusual character. At the time of their meeting there appeared no reason for my brother to query his credentials (as the judge agreed in the court action of July 1974, when Ronald Milhench was tried and convicted for forgery). His backers were the Cripps-Warburg Bank, one of the new merchant banks that had sprung up in the City during the boom years; they had a good reputation, and my brother felt that if they trusted Milhench with a loan large enough to buy the land – well, that was good enough for him. He assumed further that they would not back a man unless they had carefully checked his credentials (whether they did, or did not, has never actually been established; to this day, the Bank have neither confirmed nor denied it). It was a natural assumption to make in view of the size of the loan and the probity of the Bank.

The other character to appear in the story also seemed perfectly respectable. Birmingham businessman Mr Victor Harper had been one of the men who approached my brother over the sale of the land and the purchase of adjacent land, which naturally made a more viable whole. The large sum quoted by the *Daily Mail*, in fact, related to the combined land. In the event the sale to Milhench was only of the smaller, mainly original part, and consequently the sum for that was correspondingly much smaller. But this fact too was eventually obfuscated by later publicity, leaving everyone believing that the 'land deals' involved sums approaching £1,000,000,000: this was not so. Together with my brother, Harper was therefore involved in the Milhench transaction.

Separately Victor Harper wrote to my brother during the summer of 1973 at the House of Commons asking him if he could find out from the Warwickshire County Council some information relating to planning permission for a piece of land in their area. The letter arrived while my brother was on holiday in the Scilly Isles (the Wilson family were also there). In his absence, the Harper letter was promptly acknowledged on his behalf and, as in normal business practice, dealt with by one of the office secretaries, who wrote to Warwickshire County Council to ask them for any advice or comments about development concerning the future of some land called Jerrings Hall on which Mr Harper possessed a binding option of purchase. The matter was dealt with in the routine way for all letters of this kind coming into the office. (Many years later, Denis Thatcher's letters of a similar kind, but on Number 10 notepaper, were to attract rather less attention.)

Somehow, the correspondence about Jerrings Hall came into the hands of the *Daily Express*, who printed the letter to the Warwickshire County Council on 3 April 1973 under the headline 'Wilson man in land deal row', irrespective of the fact that ten months earlier my brother had given up his part-time, temporary and unpaid work for Harold Wilson. There was never any question but that what my brother did for Harold Wilson was done on a basis of friendship only (my brother was not even a member of the Labour Party); he was a hard-working businessman, most of whose activities were perfectly well known to a large number of people – it is inconceivable that journalists, particularly those working in the Palace of Westminster, were unaware of this.

The *Daily Express* headline prompted its rival, the *Daily Mail*, to go one better. A number of stories appeared in the *Daily Mail*, and, during the course of their investigative journalism, they came up with a new angle: a letter (shown to a *Daily Mail* reporter by Ronald Milhench) which was purported to have been signed by Harold Wilson, indicating that he, Harold Wilson, hoped that the deal which Milhench was about to be involved in would be successful. As Joe Haines pointed out in a memorandum to the Prime Minister, more than 6,000 column inches devoted to reportage, comment, analysis and photographs of leading participants in this story appeared between 3 and 11 April. One thousand one hundred column inches were similarly used between 30 April and early May. With headlines like 'Who forged Wilson's signature?' (*Daily Mail*, 3 April), 'Land deal rocks Labour' (*Daily Mail*, 4 April), 'Wilson met land dealers' (*Daily Express*, 6 April), there was, as Joe Haines pointed out in his memorandum, every likelihood that the impression of 'no smoke without fire' would be given.

And so it proved. Never at any time was it pointed out that my brother, who was not a committed Labour supporter, was doing something that was not only the natural conclusion of the running-down of his business, but a lot less notable than the activities of a large number of Labour voters and supporters – and indeed of well-known Labour MPs and Peers – whose extra-parliamentary activities were devoted almost wholly to property, land development and speculation.

Most difficult of all to counter, perhaps, was not merely the implication that my brother had been with the Prime Minister far more recently than was in fact the case, and that I and my sister were deeply involved in something undesirable, but the unspoken, underlying suggestion that Harold Wilson might himself be involved. As anyone who knows could say, this is a ridiculous idea: he has never held stocks and shares, and has never been on the board of any company for financial reward; he has earned money solely through his political and parliamentary career, and by writing and advising.

The question of the forged signature was equally difficult to counter. Harry Longmuir, an excellent investigative journalist (to whom a special award was made for the high quality of his work), interviewed Milhench a number of times. At no time (as prosecuting counsel pointed out) did Longmuir believe the letter was genuine when he saw it. He always felt the signature was forged, and he gave little credence to Milhench's story. Certainly if I myself had ever met Milhench, which

I had not either then or since, I too would have had immediate suspicions. Subsequent details learned about him in his court case confirm his unusual character. Not many British estate agents, or land developers, water ski so expertly and collect guns – even a sten gun complete with ammunition. He was larger than life – a character straight out of an American soap-opera, a J.R. business partner perhaps, but not a J.R.

Sometimes the juxtaposition of photographs and headlines in the newspapers of that period seemed to hint that a member of my family or even I myself had been a party to the forgery. For instance, the senior police officer, Alan Jones, who did most of the interviewing during the investigations into the alleged forgery of Harold Wilson's signature, was featured in the *Daily Express* on 13 April in a headline which ran: 'He also expects to interview Mr Field's forty-one-year-old sister, Mrs Marcia Williams, who is Mr Wilson's Political Secretary.' Adjacent to this was the sentence: 'Among questions that will need answering is how Mr Wilson's personal House of Commons notepaper could have been used for the forged letter.' These two stories were run together; I can only say that if I had not been the subject of one of them but an averagely intelligent reader, I would have wondered about Mrs Williams's role in the story.

Stripped of the wild imaginings of Ronald Milhench and the angled reportage in many of the papers, the story boiled down to the sale of my brother's land, after all the slag on it had been cleared and sold, to a person who was supported by a reputable merchant bank, and who had as colleagues and friends a number of prominent businessmen in the Midlands area. During the Milhench trial, prosecuting counsel (Mr James Comyn) said as much. 'The [Field] family who have figured largely in this story and introduced the original connection with Mr Wilson ... have acted with complete propriety throughout the whole of these transactions.' 'I am much obliged,' replied Mr Justice Crichton.

No one would have guessed this during the weeks leading up to Easter. In addition to the land deals stories, the press was filled with personal details – many of them inaccurate and distorted – about myself and my family. All were painful and intrusive. Journalists visited villages where my family had once lived, asking the most personal questions of people we knew, even offering money in return for a story, if one could be provided. They visited the area where my brother had worked near Wigan. No friend or foe was left unturned to obtain a story.

That time is still horribly painful to recall. The moment that the story broke, the nightmare familiar to any victim of the press on a hunt for a big story began. A large crowd of journalists appeared in the small mews where I live, and stationed themselves outside my front door and the ground-floor windows of the sitting room and dining room. These had to be kept closed and the curtains drawn in order to ensure some kind of privacy and to prevent the journalists outside hearing every single word spoken indoors. Nor did we want to have to listen to their conversations, amusing and entertaining as some of them were.

Whenever anyone came to the house, they were accosted by the journalists and interviewed on the spot. All through this whole period the journalists would take it in turns to ring the doorbell or hammer loudly with the door knocker. When this failed to bring either myself or a member of my family (my elderly mother was far from well at the time), they would sometimes offer pocket money to schoolchildren to do it for them. When friends or colleagues in the Labour Party, shocked by the furore surrounding me, sent flowers or other gifts, the press read the cards attached before they were handed in at the front door.

All of this we watched from the bedroom windows upstairs, at first with amusement, later with increasing depression. I remember watching them once clustering round a particularly beautiful bouquet with great interest; only when eventually it arrived in the house did I discover that my flowers were from James and Audrey Callaghan, kindly and considerate as ever.

During all that traumatic time when I was virtually a prisoner in my own house, I was given great support and comfort by Joe Haines, Bernard Donoughue, Albert Murray and Terence Lancaster of the *Daily Mirror*, all of whom came out regularly to see me. They too became angry when the invasion of the mews reached its height. There was a point when Bernard went upstairs, filled a small jug with water, and let it trickle slowly down on the heads of the most aggressive of the press to cool them off.

As for my neighbours, they were not only embarrassed but angry – so much so that I had to restrain close friends of mine who lived in the mews from coming out and expressing their fury with the press (towards the end of the siege one friend's student lodger boiled over, throwing a bucket of water over one journalist). The 'quality' papers, I should say here, were just as guilty as the populars: it was 'the gentlemen from *The Times*' who would bang on the door after midnight to ask us questions.

So much a prisoner in my own home was I that even trying to take a few days' holiday at Easter needed careful planning if I was to evade the incessant crowd of journalists. One night, well after midnight, some friends who lived opposite lured the smaller 'night shift' of newspapermen away momentarily, and I and my family quickly ran across the mews into my friends' home – they had left the door on the latch – and then out through their back door, which gave onto a street some distance away. In retrospect, it seemed more like a scene from a film than a departure on a quiet family vacation.

All in all, this was one of the most painful periods of my life. Most of the press gathered outside my home that spring were friendly, funny and some of them even embarrassed in their role. They do the job on which they have been sent as competently as they can, with as much courtesy as possible. Nevertheless, they are under pressure to get a story and are therefore often forced into a course of action which appears to their victims to be an intolerable invasion of privacy. It is equally true, of course, that they don't have to do the job if they don't want to, so presumably in most cases they weigh the embarrassment against the financial rewards of their occupation and opt for the latter.

Difficult and traumatic though that period was, I learned much from it, not least who my friends were. I received a large mail from all over the country, most of which was warm and friendly – there were, of course, a number of abusive letters, but I had become more used to dealing with these. It taught me that I must, however painful being a victim felt, remember that I did believe in a free press, and furthermore had all my life believed the British press to be among the best in the world. But it was hard indeed to keep to that view. Politically, it taught me the extraordinary degree of bitterness with which Parties and their supporters pursue stories for political advantage. Nevertheless, that is the name of the game. I had become a victim but I would not complain about that. What is certain is that if it had not been me that spring it would have been someone else, so someone owes me for that! The stories that subsequently appeared after the Milhench trial (rarely, I hasten to add, on the front page), which included his more bizarre characteristics and activities, implied that 'everyone' had realized from the start that he was the forger and a peculiar and pathetic person to boot. But in my family's case there was no corrective editorial the other way.

What chiefly concerned all of us was the effect this affair would have on the Labour Party and on Labour voters in the country. I am sure it did have an effect, though David Butler in his book on the October election claimed it was a subject rarely referred to by the electorate except in the north-west. Nowhere else did it surface as an issue in the next election. But I also think that the saturation press coverage was in the end counter-productive. The Conservative Party, naturally, had hoped that it would arouse hostility to Harold Wilson and the Labour Government, their objective being first to prevent him going to the country in June, and secondly to stop him being re-elected. What they did not know was that, very early on, he had already personally decided on an October election. The majority of his senior colleagues were to support him in this. There were unexpected votes – like Denis Healey and Michael Foot – in favour of June; others, like Shirley Williams and James Callaghan, backed Harold Wilson for an October election.

It is difficult to speak of this whole affair without sounding either defensive or aggressive, neither of which I want to be. The land had been bought for what stood on it six years earlier, and had been worked as a business from then on until it ran dry. My brother's idea that it might then be used as a small industrial development site along with others in the area, giving an industrial complex to an area sorely in need of industry and employment, could, properly speaking, be called 'reclamation'. Because of the furore that surrounded it at the time, this did not happen; afterwards, the economic situation had already deteriorated and it had become impossible.

What was more, the financial security I thought it would provide for my retirement was not achieved, nor has it been to this day.

Other stories circulated during that inter-election period, as I have said: the extraordinary one about Ted Short and an alleged Swiss bank account, the rumours relating to John Silkin and land speculation in South Wales, and even more bizarre and fanciful ones about Tony Benn.

I can only say that had the political positions been reversed, they would have been given short shrift by Harold Wilson. Never, when presented with personal stories of even a remotely controversial nature about Conservative opponents – and there were plenty – had he ever considered the possibility of attempting to use them against his opponents in this way.

My own view is that there is a point beyond which stories of this kind – however genuine the nugget of news at their core, however compelling the political or circulation-boosting reasons may seem to the newspaper concerned – should not go: in the end, unjustified and unrelated personal attack is itself a form of immorality.

SEVENTEEN

Interlude Between Elections

The Land Deals affair had a severe effect on the work of the Political Office in Downing Street. It took me at least four weeks after it had first blown up before I could reorganize myself to go back to my office in Number 10.

Physically, it would not have been possible any earlier. My household took a long time to settle down after the state of virtual siege which we had suffered. My mother, who had been completely devastated by the death of my father two years before, was still in poor health; the worry she felt over an affair which, as she saw it, involved her whole family collectively, depressed her still further. Nevertheless, she always sounded cheerful and responsive on the telephone, dealing with the press who rang with courtesy and kindness.

Then there was the general debris, as well as the emotional aftermath – during the press siege it had, for instance, been impossible even to watch television, such was the noise that came through our sitting-room windows. It was particularly comic and sad that one of the pair of beautiful bay trees at either side of my front door, given to me as a birthday present by my friends who lived opposite, gradually withered and died, whether from the shock of so many people standing round it or whether from being over-watered by nameless fluids, I do not know. It all seemed to confirm the premonition I had had when we won the election that I should not return to Downing Street.

The inter-election months of that year were dramatic in the extreme: there was the startling event of the attempted kidnapping of Princess Anne as she was being driven down the Mall. This took place at the end of March, shortly after Harold Wilson's return to office. I learned of it within minutes, as police and Downing Street custodians rushed into my office on the ground floor to check that its wooden shutters were closed, as they had checked all the rooms overlooking the garden at the back, Horse Guards Parade and St James's Park. They told me briefly the reason for this panic. I went straight up to the study, to find that the Prime Minister had been sitting there, unaware and therefore unconcerned, working on his boxes with the curtains drawn back and the windows half open. It was the last time he was allowed that luxury in the evening.

Fortunately, as everyone knows, no ill befell the Princess. Harold Wilson, deeply attached to the Royal Family, was greatly shocked personally at the Princess's ordeal and narrow escape; in Downing Street, its immediate consequence was a stepping up of security at Number 10. The key rooms were furnished with blast-proof curtaining, strong enough to prevent broken glass showering into the room, and the high wooden shutters were closed early on in the evening. The effect was faintly claustrophobic. Outside, in Downing Street itself, there were similar precautions, with the result that Downing Street today, with its restrictive barriers along the street and at either end, contrasts strongly with the Downing Street of the 1960s, when large crowds could assemble at will outside the front door.

We all knew, that summer, that another election was not far off. Preparing for it was an urgent matter. For myself personally, the decisive factor was Albert Murray, a man of whom I was extremely fond, and who appeared regularly at the mews with great mountains of paper that had been piling up at the office. When he came, he would ask me with a twinkle in his eye to hurry up and come in again; his urging and my own affection for him made me change my mind.

So, gradually, work at the Political Office went into top gear again. This meant, among other things, that we had to start planning for the next election. We were anxious to get through as much of the necessary work as possible beforehand rather than have to do it very quickly once the election had been announced.

Essential to this were those members of the Party's Publicity Group who had sat in on most of Harold Wilson's meetings during the February campaign. Chief among these were Dennis Lyons and Peter Lovell-Davis. One of our worries at that time was that the main points of the Prime Minister's Master Speech for the election would be left until the last minute. To obviate this, they attempted to prepare a draft outline on which Harold Wilson could work. In fact they were unsuccessful in this, as it was not easy to copy his style of presentation.

Where people were to work was always a problem in Downing Street. We tried to find a room for Dennis and Peter during this pre-election period, and eventually cleared out a room that had, during the Heath years, been allocated to the girl who had first cooked for Edward Heath and then crewed his yacht. During the 1960s, this room had been used first by Gerald Kaufman and then by Mary Wilson's successive secretaries. Somehow, though, Peter and Dennis did not really settle there. However, regular meetings were held with them throughout the summer.

During the late summer another piece of reorganization got under way, when the Liaison Committee was reformed. This committee had been started much earlier, in the 1960s. It was the brainchild of George Wigg, its first chairman. He, together with Dick Crossman (his successor), Gerald Kaufman, myself and, sometimes, Thomas Balogh, were the nucleus of a group of people who included the Publicity Officer for the Labour Party (then Percy Clark), the Head of the Research and Overseas Department, the National Agent, a representative from the General Secretary's office, and from the Chief Whip's and Lord President's offices, as well as whichever Junior Minister was appropriate to the subject under discussion.

George Wigg's original reason for starting the Liaison Committee was the political crisis prompted by the failure of Patrick Gordon Walker first to retain his seat and then to win a by-election after his appointment to the Cabinet: George had rightly identified these events as stemming in part from insufficient liaison between Number 10 and Transport House. What was needed, he correctly believed, was co-ordination between what Ministers were doing in their Departments and what Transport House was doing, and a flow of information between Transport House with its countrywide links and Number 10.

Over the years, the Liaison Committee developed to a stage where it produced an annual record of the Government's achievements in political terms; this report went to MPs and other interested parties, so that co-ordination on statements in speeches and articles was maintained. I was more than a little amused that summer in 1974, therefore, to find myself summoned to the first meeting in this new Government, and having the committee and its work explained to me. In its earlier incarnation, it met in the late 1960s under the aegis of the Lord President, Dick Crossman, in the lovely old house in which Melbourne had once lived, instead of in any of the Prime Minister's rooms. Those who attended meetings from Number 10 walked through from Downing Street via the Cabinet Office and then into the Lord President's office. By 1974 it was meeting under the aegis of the Junior Minister responsible for Government Information, John Grant, located in modern offices in Whitehall. It proved as effective during the 1970s as it had a decade earlier. I attended a number of its meetings, though gradually, during the run-up to Harold Wilson's resignation, the constitution of these meetings changed.

EIGHTEEN

'The Plot'

The Political Office in Downing Street was not only the eyes and ears of the Prime Minister in his role as Leader of the Party, but it also served as a channel of communication between him and the outside world. As I have said, I frequently found myself being asked to transmit some message to Harold Wilson by those who did not want to bother him directly, but who wanted something that they considered sufficiently important or delicate in content transmitted to him quickly and accurately.

Thus I was not surprised when in 1974 I received a message from Clive Jenkins, General Secretary of ASTMS, asking if I could call and see him. As this was Harold Wilson's own union, he had in any case built up a close relationship over the years both with Clive's predecessor as General Secretary and with Clive himself.

Accordingly, after finishing off my work at Number 10, I went round early one evening to the ASTMS union building in Camden. Most of the staff had gone home; Clive sat in solitary state in his spacious, splendid modern office. He poured me out a drink while I wondered what confidential matter I was going to be asked to transmit to Harold.

We exchanged gossip about the Party and he enquired after Geoffrey Bing, who was legal representative of the ASTMS organization. Geoffrey was a very distinguished lawyer with a long association with the far Left of the Party. In his friendships he appeared to span the whole political spectrum: they ranged from Nkrumah to Sir James Goldsmith, who knew him well.

Geoffrey had been anxious for some time to go to the Lords and had corresponded with Harold Wilson on this. He qualified just as much as various others (Tom Driberg, for instance) who were to go to the Lords. After Nkrumah, to whom Geoffrey was adviser and attorney in Ghana, was assassinated, Geoffrey had held no similar positions and it was some years since he had left the Commons. Clive gave very enthusiastic support for this idea.

The latter half of our conversation was taken up with what Clive referred to as 'The Plot', which he assumed I knew all about. It was quite true that I did know about it in that, as far as I could see, 'The Plot' was something that had been going on since devaluation in 1967. There has always been 'a plot', of course, against every single Leader by every dissident group within the Party since it was formed until today. Susan Crosland refers in her book about Tony to the grouping around Roy Jenkins whose aim was to replace Harold Wilson during the Opposition years. Its activities were well known. Politics would not be politics without 'a plot' in every political Party. I did not take this very seriously.

So I was interested to hear that there were very strong moves by David Basnett of the General and Municipal Workers' Union to get together a wider group of people whose aim was to get Harold out and Jim Callaghan in – but only, it was alleged, as a first step towards installing Roy Jenkins at Number 10.

I couldn't help finding this long-term planning – and the degree of seriousness with which Clive took it – slightly amusing. It presumed a degree of influence over the machinery for electing a Leader of a kind that seemed totally unrealistic. Later, of course, came the electoral college and with it the possibility that union leaders could put such an idea into practice; though by this time the principal personage had placed himself at the head of an entirely different army. However, this leaves the most interesting question of all unanswered: if Roy as Prime Minister was the objective of Basnett *et al.*, will we evenually see some major unions defecting to the SDP? Or did the Callaghan years destroy the strategy?

It is, I believe, a distinct possibility if the Labour Party does not resolve its problems. The Labour voter, as distinct from Party member, has always been conservative with a small 'c'. Only a Leader from the middle ground left of centre will provide the necessary stability that can prevent the continuing desertion from the Party by both MPs and voters – a flight which might well eventually include trades unions, on the grounds that to afford their membership an effective voice in Parliament it would be better to opt for the middle ground. Could then the scenario envisaged at that time by David Basnett and the other like-minded but unnamed trades unionists eventually come to pass, with Roy Jenkins in Number 10 – but leading an SDP coalition rather than the Labour Party?

At the time I quite clearly could not take this long view. I merely reported 'The Plot' to Harold Wilson, also recounting Clive's support for Geoffrey Bing as I thought Clive would have wished me to do so. In the event, Harold acted on neither.

Their personal relationship was excellent. Clive's ebullient, extrovert character appealed to Harold, who enjoys larger-than-life characters; in addition, Clive is extremely sharp with an excellent mind, and very good company. In his attitude to life, he has much in common with the other Jenkins – Roy. Although Clive comes from the Left of the Labour Party and Roy moved ever further Right until he departed from it, there is much they share.

Both live at good addresses, appreciate good food and wine, are good talkers, and enjoy the good life. At any party where you see Clive, he is enjoying himself – indeed, I would say there is only one thing he enjoys more and that is appearing on television. His circle of friends is artistic, he is very witty, dresses well – in all, is a colourful personality who contrasts sharply with the greyish figures who form the usual run of union General Secretaries.

More importantly, he has understood the radical changes that will be forced upon the working population as the microchip and other technological advances revolutionize industry and society, better than almost all trades unionists and many politicians. A long time ago he grasped what this meant not only for working men but for the unions who represent them; he sees how unions, too, will have to remodel themselves in order to adapt to the new technologies.

NINETEEN

Introduction to the Lords

Early in that summer the Prime Minister had decided that the time had come to reinforce the Labour side of the House of Lords. One of the first to be sent there was John Harris – first Gaitskell's Press Secretary, then Roy Jenkins's political assistant – and, at the same time, it was put to Terry Pitt, the Head of the Research Department at Transport House, that he too should go to the Lords. Both suggestions emanated from Number 10. (Unfortunately, Terry decided against it: they would have balanced each other nicely, one from the Right of the Party, the other from the Left.)

Later that summer, another major political list was constructed, on which my name appeared together with Sammy Fisher, Doris Fisher, Henry Kissin, Phyllis Stedman and others. On publication, it produced, for the second time in the space of four months, a press invasion of the small mews in which I lived. The scenes of chaos went on for the two or three days during which the reporters and photographers were camped there; again, most were good-natured – though I have to say that some were very difficult indeed. The most charming was James Whitaker – as was to be expected – whom I remember most from all the similar occasions because of the splendid bouquets of flowers he presented in advance of his person.

At this point I should comment on my own honour. In 1970, after Labour's defeat, Harold Wilson suggested that I might like to be more directly involved in political and parliamentary life. I was not at all interested then, and later only reluctantly. The presentational end – the theatrical side of politics – has never appealed to me. If it had, I think I would have preferred to aim for a career in the Commons.

When we won in 1974, Harold Wilson raised the question again. It was decided that such an honour was probably most appropriate for his Resignation List when it came.

However, my subsequent personal difficulties over the land deals, and the saturation press coverage these attracted, persuaded him that an earlier opportunity should be taken to enable me to concentrate on something entirely different that was, in a sense, above it all. He also hoped that it would create a pause in press attention in that I would be seen in a different context. He wanted, also, to give public acknowledge-ment to the work I had done – as Jim Callaghan was to do for his Constituency Party Agent some five years later. Harold Wilson felt that my contribution and work was being buried under a sea of irrelevant comment.

Put to me like that, I thought he might be right and that it would help. I was wrong. It could have done and I think it should have done – but it didn't. If it had worked, it would have been tremendous and I would have enjoyed it enormously. As it was I was reluctant – extremely reluctant, as I made clear to the Prime Minister (who in turn made clear his views to me, in a letter).

Lest this sound grudging, I would add that this honour was a very generous acknowledgement of his support for me and, above all, it was a recognition of the work I had done for the Party and for Harold Wilson personally over a very long period, at that time nineteen years. There was plenty of precedent: Harold Macmillan had expressed his gratitude and acknowledgement to his Private Secretary, John Wyndham (the late Lord Egremont) by ennobling him; Montague Corrie was created Lord Wroughton by Disraeli.

So I was pleased and honoured to accept a peerage in the summer of 1974 on those terms despite my grave doubts. But it did not work out as I had hoped; I was very sorry then and I still am, though I hope that perhaps one day it will. I have a proper regard for the Prime Minister's recommendation and I have every respect for present members of the House of Lords, whom I believe do a great deal of valuable work and add a dimension of important expert information and knowledge to political debate not normally offered by the Commons.

Life is a complicated business and fits together its own special pattern as you go along. If the timing goes wrong in any venture, you have to wait to put it together differently at, hopefully, some later date.

On 23 July, the day of my Introduction to the Lords, I woke to the first part of a centre page, two-part study of me in *The Times*; it was less than friendly. Much of it bore an uncanny resemblance to *Private Eye*, but behind it was the weight and authority of the Thunderer. I was particularly cheered by a warm-hearted and kindly letter from Bernard Donoughue, telling me to ignore it all – 'They won't stop today from being your day,' he said, 'so please keep your pecker up, enjoy it – and keep in trim for the battle ahead. We must line up the old winning team. With love and best wishes.'

Once at the House of Lords for the Introduction, I started by making the elementary mistake of allowing some newspaper reporters into the Moses Room, where I had to put on the appropriate robes; I was so nervous that I simply forgot to check who everyone was and whether or not they had the right to be there. Only later I learned it was discretionary: as well as publishing the normal picture of me standing between my two sponsors, they printed some of me putting on the rather peculiar headgear, a sort of three-cornered affair. The result was an image of someone greatly enjoying the occasion, when, in fact, I was longing to get the whole thing over with and go home.

As for the actual Introduction, I found this – or rather, being the focus of so many pairs of curious eyes – unnerving to say the least. The House was packed from one end to the other; the galleries were all full, with the Press Gallery crammed to bursting; and I was faced with tier upon tier of faces from the Labour side – friends I knew smiling encouragement. All I recall clearly was the stiff upright figure of Edith Summerskill, with just the faintest glimmer of a smile, a great concession from Edith. I could not see the faces on the other side. After I had been through the elaborate ritual of circumambulating the Chamber, the ceremony ended with my kneeling in front of the Lord Chancellor, Elwyn-Jones, whom I knew very well indeed socially and politically. In the 1960s, he and his wife Polly had often stayed in Essex with Beattie Plummer, where I too was a frequent guest.

As I knelt down, Elwyn whispered in my ear, 'It's not such good fun as HMS *Fearless*, is it?' – a reference to the time we had both been aboard her at Gibraltar in 1968 for the last talks on Rhodesia with Ian Smith. After kneeling to the Lord Chancellor, the newly introduced peer then bows to the Throne; when I did this I noticed that a number of Privy Counsellors had availed themselves of their privilege of sitting on the steps of the Throne. Among them was Harold Wilson.

I left the Chamber; as I did so Eric Varley, who was standing just inside the doorway – he, too, had been sitting on the steps of the Throne during the ceremony – gave me a big hug and a kiss, and I went out into the corridor where Thomas Balogh and Gerald Kaufman were also waiting for me. I remember those moments, and the faces and words of good friends from the early years, particularly well – and my dear mother, bursting with pride and in floods of tears.

Harold Wilson in discussion with
Richard Nixon, 1970

Harold and Mary Wilson standing outside
their bungalow on the Scilly Isles, 1973

Harold signs copies of his book, 1971

Back in my office at Number 10 after the election victory, 1974

A walkabout in Huddersfield during the October 1974 election campaign

Labour's 'New Look' October 1974 election campaign

Harold and Jim Callaghan with Henry Kissinger and Gerald Ford at the Helsinki conference, 1975

ABOVE *and* BELOW The Christmas party
for the disabled at Number 10, 1974

BELOW Harold being presented with a
bottle of HP sauce at an official dinner, 1975

LEFT Leaving my mews home with Gerald Kaufman on the day of my Introduction to the House of Lords, 23 July 1974

BELOW The exterior of Chequers

The Wilsons with their twin grand-
daughters after their christening, the first
ever to be held at Chequers

Harold at Grange Farm

Harold with his son Robin, daughter-in-law Joy and twin grand-daughters in the
White Parlour at Chequers on the occasion of the twins' first birthday

LEFT At the party to say
goodbye to Robin Butler

BELOW Harold and Mary
with the Queen and Prince
Philip at the resignation
dinner at Number 10,
23 March 1976

At Harold's Farewell Party for the staff
at Number 10, 29 March 1976:
ABOVE Harold with Bernard Donoughue
and Eric Morecambe; LEFT Joe Haines
with Caroline Cushing

TWENTY

The October Election

If for nothing else, I would remember the summer holiday of 1974 well for one marvellous summer's day, hot and clear, with the Scilly Isles looking magnificent – lush and semi-tropical, like Caribbean islands but set in the cold waters of the Atlantic ocean. That day, as we walked along deserted paths across Tresco, one of the most beautiful of the islands with its old Abbey and superb tropical gardens, Harold Wilson began to discuss the long-term future. Once again, he indicated that he wanted to serve only two years as Prime Minister and then to resign.

It was with this decision in mind that we talked as we crossed the island; Harold Wilson seeing as his first duty the settling of the Common Market issue through the referendum, to ensure that the Party came through the debate on Europe as a united force rather than, as had always been feared, irreparably split. After that, he said, his task was to set the Government on the path to overcoming roaring inflation, and to establish an atmosphere favourable to the proper discussion and direction of economic policy.

Our talk took place in August. The Wilsons have always gone to their bungalow on the Scilly Isles for their summer holiday, and I usually go down for part of this period with my own family. In this relaxed and happy setting, there is plenty of opportunity, over dinners or excursions to outlying islands, for leisurely discussion of past events or future ideas. That summer was no different.

Before the holiday, that summer had seen much talk in Parliament – and during the recess – of coalition. This followed the attempt by Edward Heath to form a coalition with Jeremy Thorpe after the February election; in the months that followed, discussion on the possibility of a coalition escalated. Harold Wilson had made it clear, then and on many previous occasions both publicly and in private, that he was opposed to any thought of coalition whatever the circumstances; a point of view which made many people both in the Labour Party and outside believe that any subsequent election that produced only a narrow victory for Labour would present the Party with an extremely difficult tightrope situation if forced to 'go it alone' for a long period. To do so for six months was possible, even for eighteen as in the 1960s; longer was impossible.

Once Harold Wilson had announced his resignation and left office shortly thereafter, the way was, of course, open for Jim Callaghan to remove this hazard by reaching accommodation with the Liberals – a solution which kept Labour in office until 1979. Right up until this moment, however, the survival of the Labour Government was in doubt: a week before the resignation, the Government had been defeated in the Commons when Labour MPs had voted with the Opposition; just before the day of resignation itself, there was the likelihood that a sudden financial crisis – when the pound fell below an exchange rate of two dollars – might bring the Government down. The prospect that Labour would be forced to go to the country again was ever-present if Harold Wilson continued as its Leader. For those who took a rightist or coalitionist view, the decision that he had taken some years earlier in a completely different set of circumstances was therefore, by a freak of fate, welcome in its timing. (As for the desirability of coalition, this is something upon which the Labour Party, with its memories of the Ramsay MacDonald years, is still divided.)

Although electoral security was achieved via coalition and the Lib–Lab Pact of 1977, the Labour Government's major legislative contribution was produced earlier; indeed, the total volume of legislation passed during the years 1977–9 was small compared to the earlier period from 1974 to 1976. Most of the legislation after 1976 flowed from the implementation of the Employment Protection Act in the earlier period. Indeed, it is very doubtful if any of the legislation before 1974 could have been carried through if the then Government had been dependent upon Liberal electoral support. The major legislation from 1974 had been embodied in the election manifestos and put into effect as early as possible, first by presenting a programme to the country and Parliament during the short Parliament of 1974, and then putting it through in legislative terms once re-elected in October 1974. Like the tip of the iceberg that hints at the colossus beneath, much of this was, of course, the result of extremely hard work during the years of Opposition, when the entire fabric of the Labour Party had echoed to the hammering out of policies.

One of these came to fruition only a few weeks before that summer's day talk on the Scilly Isles with Harold Wilson. It was not until the National Executive Committee and the Cabinet met at Number 10 in July to work out the details of the manifesto that the final decision to have a referendum was agreed. Until then, there had been no vote on whether the decision on Europe would be by referendum or through a general election. All that the February manifesto had said was that it would be 'through the ballot box'. Once the decision on an October election had been taken, it was clear that a referendum was the only practical alternative: to subject the country to yet another general election the following year would be, to say the least, counterproductive.

The dissenting voice was that of Roy Jenkins, who tried hard to persuade his colleagues and followers not to commit themselves to the definite, black-and-white referendum proposal, but to stick to the vaguer formula in the February manifesto. He was reluctant to use what he regarded as the 'blunt instrument' of the referendum, preferring instead what he termed 'electoral decision'. But he was overruled by his colleagues. Once we moved into the campaign period, the decision to have a referendum rather than a third election could be seen to be amply justified.

The weeks preceding Polling Day were quiet and, politically speaking, almost boring. The whole country seemed tired; people had been through the disruptions of the previous winter, an eventful election in the spring, followed by a disturbing summer set against the upheaval of Labour legislation after three and a half years of Conservative government. After being presented with policy statement after policy statement the electorate was punch-drunk. October found them unenthusiastic.

The referendum was not the only cause for dissension contained in the February manifesto. That summer also saw differences with Tony Benn over the White Paper on nationalization and industrialization. Then there was the continued growth of the separatist movements in Scotland and Wales that had caused trouble in the February election, and had resulted in the bringing in of new policies on some form of devolution for both countries.

As for the most overt threat, the Liberal vote, Conservatives as well as Labour were worried that the number of votes cast for the Liberals and the minority parties would cause difficulties. As the talk of coalition gained ground, this must have forced Edward Heath into deciding that this was the best approach for his Party to adopt; consequently, we saw the emergence of a 'national unity' battle cry. This had first been mooted at the end of the February election, but as the months unrolled it became ever more strongly heard.

Internationally, the scene that summer was equally dramatic. Britain was almost on the brink of war with Turkey over Cyprus; this international crisis gave rise to a scene at Number 10 that could have come straight from one of those Twenties 'treasure hunt' parties. Archbishop Makarios, who had fled the island, turned up at Number 10 with only the clothes he stood up in, and a complicated operation had to be set in train to produce a change of clothing. Dom Mintoff, Prime Minister of Malta, had given him a clean shirt when he stopped off there, and Harold Wilson provided reserves in London (all three shared the same collar size). The dramatic and instantly recognizable vestments, in which Makarios was invariably clad, were a different matter; most clerical clothing is easily obtainable, but acquiring Greek Orthodox vestments in London is not quite so simple. In the end, we were able to track down a priest in the Greek Orthodox Church who was tall enough to lend Makarios a spare cassock.

In the event, the political bombshell of Cyprus was defused, chiefly through the medium of last-minute appeals over the telephone to Prime Minister Ecevit of Turkey, combined with help from the United Nations. But there had been a very real danger that Britain would have had to mobilize her forces to protect her Cyprus bases, those Britons who worked there and – because it was the summer season – the large number of British tourists also on the island.

Other visitors from abroad had arrived in more orthodox fashion. That June had seen a large Socialist International conference held at Chequers, attended by all the heads of the various Socialist parties in Europe, meeting now against the backdrop of the renegotiations of Britain's membership of the EEC. Many of them are better known for the positions they subsequently occupied in the political structures of their own countries: Mario Soares of Portugal, Bruno Kreisky of Austria, François Mitterrand of France, Dom Mintoff of Malta, and Conor Cruise O'Brien, at that time connected with the Irish Government, as well as Lee Kuan Yew (Harry Lee), a close friend of Harold Wilson, and Yitzhak Rabin of Israel. Ron Hayward, the Party's General Secretary, was among Transport House representatives; Eric Miller was

there as Treasurer of the Socialist International. As with political entertaining at Downing Street, although the catering for the conference
hospitality was done by the Chequers staff in the normal way, the cost
of it was not borne by the Government or the Chequers Trust but billed
separately to the Prime Minister, and therefore in due course to the
Labour Party.

As that frenetic summer wore on, internal troubles emerged ever
more strongly within the Party. Every week saw Tony Benn taking an
increasingly robust line on industrial policy, spreading consternation
not only throughout industry generally – and the City, in particular,
where the effect on confidence was soon felt – but also among his
colleagues. There was more dissension in the Party and outside on the
question of Chile, where the change of government to a brutal and
repressive regime had caused the doctrine of Cabinet collective responsibility to be broken once again (as in 1969); the situation in
Northern Ireland had become increasingly explosive with the breakdown of power-sharing and a general strike.

A further small cloud on the political horizon related to Lord Brayley.
Harold Wilson had met Desmond Brayley some years earlier. He was a
close friend of Samuel Fisher, Bob Mellish and George Wigg (through
whom the introduction had come about), and well known to many
other members of the Labour Party. He frequently entertained distinguished Labour MPs on his yacht in the Mediterranean; he introduced
Harold Wilson to President Bourguiba of Tunisia (whose close friend
Brayley was); when the Wilsons had nowhere to live after the unexpected defeat of 1970 it was Desmond Brayley who had offered them
hospitality at his country home and London flat.

After the election victory of 1974, George Wigg suggested to the
Prime Minister that Brayley's knowledge of army affairs would make
him an ideal Army Minister; he was duly made Parliamentary Under-
Secretary of State for the Army. However, during this summer his
chronic ill-health (arising from heart trouble) worsened, and the bar-
rage of press criticism focused on the conduct of his business affairs made
his condition serious.

Some time was spent discussing Desmond Brayley's position and what
should be done. Should he be allowed to retire because of what was then
simply press criticism? One Sunday morning, when I had been summoned urgently to take coffee with the Prime Minister on the terrace at
Chequers, the Brayley question was again the subject of conversation,
the Prime Minister saying that perhaps it would be best for Lord

Brayley to resign before the autumn election that we knew was coming. On 25 September, after a meeting with Harold Wilson, Brayley did in fact resign, in order, it was said, to clear his name following the damaging press stories that had appeared about him and the companies with which he was connected.

Apart from some meetings in July with our publicity team at Number 10, the real start of that election campaign was, I suppose, incubated during that long, hot holiday on the Scilly Isles. Harold Wilson had decided to address the Trades Union Congress in September to launch Labour's campaign: his speech would set out the Government's record and plans for the future, as well as containing an unscripted appeal for the underwriting of the Social Contract with the Labour Government by the trades union movement. Work on this speech was obviously vital and, to facilitate it, we brought down Doreen Andrew, one of the girls from the Political Office. Doreen stayed at a guest house, going every day to the Customs House to work there with the Prime Minister on his speech.

As a launching pad for a major political statement, a small guest house and a converted corner of one of Her Majesty's Customs and Excise outposts may sound faintly Heath Robinson, but the reason, we were told, that the TUC speech had to be handled this way was that it was a political speech and, therefore, could not be handled by the official office. They could touch only that part of it which related to Government policy, but those sections with Party-political emphasis had to be handled by the Political Office. I feel certain that this rigid line between political and official, adhered to so firmly, was peculiar to that year – almost a freak of that fateful summer – and I am sure that it is something that would not now happen, whatever the colour of the Party in power.

Before the campaign proper began, our small group was joined, as before, by Stanley Baker; this time he brought with him the playwright John Mortimer, whose expertise was of great help in the treatment of Harold Wilson's TV programmes, and in suggesting many of the passages or themes contained therein. Apart from his knowledge of television and his ability to make the most effective use of it, there was the added bonus – for us – that John was such an amusing, clever and entertaining man, whose presence made an enjoyable addition to our small group. Along with Stanley, who had been helping us since 1973, we felt we had an impressive degree of professionalism at our command.

Once back at Number 10, our campaign team swung into action.

Peter Lovell-Davis and Dennis Lyons were, of course, a major part of the Number 10 advisory group; they concentrated on putting across the major theme of 'Labour's Winning Team', with the secondary one of 'Labour Keeps Its Promises'. Both these harked back to a view they had put forward in 1973, when the two main Party Leaders suffered from what has become known since as a 'credibility gap' – at that time it was based on the electorate's disbelief that either political Party, once elected, would keep its election promises.

Peter and Dennis believed that the only way to bridge this gulf of scepticism was to make a commitment so clear and specific that the electorate could check off what was being done action by action. Harold Wilson had done this in his Bolton speech of December 1973; this, in turn, was based on an earlier speech in 1970 after Edward Heath had taken office.

In 1970, Harold Wilson had told the country that while, of course, Edward Heath had promised to bring prices down, the electorate should keep a note, week by week, of what actually was happening to prices – and keep this note behind the clock on the mantelpiece. This started off a campaign in the *Daily Mirror*, who ran a weekly 'Prices Clock', showing the movement of prices. It was a very effective way of demonstrating the rising cost of living and bringing home the fact that the promise to bring prices down was not being kept.

At Bolton, in 1973, Harold Wilson had done something rather similar when he said that the Labour Government would be judged by what it did on ten promises within three years of taking office, and that he personally would stand to be judged by this record. Now, six months after taking office in the first election of 1974, he listed those ten promises again.

This theme was one to which Harold Wilson returned again and again (and which served him in good stead until his resignation). Now, he asked the electorate to judge for themselves on the progress that had been made during the six months since the February election. Prior to the October election announcement, White Papers had been brought out in abundance – on consumer protection, pensions, land, devolution, sex discrimination – and Harold Wilson listed these and plans for the period ahead. These were the policies, he said, on which Labour was asking for a mandate. Whether or not you agreed with them, the overriding impression was of a Government determined to plan ahead and to govern, rather than to mark time or play at politics. His speech to the Trades Union Congress was also bearing welcome electoral fruit;

during it, he had talked about the Social Contract in great detail, emphasizing that it was a contract that involved everyone, not just the trades union movement. The TUC rose to the occasion. In the October election Harold Wilson was able to draw on trades union support that was whole-hearted rather than the lukewarm affair it had been in the February election.

On the other side, Edward Heath this time round was keeping a much lower profile. At his press conferences, for instance, other members of his Party would join him, or take the conference for him, William Whitelaw in particular; but the campaign saw the first major exposure to national campaigning of Margaret Thatcher, who was given the job of putting over the Tories' dramatic commitment on domestic rating, its lowering and eventual abolition.

What made all of us nervous was the gathering momentum of the idea of coalition. We knew how the electorate disliked confrontation, we knew that in politics the middle ground invariably has the widest popular appeal – certainly as far as home affairs go. Most people are drawn towards consensus politics: the appeal of coalition appeared irresistible.

With it would come certain problems for the Parties concerned. Jeremy Thorpe shared with Harold Wilson the difficulty of stating his intentions if it became a case of a hung election: he did not want to commit himself in advance to a situation in which he might not wish to continue.

Thorpe's own sympathies were much more towards Labour than Conservative – but what if the Tories won? In the event, he got out of it neatly by saying that, of course, the Liberals would be prepared to talk – but without the (then) present Leaders of the two main Parties. This proved to be one of his brightest campaign strokes.

The fluidity of the Liberal vote was again one of the complications of this second election. In February, the big Liberal vote had been a key factor; unfortunately, much of it was a protest vote against the previous Conservative Government rather than an indication of Liberal strength. This meant that in many marginal areas where Tories had abstained or voted Liberal, a Labour candidate had slipped in. By October, though, many of those Tories who had voted Liberal as a means of signifying dissatisfaction had returned to the Conservative fold, and the Liberal vote, although still high, was no longer working to Labour's advantage in certain marginal seats.

The conundrum of the fluctuating Liberal vote is still with us, with the added complication of the arrival of the SDP. Another 1974 situation is still possible ten years later, or whenever Mrs Thatcher makes her appeal, despite the Falklands crisis. The Alliance, together with other minority parties, could create again the strange and uneasy atmosphere of 1974; then, we had no idea this depressing sequence of events would occur. What we were conscious of was the Scottish Nationalist Party; Labour had been able to circumvent some of the activities of the ScotNats by devolution proposals, which would give a certain amount of self-government to Scotland, as well as by nationalization policies that would protect Scottish oil and bring new industry to Scotland.

The campaign proper lasted twenty-two days, the same length as that of the February election, with the election being announced on 18 September and Polling Day on 10 October. Our team worked from Transport House and Lord North Street as before, although there were one or two alterations in the *modus operandi* of some of the key people.

Jean Denham, recruited by Joe from the Labour Party headquarters to the Press Office at Number 10, and now a civil servant herself, went on unpaid leave to act as one of Harold Wilson's press officers throughout the campaign. This meant that Joe could liaise closely with her, passing on invaluable advice acquired through his own experience during the February campaign. The addition of Terry Boston (now Lord Boston of Faversham) to help out on the broadcasting side of these arrangements, and to double as Press Officer for out-of-London visits, meant excellent coverage.

Once again, Joe and Bernard came to Transport House for meetings before the daily press conference, and for the Leader's own meetings at Lord North Street where, once again, we went through the planning just as we had done six months earlier. The only difference was that Joe and Bernard spent the rest of the time at Number 10 (unless specifically wanted) instead of being continuously on call. Once again, the three of us worked on the Leader's speech in the evening, in the same way as before, except that this time the venue was Number 10 rather than Transport House. We all found this arrangement far superior from the point of view of physical comfort. After working late, we would often eat in the dining room of the private flat on the second floor; Joe and Bernard would buy steaks and a bottle of wine, and Bernard, the steak expert, would prepare the meal.

I was sometimes absent from these meals or often very late getting to them: at Transport House, the General Secretary would ask me down for a drink in the early evening to watch some of the newscasts with him. It was a chance to talk through what had happened that day and what tomorrow was likely to bring. The National Agent and other senior Party officials would look in: we felt the campaign was going reasonably well and that with luck we would get our mandate, but we were aware it was going to be difficult: our expectations were of a majority somewhere between ten and thirty.

There were various sudden alarms during those three weeks. One was the 'mini-campaign' that suddenly developed on the Liberal side, with so-called major defections from Labour to the Liberals. One such was Alun Chalfont, and although his move was expected, it caused some consternation; we were not sure who would follow. The Liberals made the most of this by putting out a rumour that more big names would emerge later – in fact, the one that did was Lord St Davids, which really was, as Harold Wilson later remarked, 'a case of Bertie Wooster rides again'.

Another whom we feared would defect to the Liberal camp was Raymond Mais. Rumours of his defection were reaching us from every quarter. Harold Wilson would have regarded this as a blow, although he had experienced some difficulties with Raymond: when the latter was Lord Mayor, he had in a major speech denounced Harold Wilson's opposition to the visit to London of President Caetano, the fascist dictator of Portugal, at the height of the Angolan troubles. Despite all this, Raymond was someone Harold Wilson knew well and had nominated as a Labour Peer in 1967. He had been a member of the 1944 Association and had a long connection with the Labour Party. Later, he was to come back into the news when he took over the Peachey Property Company from Eric Miller. When we heard the rumour that Mais was going to defect, we believed it. We were sorry, not least because his daughter was working as part of the Polling Team with Bob Worcester and the group employed by the Party to produce its daily private poll.

The private poll was one of our greatest assets during those two elections, and a luxury we had never been able to afford before. It was the fine tuner we needed. Working out what questions we wanted the poll to ask became one of the key jobs of the day; Bernard, as well as Joe, was particularly adroit at wording the questions in exactly the right way to elicit the information we needed: the most difficult end of poll usage. Anyone, as Harold Wilson frequently said, can find the answer to the questions, but it is essential to get the right questions to the answers.

The need for a private poll had become clear in the 1970 election. We saw then the advantage the Tory poll had given Edward Heath. So when Heath's difficulties with the miners made an election seem likely, we again raised the issue of a Labour private poll. The Press Officer, Percy Clark, and the Publicity Group regarded it as vital. But once more the old problem raised its head: the Party could not afford it. Deadlock was averted by talks with Harry Kissin and Harold Lever; it was put to them by Harold Wilson that although the Party could itself make a small contribution towards the cost of a private poll, they would be unable to finance one completely. It was therefore up to Labour supporters to find a way round this.

Harry Kissin took on the job of organizing a group of distinguished people who would help finance a private poll once the next election was fact. At first a daily poll was too expensive and too difficult to organize in the time available. So in February it came twice or three times a week. By October it was possible to arrange for a daily poll.

A number of those approached for contributions to such a poll were anxious to have more ready access to the Leader of the Party, especially should he be returned to office. They wanted to be able to tender advice, but this could not be done through official Labour channels nor via the Political Office as not all of them were committed Labour Party supporters, nor were their reasons for desiring this greater accessibility political. What they wished was a chance to offer advice to the Government on industrial and financial questions, but again this could not be done through official channels either, since they were not representing any specific organization but acting personally.

Harry Kissin made it clear they would do everything possible to make the proposed private poll a reality, but asked Harold Wilson in exchange to take one of his acquaintances into the Leader's Private Office during the election run-up and campaign in the first instance, as an additional publicity adviser who would take charge of the organization of the poll. This turned out to be Bernard Donoughue; Harold Lever, however, was doubtful this would work and expressed some misgivings to the Leader, reminding him that Bernard had been a committed Gaitskell supporter and a founder member of the Campaign for Democratic Socialism. Harold Wilson regarded the acquisition of Bernard in exchange for the daily poll as a bargain. Harold Lever eventually agreed with him. All were to work well, harmoniously and effectively in those campaigns and after.

The poll results usually arrived around 6.30 in the evening, via a call from Bob Worcester which I normally took. Each time we carefully monitored not just our specific questions, but the key question, which was who people thought would win, often a better method of discovering people's voting intentions than a straight, 'How will you vote?' Those who are reluctant to declare who they are voting for will often reveal this by saying who they think will win. Any violent change in that figure had a profound effect.

There were several dramas during the three weeks of the October campaign. One was the ITV strike over parity of pay with the BBC. Nothing is more unnerving than a television strike during an election campaign. It means the closure of a major area of exposure for the Party's message, of film of the Leader and his colleagues campaigning, all the vital elements in modern electioneering. We had suffered in 1970 from a newspaper strike, now we were dogged by the same ill-fortune since we felt that ITN in particular gave us very fair coverage and large numbers of key Labour supporters watched Independent Television. It was a short-lived dispute, but caused enough tremors. I had had the difficult job of transmitting messages about complicated pay differentials, percentages and the rest, which I had to brief myself on, in order to make my own reports intelligible. I was greatly relieved personally when Nigel Ryan and his team resumed normal working.

Another media disturbance during the campaign was the visit by the BBC to film us at work at Transport House. At one point they asked if I would give an interview about the organization of the Leader's campaign, but Ron Hayward – the only person there at the time – advised against it, saying he thought I was too much of a 'hot potato'! I kept a straight face while I sought his advice and received it, but was unable to stop myself from doing what I always do on such occasions, namely writing up a suitable headline for the following day's papers: 'Labour's hot potato interviewed by BBC'. I wondered what sort of potato Ron was.

The major scare at the end of the campaign hinged, as one might have expected, on the Common Market. On this, the Conservatives mounted an attack difficult to counter in the morning press conferences. One day, they scored unexpectedly through the medium of Shirley Williams. At every press conference a senior member of the team was present with the Leader and General Secretary, not only to give weight but to make a contribution on their own special subject in order that every possible area of policy should be covered. That day, ironically, Shirley was there because Denis Healey had earlier got into difficulties over his 8.4 per cent inflation speech; it was thought that Shirley, with her special charisma, would help to rescue the situation and prevent a drift into a sterile, statistical slanging match between the major Party press conferences.

Suddenly Shirley was asked what she would do if the referendum vote was 'No'. Harold Wilson immediately attempted to deflect the questioning back to himself, saying that this was not something for individuals but for the team as a whole; to his astonishment, Shirley did not seize the chance to remain silent. Instead, she answered, 'I would not want to remain in active politics.'

Harold Wilson, although he did not show it at the time, was stunned by this reply, realizing its danger: from then on, every single senior member of the Party, on both sides of the Market controversy, would be asked this question. The first for whom the hunt was on was Roy Jenkins. On the other side of the Market argument Peter Shore gave a clear statement of his position: he said that he had campaigned for a long time to get this very issue put to the people, and it would, therefore, be very inconsistent if he did not stand by the people's verdict. The pro-Marketeers were not quite so helpful, Shirley having made herself into a political liability on this.

However, on the other side, Margaret Thatcher was laying up liability status for herself in the years ahead. She had been drafted in by Edward Heath to intervene on the Tory promise to tackle the problem of domestic rating; unfortunately the promise of a dramatic pegged reduction for the Tories was a pledge that boomeranged. It fell into the category of election promises marked in the mind of the electorate as 'unlikely to be fulfilled'. Nine years later, and herself leading the Government, Margaret Thatcher has still not found the time to take action in an area where she once felt action was so urgently needed.

The Tory Party had some powerful allies. (To our consternation, on 8 October Marcus Sieff made what we thought was a very pro-Heath statement on prices.) By the second week of the campaign Conservatives were stepping up the theme of national unity, and coalition in the sense of people rather than parties. Undoubtedly clever though this scheme was, it backfired on Heath: his own advisers told him that to make sure this idea had the credibility it needed, he should make it clear that if necessary he would be prepared to step down to make it a reality. Heath, like Harold Wilson, was aware of his own 'credibility gap', but he was alarmed by the reaction of close colleagues on this as he suspected it was not necessarily the result of a desire for authenticity. He was right: not long after that election he lost his job as Leader.

We spent a lot of time working out how to combat the appeal of a government of this sort; they countered by saying the Conservatives were only using this theme as a means of regaining power for themselves and their friends. Through Joe Haines and Bernard Donoughue we had a wide network of contacts; thanks to these, with their speedy transmission of information and rumours, we were able to make our own counter-dispositions quickly and effectively. When we heard that Edward Heath might be making a statement about stepping down, we were able to get the news to Harold Wilson in Birmingham straightaway, so that he would be ready with the immediate response that would be needed. The electorate would be bound to wonder, 'If Edward Heath is prepared to make a sacrifice for a principle of this kind, why isn't Harold Wilson?'

The Tories effectively countered our accusations against them of confrontation and conflict with the suggestion that such accusations were an implicit threat that if people voted Tory, Labour would give them a hard time by stirring up our allies in the Labour movement. It was a cynical but effective way of turning round our claim that we had brought industrial and social peace to the country.

There is no doubt that in both election campaigns Tory headquarters was extremely well-organized and alert, and adept as always at putting across its own messages in response to ours; it was particularly efficient in picking out the one theme that evoked a deep response in the electorate: the desire for consensus and agreement. They translated this as a Government of National Unity, we as the Social Contract; the same policy idea but viewed from completely opposing aspects.

Once again, we opened our campaign in Glasgow – for luck. Unfortunately one almost farcical memory sticks in my mind of that visit to Glasgow. As on previous occasions, Harold Wilson entertained the Lord Provost of Glasgow briefly at our headquarters hotel before going on to a rally at the Playhouse Theatre. The sitting room happened to be decorated in a style very popular at that time, with cupboard and other doors papered to match the walls – in this case a rather elaborate patterned wallpaper. While our small group – the Wilsons, the Lord Provost and his wife, and a few other Party and City dignitaries – were exchanging courtesies, Harold Wilson realized he needed some information urgently before the rally. Excusing himself for a moment, he took me to one side to ask me in a whisper to slip out for it. As I got up to leave the room there was a sudden hushed silence. I walked confidently through the door – and found myself in a dark wardrobe. I stayed put, silently savouring the absurdity of the situation and cursing the decorators for doing such a perfect job.

The whole campaign, like the preceding one, was a spirited and enjoyable affair. Morale was still very high; there was great friendliness and co-operation between all sections of the Party. But as the campaign wore on, our private polls became more and more depressing as the large hoped-for lead failed to materialize and the signs were that it was going to be an extremely close-run race. The campaign team, however, remained in good spirits from beginning to end, its teamwork even more effective than in February, despite the increased workload resulting from some of the members' other duties at Number 10.

In addition, we were convinced that, having brought the country back to industrial peace and announced our intentions on future policy and the need for co-operation with the working population, the country would give the Labour Government a clear mandate to continue.

On the eve of the poll, we all travelled up to the Adelphi Hotel in Liverpool. (Bernard and Joe, as civil servants, had taken official time off that evening.) In Harold Wilson's suite on the first floor, we listened to the results. As they started to come in, the outlook seemed quite good, with the computer predicting a twenty-seat majority for Labour – at one point, Bernard and even Joe thought that it might approach the size of that in 1966, and they began to pose the question of how we should have to handle such a massive parliamentary representation. But as the evening wore on their calculators and notebooks began to show a different pattern; the final result was an overall majority of a mere three seats, a situation that could be transformed overnight by death, disaster or by-election. It was depressing, but we had got our mandate.

TWENTY-ONE

After the Election

We had won. The overall majority was small, but we had a substantially greater number of seats than the Tories, and the minority parties were in most cases unlikely to vote with the Conservatives; our position therefore seemed to be reasonably secure.

These feelings were in my mind when we returned to London after it was all over, and we had been to Transport House both for the final result and to thank the staff. But what was missing was the feeling of elation usual after victory. When Harold Wilson went back to Number 10 after his traditional Party Headquarters visit, I decided not to return with him to my office but to go straight home. I missed the usual ceremony of the Number 10 staff clapping in the new Premier. I still don't know if it actually happened on that occasion. After all, it had only been six months since their last greeting.

I drove up Whitehall without looking at or turning into Downing Street, completely unmoved by the fact that we were back in office again. It was not simply campaign fatigue; my excitement at being in Number 10 had long since evaporated anyway.

Effectively, of course, there was to be only one more year in Downing Street for us all on Harold Wilson's staff before 1976 began with the three months that led up to the Prime Minister's resignation. But politically those twelve or so months were among the most eventful, the busiest and, perhaps, the most crucial of any I have known, not just for us but for the Party, and I would hazard with wider implications still. 1968 had been a key year; so was 1975.

Within the Party, there was continual controversy, not only on the comparatively clear-cut issue of the Common Market and the referendum, but in the fabric of the Party itself. Trotskyist influence was increasing, the Far Left was already emerging strongly within the Party in the regions and, above all, in the National Executive, now far more difficult to manage. 'I love my Cabinet but I don't love the NEC,' became one of the Prime Minister's joking remarks, as he found his meetings with the latter becoming ever more prickly.

The 1975 reshuffle was difficult enough, not least the moving of Tony Benn sideways to Energy from Industry, and the need to persuade the other half of the equation, Eric Varley, to fall into line.

That summer I remember many discussions over tea in the rose garden at Chequers, about how to save Tony, persuade Eric and keep the Government on course. Eric was exceedingly reluctant, when first approached, to exchange jobs like this. He felt he might appear to be colluding with the Prime Minister in something more sinister than a sideways move for Tony. He clearly did not wish at that point to lose favour with his left-of-centre and soft-Left friends, who were his main supporters in the Parliamentary Labour Party.

I was asked to approach Gerald Kaufman, with whom I had worked closely in the 1960s and whom I knew well, to suggest to him a means whereby Eric might be more happily persuaded to move. Eric and Gerald also knew each other well – again from the 1960s and also from Number 10, when Eric had been Parliamentary Private Secretary to the Prime Minister.

The Prime Minister asked me to say that if it made the move to Industry more appealing to Eric, the Prime Minister would give him Gerald as one of his Junior Ministers there. The Prime Minister was not entirely correct in his assumption that if the case was presented fairly and persuasively to Eric by Gerald then the former would wish to move; nor was he accurate in believing that Gerald himself would welcome the chance to join him in Industry. Gerald was, in fact, extremely reluctant to go, and only when he was convinced that the long-term security and success of the Government required it did he accept these proposals.

The move caused much hostility and suspicion on the Left, who felt that Harold Wilson was giving in to the City depiction of Tony Benn as a bogeyman. They were partly correct, in that some of Tony's wilder statements and acts at the Department of Industry, and the moves he made on the National Executive Committee – which became public debates on questions of nationalization and public ownership – had caused considerable erosion of confidence in the City on the Govern-

ment's performance as a whole. In order to hold the line, the Prime
Minister felt strongly that the best solution was to move Tony.

What Harold Wilson never had in mind was sacking Tony Benn,
since he felt Tony had a great contribution to make inside the Government, as part of the Labour team, and that it would be a good idea if he
were moved to an area where public ownership was not such a controversial issue. At Energy, it was established Party policy: and the whole
of the oil nationalization programme, which was under way, was of key
importance; it was one of the main policies on which we had just fought
an election, and we had emphasized the benefits that would accrue to
the Government and the country from a nationalized oil industry. It
would, he felt, be good to have Tony's messianic fervour on the question
of nationalization harnessed to official government policy.

Arranging this desirable state of affairs took much time. On the
crucial evening, I shuttled back and forth at the House of Commons
between Eric and Gerald on the Ministerial floor below the Prime
Minister's room and back again to Harold Wilson to report what they
had said. Finally, after argument, discussion, debate, soul-searching
and analysis, Eric agreed that he would not take unilateral action if the
Prime Minister sent for him to inform him officially that the move was
to take place; that he would not refuse the offer of the Industry job. We
had feared that he would refuse to be moved and simply leave Government for the back benches, so strong was his feeling that he did not want
to let down his centre-Left and Left supporters, or be accused of helping
to make a scapegoat of Tony. Eventually, though, he yielded, accepting
the situation after talking at length with most of Tony Benn's closest
friends and advisers.

That particular night, the corridors of the Commons were alive with
messengers darting to and fro between the various camps bearing
negotiating points for consideration between the two principals. At the
end, both men knew exactly what the score was. They were both able
to accept and survive in their new jobs. The reshuffle that had cost the
Prime Minister too much time and trouble had worked out well.

Although the Prime Minister's decision to resign during his sixtieth year
had been made much earlier, the fact that the Party was moving so
rapidly farther leftwards, and that he was finding relations with its
governing body so difficult, only served to convince him that the timing
of his resignation was fortunate. If he had been staying on, I have no
doubt he would have formulated an effective strategy to deal with it.

But other issues had paramountcy in the limited time available to him.

Criticism has been levelled at Harold Wilson because he did not tackle these growing difficulties head-on at that point. He himself, I think, accepts that he could have done more during that year, but, as I have said, at the time he concentrated on those issues that seemed to demand priority: counter-inflation, the referendum, the augmentation of policies, the whole business of preparing, presenting and putting through Parliament legislation that would implement the election pledges on which Harold Wilson had stated that he, and the Labour Government, would be judged.

On the international front, there were major overseas visits to Moscow and Leningrad on *détente* and on re-establishing our trading links with the Eastern bloc; to Jamaica, where much progress was made (the work of the Lomé Convention earned great praise later); to Helsinki, on *détente* again and on human rights, where the Soviet Union gave undertakings that were, unfortunately, to prove less than satisfactory later. All through this year, there were endless meetings in Europe (including the Rambouillet meeting and the decision to hold regular gatherings in the future), many in connection with the renegotiation of the Common Market, as well as those other meetings which were now becoming convention. International activity of this sort is both time-consuming and tiring for a Prime Minister. Most of it, in my view, is expensive and unnecessary: more for public relations than good government.

At home, the end of the year saw the convulsive argument within industry that culminated in the Chrysler dilemma during the last months of 1975 and the first of 1976, and which had been preceded by the difficulties at British Leyland – including Don Ryder's personal position.

The Chrysler problem divided the Cabinet, in a way unusual in that many of Harold Wilson's closest supporters – not least Eric Varley, the Secretary of State in charge – were deeply disappointed with the line finally adopted. The feeling was that the Prime Minister had been 'got at' by some of the more unorthodox thinkers, who took a risk-filled approach to Chrysler, believing the Government should intervene to save the company. Others felt Chrysler should probably have been allowed to die and the expensive rescue operation avoided.

So full of plot and counter-plot was the Chrysler saga that Eric Varley finally reached the point of contemplating resignation. This was almost as much because of the way in which the final decision had been reached as in protest against it. In the event, he was prevailed upon by his own intuition as well as by the advice of Junior Ministers, including his own, Gerald Kaufman, that such an action would be counter-productive – not least because there was now the constant rumour of impending change at Number 10.

When Harold Wilson was given the Freedom of the City of London, Gerald came to collect me to take me to the Guildhall; during the car journey, we discussed exactly what had been happening in Cabinet, where there had been a sizeable plot against the Secretary of State, so that the line he wished to follow had been overruled. It was a strange situation, especially against the background of a Labour majority dwindling almost to vanishing point – from two down, finally, to one.

Despite this – or perhaps because of his House of Commons difficulties – the Chief Whip, Bob Mellish, was becoming temperamental. On one occasion I arrived at Number 10 to find Joe Haines waiting for me in my room to ask whether I knew that Bob Mellish had resigned. No, I replied, I didn't, upon which Joe informed me that Harold Wilson had just received his resignation letter and it was, therefore, all over. Was it not terrible? said Joe, and, of course, it was.

At this point came, as I see it, justification in almost classic form for the key role of the political adviser (*any* political adviser!). The man or woman in this post who knows the principals, who has worked with them and knows how they think and how they react, has a specialist knowledge in an affair of this kind that can often bring it to resolution.

So it was now. My instinctive reaction was to ask, 'Has Harold Wilson seen Bob Mellish in person?' Face-to-face confrontation at a moment of crisis often produces a situation quite different from one reached by the second-hand means of intervention by others or even personal letters. No, replied Joe, he had not. I suggested that the best thing would be for the Prime Minister to send for Bob Mellish and to ask him what was worrying him and whether he would reconsider, explaining to him how important it was for the Party that he remain in his post. No letter, and no statement, could give a truly comprehensive and accurate picture of all that Bob was feeling. When Bob arrived soon after, the length of time he spent in the Prime Minister's study bore witness to this. When he eventually emerged, Harold Wilson joined me in my room and, wiping an imaginary tear from his eye, told me that they had both, in fact, left the study with tears in their eyes, having agreed that the Party desperately needed their experienced Chief Whip during the difficult period they were going through, and thus could ill afford to lose Bob. The Prime Minister said that although he knew that Bob would prefer to move to a position that seemed more personally creative, such as the Housing Department, as far as the Party was concerned he was in the most constructive of jobs. Would Bob, therefore, change his mind about going? After the Prime Minister had talked for some time on these lines, Bob finally and nobly withdrew his resignation.

For me, some of the most agreeable hours of that eventful year were spent working on the John Terry Working Party on the film industry. I had become a member of this body in order that I could act as a deputy for Harold Wilson. As his eyes and ears on the committee, I learned much and enjoyed it enormously.

The work went with speed, and we were able to finish our report on the state of the film industry and our recommendations for its future by Christmas. We made a small party of its presentation to the Prime Minister, handing it over to him personally in the White Drawing Room at Number 10 immediately prior to the staff Christmas party, and celebrating with a glass of champagne. We all – I was sitting with Alasdair Milne, Richard Attenborough, Bernard Delfont and Don Ryder – hoped that action would be taken on the recommendations contained in our report, especially on the main one of setting up a British Film Authority – something still not achieved. (Indeed, it is arguable now whether such an Authority would be too limited and whether the real need is now for a Communications Agency or Authority to act as an umbrella for all the developing new technologies including film.) After the party, I went down to my office to clear my desk before going home; then decided that perhaps I should look in at the Number 10 staff party for a moment. It was the last Christmas party for those who lived and worked in Number 10 that I attended.

The festivity that followed took place in the Pillared Room and, by the time I managed to get there, it had reached a stage of considerable joviality. For the first time, a piano had been brought into Number 10 (apart, that is, from the pianos that were the personal property of other Prime Ministers). It had, in fact, been brought in the day before for the party for disabled children I had again organized. The staff, especially of the Private Office and the Press Office, were gathered round it, singing snatches of Gilbert and Sullivan. This was in large part for the benefit of Harold Wilson, who is particularly fond of these operettas. The two 'stars' turned out to be Janet Hewlett-Davis, the efficient, talented and energetic Deputy Press Secretary, now a senior Government Information Officer, and Jean Denham, now Information Officer at the BBC. Their rendering of 'A Policeman's Lot is not a Happy One' gained much applause from the members of the Special Branch present, as well as from the rest of the staff and, of course, the Prime Minister. Behind all this merriment, however, lay a certain poignancy for those who knew that this was to be the last occasion that he would share these Christmas festivities with the staff of Number 10.

For the Wilsons themselves, 1975 had been a personally memorable year. Their twin grand-daughters were born in March – giving rise, incidentally, to a Downing Street 'first'. Robin Wilson and his wife Joy had been wanting a baby for some time and when, during that inter-election summer of 1974, the Wilsons learned that their daughter-in-law was pregnant they were naturally delighted. Mary Wilson in particular had been looking forward to the birth of a grandchild. I think I first learned the good news in the Scilly Isles in late August. On 13 March 1975, during a Cabinet meeting, the Prime Minister was told that Mary wished to speak to him; he emerged from the Cabinet Room to be told the good news about the birth of the twin girls; he went back in and announced this to the Cabinet, who were delighted for him. This is the only instance I can recall of a Cabinet Meeting being interrupted for personal reasons, though Margot Asquith was given to the habit.

The babies were christened at Chequers in a special ceremony in the Long Gallery during the Christmas holiday – the last Christmas that the Wilsons were to spend at Chequers. Their first birthday also, on 13 March 1976, was spent there just before their grandfather resigned. For him, those first months of 1976, like the previous year, were, I think, among the most dramatic and memorable days of his life.

In world terms, 1975 was indeed a year notable for the extraordinary number of issues and developments it contained – some that were speedily settled, some that appeared only in embryonic form, and some that cast a long shadow. That period saw the end of Richard Nixon's time in the White House and the whole Watergate affair, but not of its ramifications throughout American politics, nor for that matter in the media world-wide; the Referendum and the Common Market problems; the new financial arrangements within Europe; the North–South arguments in the Third World; the development of *détente* after Brandt; the decisions to hold regular meetings of European leaders; and the sharpening Israeli situation.

Most of the 1974–6 period saw Gerald Ford as President of the United States, though Harold Wilson had renewed his acquaintance with Richard Nixon before Nixon's final departure.

At a summit meeting in Paris, Harold Wilson's advisers had persuaded him against his own better judgement to dodge a meeting with Nixon, with the media watching, by hiding in the rose bushes in the garden of the British Embassy. That was a pity, since in his dealings with Nixon he had found him to be a most able and experienced President, not least in his handling of international politics, for which Harold Wilson greatly admired and respected him.

Richard Nixon had also the unusual quality of being exactly the same in his personal contacts in office and out. When Harold Wilson visited Washington as Opposition Leader, Richard Nixon had insisted on a meeting with him at the White House even though Edward Heath looked set for a long time as Prime Minister, and the Tories in office for the foreseeable future.

On a similar occasion, before Richard Nixon went to the White House, when Harold Wilson was at Number 10, he had insisted on receiving Nixon: a meeting that nearly did not come off. It was to be held at the PM's office in the House of Commons. Nixon duly arrived with his aides and was requested to take a seat on the sofa in the waiting area outside the Prime Minister's room. A Cabinet committee meeting was in progress, which was rather important and urgent, and the Garden Room girl on duty was reluctant to interrupt it and announce the next appointment. In the end, she summoned up the courage and went in to tell him that the gentleman had arrived. 'Your next appointment is here, Prime Minister,' she said. 'Who is it?' he enquired. 'Someone called Richard Nixon,' the innocent girl replied. Afterwards the two of them laughed about it. Indeed, their relationship was easy and relaxed, and discussions always wide-ranging and deep. There were, of course, the lighter moments when Prime Minister and President could join together in singing, word perfect, a chorus from Gilbert and Sullivan's *Iolanthe* over dinner.

In the years of his Leadership, Harold Wilson probably saw more achieved in international relationships when Nixon was President than in the years he had dealt with Kennedy and Lyndon Johnson before him, or Gerald Ford after, though he developed a healthy respect for the latter, despite the unending cracks made by the media about his accident-prone handicap. At Helsinki, in particular, he was surprised by President Ford's grasp of the implications of the *détente* developments, whilst at the same time unnerved by a certain shift in the attitude of the USA towards Israel.

TWENTY-TWO

Israel

Harold Wilson's relationship with Israel has always been special. When he resigned, his valedictory words were, 'Once I leave, I leave. I am not going to speak to the man on the bridge and I am not going to spit on the deck'; but they would not, he told his successor James Callaghan when saying goodbye, apply to the subject of Israel. Here he intended to pursue his own robust, independent and often courageous line, and to speak where he felt it necessary. As James Callaghan largely shared Harold Wilson's views on Israel, he was quite content with this state of affairs.

Harold Wilson's attachment to the State of Israel dates from the days of Nye Bevan and their early friendship with Yigal Allon in the 1950s. Since then, he has been on friendly terms with many leading Israeli figures – Golda Meir, Yitzhak Rabin, Abba Eban, Shimon Peres and others, including two of the foremost Israeli diplomats, Gideon Rafael and Eppie Evron (once Minister at the Israeli Embassy in London, later to be a most effective Ambassador in Washington).

Harold Wilson viewed the creation of the State of Israel as a unique and extraordinary milestone in the history of the western world: a nation, set down in an area of difficult physical geography, producing a modern, highly sophisticated democracy amid a sea of, to say the least, non-democratic neighbours. What is more, it owed its prosperity not to the oil that flowed so freely beneath the soil of its neighbour, but to the devotion and hard work of the Israelis and the loyalty of the Jewish communities around the world. Before Menachem Begin, Israel was, too, not only democratic but socialist: a double plus for its admirers within the Labour Party.

The period 1974 to 1976 was one of considerable difficulty for the Israelis, coming as it did on the heels of the Yom Kippur War of 1973.

As few Prime Ministers in recent years have had a pro-Israel bias, there has seldom been reason for them to disagree with the naturally pro-Arab posture of the Foreign Office; if, however, a Prime Minister or Foreign Secretary feels an affinity for the State of Israel, he first has to correct or circumvent this inbuilt imbalance in the Foreign Office. In Harold Wilson's case, although it is difficult to judge how big a handicap his sympathies for Israel were, they undoubtedly exposed him to much criticism while in office, and afterwards. Partly this was because his support for Israel was so closely linked to his connections with the Jewish community here; but for his sentiments towards Israel, those links would certainly have been fewer.

As it was, Harold Wilson's pro-Israel attitude meant especial vigilance on the part of those around him: often issues would arise at the United Nations on which the Foreign Office would fail to inform the Prime Minister what had happened, or what line our representative at the UN would be taking. Sometimes information came more privately; it quite often fell to me, sometimes to Bernard Donoughue – who shared Harold Wilson's attitude to Israel – or to Joe Haines to act as go-between for Israeli representatives, friends and supporters, passing on information that the Prime Minister was not receiving through official channels.

One of these occasions occurred when the Prime Minister was in Helsinki in July 1975 for the special conference on *détente* and disarmament. At that time there were difficulties between the Americans and the Israelis, and it had become clear that the Americans were distancing themselves from current Israeli policy. The Prime Minister was anxious in case the Israelis, who were about to send their own Prime Minister to Washington, were not fully aware of this subtle change in the American position. Harold Wilson, who had been able to talk at length to President Ford, wanted the Israelis brought up to date without the Foreign Office in London being alerted.

He therefore rang me in London in order to get a message to the Israelis to tell them he needed to brief them. I, who knew nothing of the situation that had arisen or what was involved, was at something of a disadvantage. I was only told over the telephone that I was to contact 'a good friend of the friend I had been dining with the night before', and tell him that the Prime Minister needed to discuss something important with him. What he preferred was a direct talk with the Israeli

Prime Minister Yitzhak Rabin in Stockholm, where both were to attend a Socialist International Conference before the one returned to London, the other to Washington, but this could not be spelt out on the open line. Fortunately, knowing that the 'friend' I had dined with the night before was George Weidenfeld, I guessed that his 'friend' might be the Israeli Ambassador. So I rang the latter with the message, hoping I had deciphered it correctly; he thanked me briefly and cryptically.

Later, I was to learn that the Ambassador contacted Jerusalem immediately, with the upshot that Eppie Evron – then a roving Israeli Ambassador, scheduled to attend the Stockholm conference with Rabin – was instead despatched forthwith to Helsinki. Here he had urgent talks with the Prime Minister, who gave him an up-to-date assessment of the United States' position on the Middle East.

Whether all this contributed towards or improved the chances of peace in the Middle East and thus world peace, I do not know. Certainly, such activities were understandably viewed with hostility and irritation by the Foreign Office and caused great difficulties both then and subsequently. For the Israelis, it was an exceptionally fortunate period: never before had they had a Prime Minister of Great Britain so prepared to listen to their case and to support it where he thought it justified. It was not to happen again quite like that.

TWENTY-THREE

The Referendum

Many problems solve themselves by the mere passage of time. But the question of whether or not to enter Europe was not one; and the passionate and partisan convictions of those on either side ensured that the argument would rage during the years of Opposition unless some formula were found to restore harmony. The irony was that the eventual solution – the Referendum – was not only European, but chosen by that fervent anti-Marketeer, Tony Benn. As it was, even the idea of using a referendum caused a further split in the Party; ironic again in that it was the pro-Europe minority, led by Roy Jenkins, who were alienated by this European device, to the extent of Roy's resigning the Deputy Leadership during the Opposition years.

Their reason for so behaving was that they felt that the only possible instrument for achieving entry into Europe was the will of the nation – as expressed via the ballot box in support of a Party committed to it in their election manifesto. Underlining their attitude was the hard fact that as we were already in Europe – thanks to Mr Heath – they did not feel particularly inclined to allow a debate on the principle of coming out.

However, despite the original outcry, the idea of a referendum gradually gained acceptance; despite, also, the discomfort caused by lack of experience of this particular method – new constitutionally to the UK. By the end of 1973, after both Party conferences and the Trades Union Congress, a formula had been hammered out: not precisely that of a referendum on the strictly European model, but of a 'Yes' or 'No' answer via the ballot box that left the next Labour Government free to renegotiate terms. (When a Labour Government was returned the following year, one of the first acts of the new Foreign Secretary, James Callaghan, was to announce to Parliament that the terms on which the Heath Government had taken us in were to be renegotiated. This announcement was followed by the statement that after the proposed renegotiation, both Parliament and the people would have to see whether this, in turn, was acceptable.)

It is almost impossible to describe just how complicated an issue the Market renegotiation was. There were, first, all the technicalities involved in finding ground for agreement between Britain and Europe, with the endless meetings that had to be planned between various different departments of government – let alone those in Brussels – the numerous summits and mini-summits, all designed to try and find a formula for agreement. A completely different but equally important dimension was how the question of the Market renegotiation was viewed by the Labour Party as a whole – embracing as it did the widely differing views of the trades unions, the Parliamentary Labour Party, Members of Parliament, constituency parties and, last but very much not least, the ordinary Labour voter. Finally, there was the time and debate that had to be devoted to finding a device by which a majority vote could be made known on all these highly technical issues.

For a newly elected Prime Minister whose first priority was to grapple with the industrial breakdown bequeathed to him by his predecessor, and an economy brought to crisis point by the oil crisis and the consequent world situation, it was a formidable extra burden. From my seat at the ringside, I think I can say that the months from his election in February 1974 until the Common Market question was resolved in June 1975 were the most hectic and hard-working of Harold Wilson's life.

Difficult and fraught though these months were for him, they were also a period of 'marking time', in the sense that no firm decisions could be taken until the Government's mandate was – we hoped – confirmed by going to the country again. Until then, all that could be done was to arrange the necessary fact-finding meetings between the various Ministers involved, the discovery of essential facts, the delineating of the issues on which Britain would insist on some form of new deal. A great deal of ground was covered.

After the Government was given a second mandate in October 1974, the wheels began to turn faster and more purposefully. The most obvious manifestation was a series of mini-summits culminating in the Paris Summit, where Giscard d'Estaing established the principle of the European Council – the regular meeting of all the European heads of government three times a year.

By January 1975, Harold Wilson was able to announce in Parliament that a referendum within six months was envisaged. Shortly after this, Edward Heath, who had questioned the Prime Minister closely on the referendum itself and the precedent it would set, and on procedures to be followed, was replaced as Conservative Party Leader by Margaret Thatcher. From then on, Mr Heath sat just below the gangway, from which position he was free to make the running on Europe, the cause so dear to his heart. For Harold Wilson there was a slight easement because Margaret Thatcher, although pro-European, was not dedicated to the Market in the same personally passionate way.

The final summit took place in Dublin, memorable for Harold Wilson not only because of the co-operation of the Irish in ironing out the last difficulties that existed between the Six and the new entrants, but because it was his fifty-ninth birthday, for which he was given a surprise celebration. At midnight on the evening of 11 March 1975, Jim Callaghan suddenly interrupted the talks that were still going on to say 'Happy Birthday!'. Upon this signal, a big cake with candles was brought in, everyone sang 'Happy Birthday', and Jim handed Harold the present of a new tie, which I had purchased for him earlier.

By now we were near agreement. There only remained one stumbling-block: The Party was still divided in its views on the Market in Government as it had been in Opposition. There was still a sizeable minority who were very pro-Market, a similar group equally strongly against it, and a large number in the middle who had not made up their minds either way. The 'pro' group had increased slightly in size, thanks to the addition of a few converts who had been doing jobs that involved them closely with Europe, like Fred Peart of Agriculture.

These divisions meant that no clear recommendation from a united Government – or Cabinet – could go forward. So another formula had to be found and, despite the care that was taken, even here there was a final hiccup. The arrangement was that Members of the Cabinet, should they disagree, would be allowed the right to differ, their identities being made known in due course.

Unfortunately, just as Parliament was about to debate the new Market position, Harold Wilson had to go to Northern Ireland; and while he was away, the Cabinet agreed that the same arrangement would apply also to Ministers in the Government. This meant that a large number of those in government were licensed to express dissent.

And this they did, in the vote that followed a long parliamentary debate. It was at this point that Eric Heffer expressed his own dissent from the 'arrangements to differ' and had to leave the Government. Even this proved fraught with awkwardness: the man sent to Eric's flat to bring him to Number 10 in order that the Prime Minister could discuss his position with him did not know what Eric looked like, and was naturally worried that his unpleasant errand would be complicated if he failed to recognize him. It was sad that Eric, at that time believed by the Prime Minister to be one of the cleverest and most talented of the Labour Left, had to go. Indeed, as of the time of writing, Eric Heffer is a leading contender for high office in the Party.

Taken all round, however, the whole atmosphere surrounding the Market question became more comfortable with official permission to differ. In this more relaxed mood we entered the run-up to the Referendum. While the campaigns in the country both for and against Britain's membership were fully and very effectively organized, I hesitate to call what happened from Number 10 a campaign. It was not one certainly in the accepted sense, if only because no one was responsible for the machinery to organize it. As it wasn't a Government campaign, the Civil Service couldn't be called on in the normal way to help with meetings, broadcasts or speeches. The Labour Party was committed against the Market, so they could not be called upon for help either. In the end, help for the Prime Minister came from his Political Office, which was independent both of the Labour Party machine and of the Government. We sought assistance from the few unions, like the General and Municipal Workers' Union, his own union, who were pro-Market, and from those pro-Market people in the Party who knew how to organize meetings, public relations, back-up literature and all the paraphernalia of campaigning. Lord Harris of Greenwich was called in to give advice on the Prime Minister's personal campaign presentation.

The Referendum had been arranged for the middle of the summer holiday period in order to give those who wanted to be involved the chance to campaign, which meant that quite a number of people were on holiday. Both Bernard Donoughue and Joe Haines were away since both were civil servants and therefore not technically allowed to be involved in the campaign. Earlier they had asked me to make sure that the Prime Minister himself did not go on his usual holiday to the Scilly Isles during the campaign period. He wanted a brief break after such a hectic year; they, however, felt it vital that he should be near at hand and quickly contactable if necessary, but preferred not to ask him to remain near to London themselves. In the end he went to Chequers.

Although we were fairly confident from the start that there would be a 'Yes' vote, as the actual day drew nearer there was – as with all elections – the worry that it was all going to go wrong at the last minute.

One morning, Jim Callaghan came into my room and said, 'I do hope you will make it clear to Harold that he should resign if the vote goes the wrong way. I shall resign.' To this extraordinary remark I made no reply at all. He went on to insist that I understand the seriousness attached to the Referendum vote, saying that both he and Harold should feel it was their duty to resign if the country recorded a 'No' vote: so strongly were they committed to an affirmative that anything else would be a vote of no confidence.

Looking back, I think that what Jim was asking was for me to add my voice to those who would be saying, 'You must resign now' in the event of a 'No' vote. Even then this rather surprised me; I myself was a committed anti-Marketeer (and had made no secret of the fact), but the whole principle of the Referendum, established after a lot of heart-searching, was that people were allowed to differ – and this should be as true for the Prime Minister as for anyone else.

However, on the day that the results of the Referendum were announced, a 2–1 vote in favour, Jim Callaghan came into my room again, this time to say how pleased he was it had gone well. The Prime Minister, Jim and myself drank a champagne toast to its success – 'A job well done' were, I think, the exact words.

More precise we could hardly be as, to those involved in European politics, the Market is something like the Irish question, in that it is always there as a question mark. To this day, the Party not only argues over it, but official policy has swung full circle: the Labour Party is now committed against Europe and to bringing Britain out of the Market. That Thursday, the glass of champagne I drank before setting off home seemed as much a toast to a final conclusion of this long-drawn-out issue as to the success of the official Government line.

TWENTY-FOUR

Inflation

The economic situation inherited from Edward Heath was one of terrifying and rapidly increasing inflation. In a less violently volatile economic climate, it is arguable that Mr Heath's statutory prices and incomes policy might probably, given no large-scale confrontation with any of the big trades unions, have achieved its desired objective. But with the cost of oil soaring overnight and in its turn generating massive price rises worldwide, the 'threshold' formula for wages built into the Heath incomes policy produced a ratchet effect that was ferocious, to say the least. It also provided Labour with a savage inflationary inheritance after it took office. Within this maelstrom Harold Wilson believed the first priority was to get Britain back to work and the labour force at peace with the Government, and then to achieve an early solution on the Common Market, problems which otherwise would continue as a disunifying and destabilizing element. Similarly, he felt no sense was to be made out of the economic situation at home until both Great Britain and Europe knew where each other stood. Without unity on this vital question, a Party and a Government at odds with itself could hardly tackle the major issue of inflation and economic distress with conviction. So, rightly or wrongly – and there are plenty to speak on both sides – he decided to settle the Market question before devoting himself one hundred per cent to the general economic situation.

Nevertheless time was not on his side and he was forced to devote a great deal of his time and effort to holding the line on the economic front. By the summer of 1975 inflation had escalated so dramatically and the pound had once more, as in earlier Labour Governments, come under such pressure that crisis point was reached. Without prior indication or warning late one night the Treasury advocated the immediate introduction of another statutory prices and incomes policy. Their reaction was predictable. Indeed they were in a sense behaving responsibly and, with the Heath years recently behind them, as they thought correctly. Their advice was once again based on experience of the last Government with no recognition of the political difficulties the new Government would find in accepting such advice. Harold Wilson was faced with this critical situation late at night during an official visit of the Belgian Prime Minister, Leo Tindemanns.

He needed little persuasion against the Treasury advice. He had learned from bitter experience over five years in office earlier that such advice contrary to Party policy was to be resisted. His Cabinet colleagues, equally experienced, knew the score too. The situation was similarly contained by advice he received personally within Number 10. I was myself present for the Tindemanns dinner, and then joined the Prime Minister in his study afterwards where he received advice from his colleagues and from his policy adviser as was appropriate. Their reaction was the same as his own to the Treasury warlords.

The Treasury's advice was orthodox; once Harold Wilson had resisted it, government concentration on making a voluntary policy operable was essential. The immediate target was the goodwill of the large trades unions. At the union conferences held that summer they were reminded of their special relationship with the Labour Government and of the Social Contract to which they had given their endorsement, and told in uncompromising terms of the difficulties the Government faced following the collapse of the Heath Government. They were asked for their co-operation on a policy of voluntary wage restraint. In return, the Government pointed not only to the social legislation on which they set such a high value, but to other legislation, particularly the Employment Protection Act, which would give them increasing benefits and protection.

This was put – much of it personally by Harold Wilson – to trades union conferences throughout that summer. At the miners' conference a personal, albeit perhaps back-handed, compliment was paid to the Prime Minister when he sat down after delivering a speech urging restraint and giving the reasons why; the Scottish NUM leader, Mick McGahey, said to him, 'I suppose you got what you came for, then.' McGahey, like Harold Wilson, knew that if the Government could sway the miners, the chances were that the rest of the trades union movement would follow suit. Both were proved right: the other unions fell into line one by one.

As head of the Government, Harold Wilson was determined to take an obvious lead in putting the message of restraint across to the country as a whole, and this he did in his Prime Minister's broadcast.

Simultaneously with the launching of the voluntary restraints policy came the setting up of the Counter-Inflation Unit (ciu), a small think-tank physically sited in the Cabinet Office, but with a watching brief over every Whitehall department. The ciu's work was partly policy and partly propaganda: it aimed to discover the economic weak spots both within the Government and outside, work out how they could best be plugged, and present both the need for this and the method chosen in the best and most encouraging light to all concerned.

Two more suitable (though in view of their basic profession surprising) people to run it could hardly have been found. These were Sydney Jacobson, former Editor-in-Chief of the *Daily Mirror*, and another *Mirror* man, Geoffrey Goodman (now Industrial Editor). Sydney, like many other *Mirror* employees – sometimes it seemed almost all of them – had become a member of the House of Lords. Cecil King was one who had refrained: he refused a life peerage, asking instead for an earldom. Perhaps he did not wish to be like all the other proprietors who went to the House of Lords. Along with Sydney in the Upper Chamber were Don Ryder and John Beavan (who became Lord Ardwick). At around this time representations were also made to make the talented lawyer, businessman and member of the *Mirror* Board – Ellis Birk – a life peer. But this was turned down on the grounds that there were already three peers among *Mirror* employees (the other newspaper peers were all proprietors).

The *Daily Mirror* has (almost) always supported Labour editorially, but perhaps not everyone knows what a key role the paper played, in terms of the active involvement of its personnel rather than column-inches of newsprint, in Labour Party politics; in particular, from 1974 onwards.

Mirror dinners, or luncheons, were frequently held at Number 10, attended by members of the *Mirror* Board – in early years Cecil King, later Don Ryder, Hugh Cudlipp, Sydney Jacobson, Alex Jarrett, Tony Miles, and their principal political writer Terence Lancaster. Their advice would be sought, soundings taken, opinions given, help promised. It was therefore a natural progression that the ciu should be put in the charge of Lord Jacobson and Geoffrey Goodman (on secondment from the *Daily Mirror*), with access to the Prime Minister to give and receive advice: always channelled efficiently, as it worked out, through Joe Haines. It was vital to get across the importance of the counter-inflation policy and to achieve electoral support for it, and both Goodman and Jacobson were expert and experienced in this field.

The intentions, that summer of 1975, were excellent. But as so often, the unexpected intervened: gradually it became apparent that the Prime Minister really *was* going to resign on or near his sixtieth birthday, as he had said all those years ago. By the beginning of 1976, those of us close to Harold Wilson who knew that he was going had begun to feel ourselves in a curious political no-man's-land – a sort of twilight period before the end.

In my case, the knowledge that I was, so to speak, working myself out of a job tended to make me feel less and less involved; the excitement of my work steadily diminished as the moment when it would end drew nearer. As for the Political Office, sensing what was happening they became increasingly concerned in this interim period with what would happen afterwards rather than exhibiting their usual enthusiasm and involvement in various aspects of policy for which, they now knew, they would soon have no further responsibility. Each part of the machine functioned, but the vitality, the sense of intimate, interlocking concern was missing. Everyone was preoccupied with an easy transition and with the future.

So I was more than slightly surprised to be invited at the beginning of 1976 to a dinner for Geoffrey Goodman and Sydney Jacobson, under whose guidance the CIU appeared to be extremely successful: its message was being got across to the country, Harold Wilson's speeches were all formulated round the agreed presentation of the counter-inflation policy, the policy itself was working.

No overt reason was given for the dinner; all I knew was that Peter Lovell-Davis, Joe Haines, Albert Murray and, of course, Sydney Jacobson and Geoffrey Goodman were invited as well as the Prime Minister. Only Bernard Donoughue, in the event, was unable to attend.

It was a superb dinner – though in view of what transpired it could more aptly have been called the Last Supper. The small State Dining Room provided an elegant setting for the polished dining table, the bowls of flowers, the gleaming silver and china, the printed menus. The elaborate food, like the marvellous wines, was all from Government Hospitality. Peter Lovell-Davis, the only outside guest – apart from the guests-of-honour Sydney Jacobson and Geoffrey Goodman – had, like myself, no idea for the reason behind this feast; but we were both happy to be there to celebrate, as we assumed, past success, and to hear the outline of future strategy.

We were soon to be undeceived. Very quickly the conversation took an extraordinary turn. 'Geoffrey Must Go' seemed to be its theme, but I could hardly believe my ears until Peter Lovell-Davis leaned towards me and whispered, 'This is the most elaborate way I've ever seen of sacking someone.' 'Yes,' I agreed, 'we're not at a dinner – we're at an execution.'

So difficult was it to believe something so unlikely that I still wasn't quite sure. But during coffee, Harold Wilson excused himself, and Geoffrey Goodman and Sydney Jacobson went off to the Gents with him.

'We must let Geoffrey go back to the *Daily Mirror*,' Joe urged, in support, it seemed, of what we thought was happening. 'They need him desperately because they're in such a bad way – the circulation is down and the paper is very badly run. We must do *everything we can* to facilitate his return.'

Peter and I were stunned. We had no idea either that the *Mirror* was in such a bad way or that Geoffrey's return to it would make the necessary vital difference; nor had we understood that the CIU had reached a point in its career at which it could easily afford to give up both its head (Sydney Jacobson) and its principal administrator all in one go. Sydney was anxious to withdraw gradually because of ill-health.

Both Peter and I assumed, of course, that Harold Wilson had retired briefly with the two *Mirror* men in order to make it quite plain to them, in total privacy, that Geoffrey had, indeed, got to go back to the *Daily Mirror*.

So when the three of them returned to the table, we began to discuss what would happen when Geoffrey went back to the *Daily Mirror*. The Unit, everyone agreed, would have to go on, and perhaps Sydney might consent to give two days a week to oversee it. As everyone had said repeatedly through the earlier part of dinner, its work had been invaluable during the six months of its existence and it must be kept going. Who should now head it? It had to be someone competent, with a direct line to the Prime Minister; after much discussion, Joe suggested, quite rightly and with all our support, that perhaps this someone should be a member of the Press Office.

At this point in the evening, Geoffrey's desire to return to the *Daily Mirror* had been accepted. The first time it had been put forward I glanced at the other faces round the table for some clue as to this puzzling situation. But expressions varied from blank to non-committal; nobody was prepared to admit that they either knew, or did not know, anything about Geoffrey's now inevitable-seeming departure.

Eventually dinner broke up. As I went out of the door I said to the Prime Minister, 'I didn't know you were letting Geoffrey go?' 'No,' he replied, 'neither did I! It was news to me.'

I walked downstairs with Peter Lovell-Davis, discussing the evening. To Peter I commented: 'Obviously, this must be what Geoffrey wants.' It was understandable, we both felt, that the Prime Minister had not been aware of Geoffrey's wish to return to the *Daily Mirror* because he was an extremely busy man. He would not have been bothered with it until it was firm decision rather than mere possibility. We parted, satisfied that we had worked everything out.

However, we were apparently wide of the mark. That night, Peter telephoned Geoffrey, only to be told that Geoffrey's departure was not really what Geoffrey wanted. He did have a very strong and good working relationship with the trades unions, who trusted him and with whom he was popular. But he was also concerned and agreed with Joe that the *Mirror* was in difficulties and, obviously, he wanted to do anything he could to help. His devotion to the *Mirror* was beyond question. Notwithstanding, he enjoyed the CIU and he wanted to go on doing a good job there.

Peter then rang me and I communicated the gist of all this to Harold Wilson. He asked Geoffrey to come and see him and talk the whole thing through. The joint conclusion they reached was that the best thing, on balance, was for Geoffrey to return fairly soon to the *Daily Mirror*, which undoubtedly needed his talents as Industrial Editor, and that the Unit would be run by one of Joe Haines's assistants from the Press Office, so that it continued on a slightly lower key than before, but under Joe's expert and fatherly guidance.

Looking back, the only reasonable explanation for this bizarre episode was that the *Mirror* men knew then that Harold Wilson was going to resign and that it would therefore be a timely moment for them to return to the fold of Fleet Street, as his successor might not want a Counter-Inflation Unit, or might have other ideas on who would run it. At that time, the Prime Minister had, we are told, informed only two people at that table of his decision to resign: myself and Joe Haines.

With hindsight, my own view is that the Unit should have been built up and strengthened and that Joe Haines himself should have taken it over. His close relationship with the incoming Prime Minister and his personal staff would have ensured the efficient and effective working of the Unit. Who knows, perhaps the 'Winter of Discontent' might subsequently have been avoided.

TWENTY-FIVE

Harold Wilson

His favourite colour is green, he is a great champion of the female sex, he can read a government report on finance as quickly as a novel, I have rarely known him to bear a grudge or lose his temper, and I suspect he is the only Prime Minister to have been a King's Scout. Harold Wilson is a man both complex and simple; a man whom I have known and worked with for twenty-six years. Yet he remains an enigma.

The reason, I believe, is because of the contradictions between his mental make-up and his personality. Most people are 'all of a piece'; Harold Wilson is not.

He is undoubtedly a most brilliant man and a master politician. He is a first-class economist – at Oxford he got a First in Politics, Philosophy and Economics – and a trained historian who took the Gladstone Memorial Prize with an essay on the railways. He became a don very young – from time to time, various distinguished people turn out to have been his pupils. As a politician, he is one of the best and most capable and, in my view, one of the most successful peacetime Prime Ministers. He could be called devious, even Machiavellian, on occasions; his mind is complex and far-seeing.

Yet his tastes are simple. To meet, he is the exact opposite of what people know him to be – the complicated, wily politician, the economic expert, the sophisticated master of the political manœuvre; he is someone kindly, direct, unassuming, friendly, amusing and very charming.

These qualities of personality have remained true of Harold Wilson all his life. Possibly the most outstanding of them, and certainly the one that overlapped into his political life, is his sense of humour. He can laugh about himself, and take a joke against himself – something which few politicians are able to do. Hence his delight in watching Mike Yarwood on television, or listening to him at a luncheon or dinner to which both have been invited.

Funniness, in the form of wit, infused many of his public utterances. He was one of the greatest of parliamentary speakers, dominating the House of Commons for very many years. A great deal of the groundwork for this was achieved when, as Shadow Chancellor of the Exchequer, he had excellent opportunities for testing his debating skills with such legendary rivals as Harold Macmillan and Rab Butler.

When Harold Wilson spoke, he would fill the House. The attention he drew during the economic debates was such that, if he had been given the task of winding up the Opposition late at night, the dining rooms and smoke rooms would empty as Members rushed to take their seats. Press men would vacate their bars and dining room, and the Galleries round the Chamber would be packed with people leaning forward to get a better view of the action below – if it was very late at night, there was the added dimension of post-prandial euphoria.

The speeches which attracted such attention were a unique blend of political irony and satire, interwoven with cool, calculated, and constructive or destructive argument. No matter how loud and raucous the debate, he revelled in it and, as a naturally witty speaker, his arguments had an extra cutting edge and point that raised the entire level of the debate, so it was not perhaps surprising that he was listened to with equal attentiveness on both sides of the House. Style is apolitical. His chief opponents, Rab Butler and Harold Macmillan, especially enjoyed hearing him speak (and both would relish it when he flung a barbed remark at the other). Any sally against Macmillan would have Butler slapping his thighs in delight. But hostilities were confined to the floor of the House; after a debate was over, it was common for Harold Wilson to receive a note from one of these two parliamentary giants to say how much they had enjoyed his speech, the finer points of which would be discussed over a drink in the smoke room.

So well known was this sharpness and wit that on one occasion a cartoon appeared in the *Daily Mail* showing Harold Wilson leaving the House of Commons with a great pile of papers under his arm, while a custodian replied to the query of an American tourist, 'That's the Mort Sahl of the House of Commons' (Mort Sahl being one of the funniest American comedians of the 1950s, renowned for his sharp tongue).

When he became Prime Minister, this comment could no longer be made. Only occasionally did a shaft of humour illumine the long passages of Civil Service briefs (it had been the same when he was President of the Board of Trade; his speeches then, he assures me, were dull in the extreme), although there were flashes of the old style in Question Time. His style deteriorated in office – without its cares and responsibilities he has always been able to relax sufficiently to allow his natural wit and humour to come through. For this reason, he has always been an excellent after-dinner speaker.

He undoubtedly inherits his sense of humour from his mother, who was for years probably the strongest influence in his life – someone who gave him support, and to whom he turned for advice. The closeness of this bond was inevitably strained by marriage: his mother was upset that he was marrying very young before his career had had a chance to 'take off', but the new situation was adjusted to. From his father he inherited his encyclopedic memory and application to detail. Family life, both in the sense of his own family and background as well as his marriage, has shaped the career of Harold Wilson no less than his personality.

The Wilsons have always been Yorkshire people. Although Herbert Wilson (a clever man with an able political brain) moved his family from Manchester to Cornwall, where he had a job as an industrial chemist, during the Depression, Harold has retained close links with his birthplace, Huddersfield. Many of the friends who were at school with him still keep in touch; recently, this correspondence has increased: people who were too shy to write to the Prime Minister have overcome their nervousness sufficiently to renew contact with him in his retirement, and particularly during his illness. Their letters show one aspect of a man whose roots in his background go very deep. With their recollections of days spent together and childhood episodes, they help to build up a picture of a man who in many ways can be called a 'typical Yorkshireman' – unemotional on the surface, reluctant to show feeling or sentiment of any kind, yet underneath gentle and, if I may use the word, soft.

To anyone brought up outside this seemingly hard Yorkshire tradition, the Wilsons can sometimes appear to carry lack of demonstrativeness to excess. When Herbert Wilson, to whom they were all devoted, died, there were no tears or weeping; embraces, also, are a rarity. When Harold's sister Marjorie greeted him after the major operation he had undergone after a serious illness, she remarked on how seldom they had kissed each other at any point in their lives. This was a prelude to stating that on this occasion she was going to make an exception to her normal behaviour. Subsequently, to Harold's great embarrassment, she planted a kiss on his forehead.

This sister, Marjorie, now seventy-three to Harold's sixty-six, has always been a powerful influence on him. Always he has tended to heed her wishes, frequently behaving as if the years had not passed and they were still children back in Yorkshire. One of his favourite stories is how, when they were taken by their parents on a day trip to Scarborough, Marjorie insisted on taking him for a paddle quite far out despite the roughness of the sea. His new and beautiful sailor suit was not only drenched but ruined; his father had to take him into the town to buy a makeshift suit of clothes – these were of peculiarly rough, thick tweed, with trousers that were far too long – so that the whole day proved to be one of extreme discomfort.

When Harold Wilson married, his personal life became an even more private affair. Harold and Mary had met at a local tennis club when both were very young: Harold was still an undergraduate, and Mary, extremely pretty, who had left school early, was doing secretarial work at Port Sunlight on the Wirral. Once they had decided to marry, Mary left her job and went home to live with her parents for a year, while she learned housekeeping and prepared for their marriage.

The wedding, in January 1941, took place at Mansfield College, Oxford. To Mary's amusement, even during their brief honeymoon in an Oxfordshire hotel, Harold produced an enormous suitcase full of books relevant to the research work he was doing at the time for Beveridge – she would not have been so amused had she realized that this was a foretaste of the 'boxes' that accompany the Prime Minister everywhere.

For Mary has never made any secret of the fact that politics do not particularly appeal to her. The man she married, as she has said on more than one occasion, was an Oxford don, and the life of an Oxford don's wife was what she was expecting – and what she was happily prepared for. She quite rightly loved the elegant quietude of Oxford, where she settled down extremely well into the life of a university town, and made many friends. Indeed, I would go as far as saying that she was probably happiest of all in those years, with the very special friends she had in Oxford.

It was with understandable reluctance, therefore, that she saw the emergence of her husband's real ambitions, and realized that the pull of politics was stronger than that of the academic world. What she did retain, however, was the habit of privacy: she is very protective about her home, never encouraging people to treat it in any way as a social or political centre, always insisting that their family life be kept apart and separate from Harold's work.

The keynote of the Wilsons' home life is simplicity. Harold Wilson's own tastes are simple: he likes to listen to the radio, he watches a little – but only a little – TV, he likes walking in the country. He seldom goes to the theatre, but enjoys films, chiefly because he has had such a close relationship with the film industry over the years. He enjoys music, particularly Beethoven and military marches, and, as is well known, he is a great devotee of Gilbert and Sullivan. Even his taste in paintings reflects his 'Englishness': his favourite painter is Lowry – again, because Lowry's world is a world Harold Wilson understands, knowing it both from his father's recollections and from his own vivid childhood memories.

Far from regarding his wife's determined lack of involvement in his work as a drawback, Harold Wilson turned it into one of his strongest assets, especially when he became Leader of the Party. Events proved him right. Where Hugh Gaitskell had led the Party 'by coterie', in Harold's phrase, from his home in Hampstead, through meetings in various drawing rooms or at dinner tables around London, he, Harold, would have a door that was open to everyone – his *office* door. No longer would there be jealousies among those who had not been invited to wine and dine; there would be no accolade of a visit to the Leader's home bestowed upon a chosen few; all were treated alike, and all would have equal right of access – irrespective of their relationship with him before he succeeded to the Leadership.

This approach is one that he has always maintained, and it is almost entirely due to his wife – if Mary had been a woman who enjoyed entertaining, who had wanted to play a large part in her husband's working life, Harold would inevitably have built up a different sort of reputation for himself, especially over his dealings with colleagues.

Although he has, perforce, adopted Mary's standpoint over the privacy of their home, her retiring nature has in no way rubbed off on him. He is extremely friendly, gets on well with people, enjoys parties and, socially, likes the softening effect women have on any group; unless someone like Harold Macmillan were at the same social gathering, he would much rather spend his time talking to a charming or intelligent woman.

Women, in turn, like him. In the Labour Party he was always very popular with the women's sections, because he not only so obviously enjoyed their company but always remembered details about their lives and families. Perhaps part of his appeal to women is that he possesses a quality that most women rate highly: great natural kindliness. Then, too – unlike many men from his rather traditional, unsophisticated North-Country background – Harold Wilson is not in the slightest degree a male chauvinist, and in this he owes a great deal to his wife, who is strongly feminist in her attitudes. This reflects in his working life as in his private attitudes.

He feels very strongly that, as the human race is a fifty-fifty mix of men and women, unless you get a good balance of both in any area of work there will not be either a true reflection of what is required, or the sort of action that should be taken on specific problems. It is fair to say, I believe, that he put this view into practice more than any other Prime Minister. He was ready and anxious to promote women into government and into the Cabinet; and although he did not, in the event, appoint very many (probably not enough), he did break new ground by giving them jobs they had not held before – Transport and Employment to Barbara Castle, for example (for a fuller account, see Chapter 27), and the Overseas Development Ministry, which went to Judith Hart.

To those of either sex in whom he takes an interest he is a good friend, and hand in hand with his natural kindliness goes a tolerance that can sometimes seem excessive: not only can he recognize and accept merit both in people and in fields that he finds unsympathetic, but he is also able to overlook the fact that someone has behaved badly to him in the past – to the point that he did not merely refrain from impeding their career, but actively incorporated them in the hierarchy of government. Sometimes his ability not to bear a grudge caused accusations of softness – some individuals respond to generosity of conduct, others simply see it as a sign of weakness.

A worse fault, I would say, is that he expects rather too much of those around him. In a crisis, everyone can perform the impossible: Harold Wilson wants the impossible every day. During the early part of his career, he worked extremely long hours, seldom took weekends off, and had only brief holidays. His staff, he assumed, would be similarly generous with their time; even now, he cannot understand if anyone close to him is not immediately available when he needs them.

These high expectations spill over into his immediate surroundings. Although his work methods are extremely organized and neat – in the sense of annotating papers and so forth – there is only one word to describe the room in which he worked: untidy. His study, both at Number 10 and in Opposition, was littered with books and papers – all of which he expected to find in proper order, neatly arranged and easily available, first thing the next day. As he frequently worked late, this was not always as easy to manage as it sounds!

Despite his effect on his immediate working surroundings, Harold Wilson has the highly organized mind of the efficient civil servant he once was – a background that had an immense effect upon him. Indeed, there is a large part of his character that is more civil servant than politician. By nature, he is much more likely to do well in a structured background than when working on his own initiative; hence the years that he recalls as happy are those when he was working in a context within, or related to, some clearly defined organization – such as Downing Street itself, the Board of Trade, and his work during the war years attached to the Cabinet Office and other areas of Whitehall.

When war broke out, he had registered for the army but, because the authorities wished to keep those with particular expertise in key jobs, he was directed instead to Whitehall. The Wilsons moved to a flat in Richmond, where they lived with their son, Robin, then a baby.

When the war ended, his political beliefs and his desire to work for the changes that would bring about greater social justice were strong enough to force him out of the role of permanent civil servant to which he seemed so well suited.

The first step was to be elected to Parliament. In 1945, he was first selected, then successfully elected for the constituency of Ormskirk in Lancashire; later part of this was merged to form the new constituency of Huyton.

Harold Wilson has been an extremely good constituency Member of Parliament – diligent, hard-working and concerned. Over the years, he built up a very strong rapport with his constituents; his surgeries were regular and detailed, his concern for those he represented was of paramount importance to him. Similarly, he evolved strong links with all the Agents who have acted for him, not least Arthur Smith, a very special man who tragically died in 1979, and his present Agent, the excellent Phil Robinson.

Arthur, who had looked after Harold Wilson throughout the years of Government, became a close family friend as well as Agent; he was one of the few people invited to the Wilsons' family home. Harold took him to the Cup Final at Wembley every year, and he would come south from time to time to spend weekends at Chequers or Grange Farm.

When writing about Harold Wilson, it is tempting to deal with his career only in terms of his Leadership of the Party: of all the Party Leaders since the war, Harold Wilson was probably the most skilled both as politician and political tactician. He had what other Labour Leaders had lacked: an acute and instinctive sense of what the Party needed at exactly the right time, what it wanted, and how much it could expect at any given moment.

The Party that he inherited in 1963 was only recently at peace – a peace arrived at mainly because the minds therein had been wonderfully concentrated by the impending election. Prior to that, he had lived through a particularly trying period of internecine warfare, when to be left of centre (as Harold Wilson was) was to be regarded as a communist, and when any link with a leftist organization, or individual known, however remotely, to be connected with the Communist Party, was considered proof of guilt by association. This particularly obnoxious form of personal harassment was prevalent in the Labour Party of the 1950s. With hindsight it is easy to see not just how it happened, but why.

Those were, after all, the years of Burgess and Maclean, when the Establishment as a whole was on the defensive at any hint of communism, or deviation. It was also the era of the Cold War and the Berlin Wall, of John Foster Dulles and Senator McCarthy. Governments and organizations in the West were anxious to appear tough, and in Britain, with the blot on its record of first two, and then a third man, who were quintessentially Establishment figures discovered to have been working within that very Establishment against their own country, there was an extreme sensitivity. This was reflected in the degree of aggression exhibited by the Tory-owned media towards the Labour Party – where it would, after all, have been more logical to find a Burgess, a Maclean or a Philby, rather than in the Foreign Office or an Embassy overseas (attack being the best form of defence).

In the Labour Party itself, there was even more embarrassment. Many highly respectable Party members had been directly or indirectly associated with Burgess and Maclean at some time – Hector McNeill, one of Gaitskell's closest friends, employed Burgess in the Foreign Office, Gaitskell himself had spent some time when young in Philby's company in Austria, and Attlee had employed a close colleague of both Burgess and Maclean as his Press Officer. But quite apart from this there was a general consciousness of vague but definite menace via the far Left, and a feeling that the slightest whiff of communism or fellow-travelling had to be eliminated. The media's accusations that the Labour movement as a whole was being infiltrated by communists, and that the Party had become a vehicle for communism, was a cruel though probably accurate assessment of what was (and is still) happening; those communists owe more to Trotsky than to Marx or Lenin.

Against this damaging embarrassment the Labour Right reacted violently. They felt it their duty to stamp out any hint of left-wing sympathy; an attitude reinforced by what was happening on the other side of the Atlantic. Thus, just as many liberals in the United States became a target for purge and persecution, so in Britain did the Labour Left.

Harold Wilson sought to end that blind and unreasoning condemnation. As Party Chairman at Brighton in 1962 (when Gaitskell was still Leader of the Party), he effectively put a stop to the idea of guilt by association; with his election to the Leadership of the Party a year later, the decision was made more emphatic still, and the Left and Right of the Party were made to accept each other.

This desire for the preservation of unity was a constant factor. From the moment he became Prime Minister – as during his rise to power – his pattern of action was largely related to preserving the Party as a united body. To him, the Leader was a chairman who held its varied and often opposing shades of opinion together, guiding it gently in the direction in which he wanted to go.

This approach was one to which his own tolerant and undogmatic character is peculiarly suited. He is calm, unemotional, and a great believer in seeing the other person's point of view, qualities that aided him in his frequent searches for some middle ground on which everyone could agree and which would preserve the unity of the Party, rather than alienating it by insistence on some piece of Party dogma. From the beginning, he worked hard at Party politics – in the narrow sense of keeping a united Party behind agreed policies – and, after the divisive Gaitskell years, allowed every voice to be heard rather than just a minority.

His first foray into leadership had occurred during Hugh Gaitskell's last years. The battleground was the arguments on unilateralism and nationalization – the abolition of Clause IV of the Party's constitution – that first surfaced during the election of 1959, and afterwards broke out with fresh and bitter vigour.

After the 1959 defeat, Gaitskell embarked on a vast programme of trying to bring the Labour Party up to date and to modernize it, particularly in terms of policy. As he saw it, this meant a moderate stance in line with today's Social Democratic Party. Those were the years that saw the birth of the Campaign for Democratic Socialism, which was, of course, the first manifestation of today's SDP – indeed, many leading Alliance members were, as Gaitskell aides, organizers and secretarial staff of the Campaign in their younger days. With almost religious fervour they threw themselves whole-heartedly into the Campaign.

Their stance on the two issues of unilateralism and nationalization was so uncompromising that all those who disagreed with them were dubbed not only traitors to the Labour Party but often communists into the bargain. This meant that a very large section of the Party, not only on the Left and the far Left, but also from the centre – and inclusive of a wide area of trades union representation – was designated as either unreliable or fellow-travellers, and not infrequently both. It was clear that not only was a head-on collision looming, but that such a split would force the Party into the wilderness for a very long time. The defeat of 1959 had been cataclysmic, with Macmillan emerging with a majority of 106; no one wanted to see that happen again.

Harold Wilson could see that the arguments on both sides of the Party, on both issues, were unnecessarily divisive, and that there was a middle ground on which the majority could meet. It became equally clear to him that, believing this, he had no option but to challenge Hugh Gaitskell for the Leadership. This required considerable courage: he was laying his career on the line, and could have found himself 'out in the cold' for a long time. At that moment in 1960 no one could have foreseen the tragic and unexpected death of Gaitskell, at such an early age, three years later; to all intents and purposes Harold had sacrificed a great deal to make the point that Gaitskell's policies were divisive.

When Gaitskell died, however, Harold Wilson was an obvious candidate for the Leadership, although he had a hard fight with George Brown and the third candidate, James Callaghan. He emerged the clear winner; so much so that Vicky drew a touching cartoon of a knight in full regalia on horseback with the Shakespearean caption, 'Now is the winter of our discontent made glorious summer by this son of York'. In other words, gone were the days of quarrels and argument, to be replaced by an era of peace with a Yorkshireman.

At this moment, when the welding of the Party into a cohesive whole was vital, Harold Wilson's characteristic lack of malice and his generosity of approach were of inestimable importance. His natural gift for peace-making was brought into full play – so much so that many people on the Left thought that former enemies had acquired too dominant a role in the Wilson Government. Not that it could properly be called a 'Wilson' Government: most of its members (as in 1966) were former Gaitskellites, with the left wing of the Party very lightly represented indeed. One consequence of this was that when confronted with the problems, difficulties and crises that all Prime Ministers have to face (especially a Labour Prime Minister at that time), he had no clearly defined band of loyal supporters on whom he could instinctively count.

Although today Harold Wilson could in no sense be said to belong to the left wing of the Party, he then took up a Centre Left position. As at the present moment, there was a similar battle between Left and Right; then, the Right was dominated by the trades union movement. The block votes of the big union leaders, like Arthur Deakin, Sam Watson and Bill Carron, swayed Conference and controlled the levers of power within the Labour Party Establishment. Harold Wilson, though not a figure of the Left, was nevertheless sympathetic to it, and certainly regarded, as Clem Attlee had been, as left of centre.

By contrast, at Transport House – the pivotal point of the Party Establishment – the majority of the senior staff were committed right-wingers, supporters of Hugh Gaitskell and Herbert Morrison who regarded anyone left of centre, or even associated with the Left, as beyond the pale.

This attitude led to one of my earliest contacts with Harold Wilson.

The General Secretary's office had the responsibility of co-ordinating all the committees on the NEC, and much of the work towards this end was naturally carried out by his staff. I used to hear senior members quite openly planning to keep all the principal committees under the chairmanship of a right-wing, Party Establishment figure. After the 1955 defeat, this polarization of Right and Left became even more pronounced; and the power figures of Transport House were more convinced than ever that anyone who did not fit their by now rigid definition of 'suitable' should be excluded from all chairmanships.

Harold Wilson was definitely 'unsuitable' in their eyes. He was chairman of the Party's Organization Committee – and reorganization and restructuring of the Party was vitally necessary if future electoral success was to be possible. But his public disapproval of the right-wing 'dictatorship' was enough to make him anathema to certain sections of Transport House.

When I noticed that plotting had reached such a pitch that these senior Transport House brethren were actually urging right-wing members of the committees to come extra early to committee meetings, so that voting for a new chairman (who had to be present during the vote) had taken place before those they deemed 'unsuitable' had arrived, I thought it was time to act. I wrote to Harold Wilson to suggest that he, too, arrived a bit earlier.

Although I have now worked for him for twenty-six years, I cannot say that our first meeting was in any way memorable to either of us. I was then working as a secretary to Morgan Phillips, the General Secretary of the Labour Party (my first job after graduating from university), and Harold Wilson, as a member of the National Executive Committee, would come to Transport House for the Executive's committee meetings. It was the job of the Secretariat to set out the necessary papers and documents beforehand and then, if the meeting went on a long time, to take in coffee. In this informal way I met all the then leading members of the Party, from Clement Attlee and Herbert Morrison to Nye Bevan and Harold Wilson.

The first time I met Harold Wilson to speak to at any length was during a big Labour Party dinner at the House of Commons in honour of the Russian leaders, Bulganin and Khrushchev, on 23 April 1956. As it was a political as well as a social occasion, senior Labour leaders intended to speak somewhat toughly to the Russians; in the event, an enormous row broke out which dominated the following day's press headlines, the central figure in which was George Brown. But it was left-wing Party leaders too who fell out with the Russians, Nye Bevan in particular becoming incensed when neither Soviet supremo would answer questions about the imprisonment of Democratic Socialists in Russia.

Along with a senior colleague, Irene Leatherhead, I had the job of making a shorthand note of all that happened at that dinner. It was a tough assignment, and I was frozen with fear one minute and covered with nervous perspiration the next. Harold Wilson, who sat at the end of the top table a short distance away from my seat, sensed my nervousness and was extremely sympathetic. I never forgot his kindness that evening.

I suppose I had first heard of him when I was still at school and he was at the Board of Trade. I could vaguely remember hearing his name associated with clothes rationing. At college I knew of him because, as secretary of the Labour Society in Queen Mary College, London

University, it was my job – along with the chairmen of the Conservative and Liberal Societies – to organize regular debates, to which we used to invite leading guest speakers of all the Parties. (My own great *coup* was to persuade Jim Callaghan, whom I greatly admired, to come.)

To me Harold Wilson seems to have changed little since those days. One of his boasts is that he can still wear the suits he had then. As a Yorkshireman, he appreciates good cloth; one of his favourite suits is a tough, nobbly tweed that has been going strong from that day to this. His weight has hardly varied, his face has always been round, almost cherubic, with a faintly enigmatic expression. Even when I first knew him (when he was thirty-nine), he had grey hair and the appearance of a distinguished senior politician. He has always had a stoop, a legacy from a very bad attack of typhoid fever suffered as a child, which makes him seem shorter than his height of 5 ft 9 ins.

I went to work for him originally through the good offices of another member of the National Executive Committee, a nice jolly man called Arthur Skeffington, who represented the Co-operative Societies on the Executive. I had been at Transport House for eighteen months when he said to me one day, 'You know, Marcia, Harold Wilson's secretary is leaving to have a baby, and he's looking for another. Would you be interested?'

I had already turned down a job in Hugh Gaitskell's office, but I liked the idea of working for Harold Wilson: he was obviously a coming man, and I thought it would be more interesting to work for someone younger, who was outside the Party Establishment.

When Arthur offered to put in a good word for me, I was delighted. When I heard I had got the job I thought myself extremely lucky, as my rival was a girl who later became a senior committee clerk for the Parliamentary Labour Party, who was then employed in one of the Party's regional offices, and who knew Harold Wilson and his family personally. I was twenty-four when I began to work for him for the princely salary of £15 a week – a big jump from the £6.50 I received when I first joined Transport House.

As a politician, Harold Wilson has always been a reformer, and on many issues a passionate one, but he is no revolutionary. One of his boasts is that he has never read Marx. His background belongs to the nonconformist tradition within the Labour Party; hence there is no contradiction between his socialist principles and his staunch defence of most British institutions. He is first and foremost a democrat and has a deep respect and affection for Parliament. He respects and loves the monarchy, and enjoys the ceremonial. His political heroes, too, do not come from the conventional socialist pantheon of the Marxists; chief among them is Sir Winston Churchill, whom he admires not only because of his public qualities but also because of Churchill's understanding and warmth on a personal level. When Harold Wilson resigned in 1951 from the Labour Government of the day, Winston Churchill – who himself had crossed the floor of the House – realized how painful the situation was for Harold. He went out of his way to say comforting and compassionate words not only to Harold but also to Mary.

His principal historical hero is Gladstone. Admittedly, Gladstone was not the gloomy, serious, sombre character that he is usually painted, but a sociable man who loved the warmth and repartee of the dinner table. Nevertheless, 'solid', 'worthy', 'dull' are adjectives that seem more at home in any description of him – possibly because he introduced so many budgets. This was the aspect that fascinated Harold Wilson: it was Gladstone, the financial wizard, that he sought to emulate. In the early days of his career, his great ambition was to introduce as many budgets in the House of Commons as had Gladstone.

Like Harold Macmillan, another of the politicians he most admires, Harold Wilson learned to use the television camera to his advantage, with style and enthusiasm. He understands the art of communication, in all its forms, and its importance in the world in which we live today.

After he became Prime Minister he underwent, it seems to me, a sea change. The reforming zeal was still there, but the hard experience of governing, with its crises and disappointments, watered down his innate radicalism. Another factor was that – like so many before him and since – the trappings of power gave him pleasure. He *enjoyed* being Prime Minister – in particular his last spell of office at Number 10, from 1974 to 1976, with Ministers of long experience who had served in his earlier Governments and to whom he could delegate easily. Although he was still to complain, with reason, of the ever-increasing volume of work, he often refers to these years as the happiest of his life. Even so, he was ready to give up the burdens of office (and to confound his critics by going at a time of his own choosing).

What is Sir Harold Wilson's memorial as a Prime Minister? When he resigned in 1976, there was little he could point to in the last two years and say, 'There is a positive achievement.' There was much in terms of legislation that was subsequently passed through Parliament, but his greatest contribution was undoubtedly to bring back peace after the last months of the Heath Government, to make an ungovernable nation governable once more, and to restore Labour as the governing Party – as he saw it then the 'natural Party of Government'.

Crisis was then all around. The interlocking structure of world finance had finally collapsed under the strains of the international oil crisis, rocketing inflation and trade depression. The new Labour Government had to come to terms with this against a domestic background of confrontation with organized labour – not just in the mining community but in other areas as well.

Harold Wilson succeeded in doing this, while at the same time preserving a harmonious relationship with industry and the City. As Mrs Thatcher herself said in a broadcast, 'Look who's reflated in the past!', referring to the big reflation of 1973 by the Government of which she was a member: 'it led ultimately to the highest rate of inflation this country has ever had. And we were panic stricken.' In short, she acknowledged the Tory Government's responsibility.

Thus, when Harold Wilson took over in 1974, his achievement was to get the country back to work, then to avert catastrophe in the City and a consequent total collapse of the banks. Against this background he dealt with the constitutional nightmare of the Common Market, and initiated the voluntary wages and prices policy which was, by the end of Jim Callaghan's term of office, one of the most effective prices and incomes policies ever attempted.

Harold Wilson's own special qualities as a peace-maker meant that he was able to restore all-essential unity to the Labour Party, without which it would inevitably have fragmented. Nevertheless, his fourteen years as Leader are now largely ignored, almost as if they had never happened, including almost eight years in government (a longer period than the Party had ever enjoyed before at any point in its history). Thanks to his Leadership, he left a successor who had the necessary skills and abilities, and a Party with both Left and Right working together agreeing a common line. The Right continue to argue that his was the responsibility for the rising power of the Left. It is a fact, of course, that from 1964 onwards the Left has gained power in every other country in Europe. Britain has been no exception; it is to our advantage – and our credit – that, unlike Europe, none of this has so far manifested itself in Parliament with direct communist representation. From 1963 to 1976 the balance between Labour Left and Labour Right, however precariously, was maintained. Of course it can be argued that the separation of the two was necessary, but that is a different argument. Harold Wilson inherited a Party in which both streams were strongly represented from the Party's first beginnings in the days of Keir Hardie through to the years of Clement Attlee. The balancing act had always been performed, sometimes brilliantly as with Attlee, sometimes disastrously unsuccessfully as with Ramsay MacDonald. Harold Wilson carried on the Attlee tradition.

His own natural philosophy was that electors seldom wish to be involved at every turn with what Parliament is doing; when a Government is elected, the man and woman in the street profoundly hope that that is that for the next five years. However, coupled with his conviction of the need for electoral peace and his own talent for promoting harmony within the Party, went a pugnacity and fighting spirit against opponents both at home and overseas that made him not just a great politician (a description frequently used pejoratively) but a great peace-time Prime Minister.

Add to this his advocacy of technological change, of the need for innovation in industry and work methods, and it can be seen how his Leadership welded the Labour Party into an effective modern fighting unit. In one speech at Scarborough in 1963, just six months after his election as Labour Leader, he shifted the Party away from the frustrating, theological arguments about Party dogma of the 1950s, and in one big step brought Labour and the electorate up to date with the technological changes of the modern world. It was inspired, unexpected and, despite the criticisms and subsequent denunciations about the 'white heat of the technological revolution', ensured that politics in Britain kept pace with industrial, social and educational changes. He advanced those same changes to the point where, for good or ill, what a short time before would have been something to aspire to, was something to be taken for granted. It needed imagination and courage that October in 1963 to depart from the traditional ground adopted by the Party, and to strike out for a wider, more exciting and riskier territory; but it succeeded.

Essentially a compassionate and ordinary man, albeit a clever one, he gave to every individual elector the vision of the reality of a Britain where the ordinary man could take his place naturally beside the privileged in every walk of life, from Government down: a man in short they could all identify with. He was a true representative of the New Britain – a Britain which emerged, finally, with that first generation after the war years had ended, and a new affluence had made change essential – and of his Party. History, I am confident, will judge him as the man who gave effect to these changes, and who brought the Labour

Party and the country in the main harmoniously through some of the most difficult and testing peacetime years.

After his retirement the Queen awarded him a Garter Knighthood, a very special and personal award from the Sovereign to a First Minister. His coat of arms was typical of the man. There to see is the Labour Party's symbol of pen and spade – workers by brain and hand; the white rose for Yorkshire, his birthplace; the red rose for Lancashire, which he represents in Parliament; in the centre is the Trinity House ship to show he is one of the Elder Brethren, and the arms of the Abbot of Rievaulx to show his Yorkshire roots, and above it all rises the Bishop Rock lighthouse, to show his deep attachment to the Scilly Isles, where he has spent so many tranquil and spiritually and physically rewarding days with his family. Beneath it all is his motto, *Tempus Rerum Imperator*, which very roughly translated means 'Timing is Everything'.

TWENTY-SIX

Leading Labour Personalities: Men

Tony Benn has become a cult hate figure almost in the way that Shirley Williams became a cult love figure. In his case there is, of course, more reason: as well as his political opinions and the method and timing with which he expresses them, there is also the fact that he is a combination of figurehead and focus for the far Left.

Even so, I am amazed at the sheer extent of this hatred. Never before have I seen antagonism to a leading political figure so openly expressed within his own Party. The prime reason for this is not so much his views – there are many extreme left-wingers within the Party – but his failure to keep the rule of political *omerta*. There are plenty of people who do, and think, as Tony does, but not in a public fashion; whereas he expresses his views not so much openly as in a way calculated to induce the maximum publicity. The result is that there are people who used, ten or fifteen years ago, to be extremely attached to him, but who now have hardly a good word for him.

To meet socially, though, he is still the same Tony Benn as always: very good company, likeable, friendly, funny. On television, however, Tony's wit and entertaining personality simply do not come across; partly this is because he is not, thanks to his views, ever asked the sort of questions to which the appropriate answer is a witty one, and partly because – again thanks to these views – he has been under attack for such a long time now that his response is, and has to be, a serious one.

In one important sense this is a great pity: ordinary people – the very people to whom he wants to appeal – believe much more strongly in the person who has a streak of humour, because that is part of life as they – we – know it. For the average person, a certain amount of humour and laughter are a necessary part of everyday life; this apparent lack in Tony Benn makes them suspicious.

Like all top politicians, Tony is ambitious, and the years have only served to increase this – as has the fact that he has had to fight within his own Party for a number of controversial and unpopular causes (many of which have, thanks to his championship, later been endorsed with a handsome majority by the Party). For them to succeed, he has had to practise a certain amount of self-hypnosis: persuading himself with ever-greater conviction that the causes in which he believes are essential to the nation's survival. No wonder that his characteristic expression is the faintly obsessive look of the over-ambitious person who sees much of the world around him in terms of conflict.

This quality of self-persuasion is a clue to much that may appear puzzling about Tony. He is a fantasist, but an unusual one. The day-dreams, the flights of imagination of most men and women hinge upon some happening that is heroic, desirable, glamorous, even exotic, however unattainable in reality. Tony's fantasies are about workers' co-operatives, the rule of the Ordinary Man – but an Ordinary Man transformed into a superhuman creature of sparkling intelligence, total integrity and overflowing loving-kindness; not for Tony the Hobbesian theory of mankind.

How that miracle is going to come about is never explained. Nevertheless, despite the evidence of the various socialist egalitarian states around the world that are not notable for their outpourings of brotherly love, Tony continues to believe that if you elevate the conditions of his working man to a national philosophy, all will be well.

Despite his own background and upbringing, there is nothing forced about Tony's liking for the ordinary man; that is, it is not a deliberate act of will resulting from his political convictions. The liking and the convictions are co-existent, and the reason is not far to seek. Just as the working man has no 'side' to him and never seeks to impress anyone, so Tony himself is an extremely natural person who delights in a lack of pretentiousness. He likes to be accepted for what he is; he dislikes – though he will conform to – the social and ritual side of politics.

This dislike for socializing has, however, nothing to do with shyness. Tony is not a shy man. Indeed, he is someone who gets on extremely well with people. He is not at all the bogeyman conjured up by the media (and by his own reactions to them), but charming, kindly and friendly.

This impression of approachability is enhanced by his particular brand of good looks, which I would describe as 'all-American-boy'. Tony is one of those people who always look boyish, his features are regular, and that there is something faintly transatlantic about his style is no doubt due to his American wife, who clearly has a strong influence over him. This impression would be even stronger were it not for the pipe without which he is seldom seen, and which – like that of Harold Wilson – is partly ploy.

Pipes, in politics, are extremely useful: they can be filled, lit, tamped down or sucked in while the owner is thinking out a reply to a tricky question; they can be waved about for emphasis, or they can be sucked slowly to give a reassuring, thoughtful and trustworthy effect. With Tony, I suspect that it is also a safety device; and that if he were deprived of it, his first responses might be much more impulsive and less controlled.

Few people realized how deeply Tony was affected by the 1975 Cabinet reshuffle; one of them was Harold Wilson. For many years, Tony had been part of Harold's small entourage although, despite their closeness over the decades, Tony always said quite openly (at least after 1976) that he got on better with Jim Callaghan.

Harold Wilson had decided to move Tony Benn from the Department of Industry for an accumulation of different reasons. There were his discussions of Party policy (as distinct from Government policy) in the meetings of the National Executive Committee: his views attracted wide publicity and damaged the concept of collective responsibility upon which all Cabinets operate. There were his new plans for further nationalization, for worker co-operation, for the collectives which were seen as money-losers, all of which happened against a background of continuing weakness in the City. The result was a loss of confidence in the very people – the heads of industry – who were needed to back both the Secretary of State for Industry and the Government itself. (The same thing happened to Sir Keith Joseph.)

It became more and more dangerous for the Government as a whole to allow Tony to continue in the same job. With sterling as it then stood, confidence was essential. Tony did not have the trust of industry nor was he a man with established TUC backing; and he certainly did not have a following in the City.

Thus, the Government as a whole was losing ground through the medium of one particular job. It was impossible to have someone running industry in whom industry, the business community and overseas interests had no confidence. Tony had to be moved. Harold Wilson, who felt that Tony had much to offer as a Minister, especially in the fields of ideas and enthusiasm, gave much thought to the finding of a new, appealing job for him. He did not wish to see Tony leave the Government. Energy, for a number of reasons – not least the fascination technology held for Tony – was an imaginative choice; and to most people, however bruised or offended they might be by a switching of jobs, this was better than outright sacking.

But Tony's reaction when Harold sent for him was not that of most people. He was enormously affected, and this took the form of a 'lecture'. He harangued Harold for what seemed hours; he began on the history of the Party, dwelling particularly on the 1931 crisis and the fall of the Labour Government because of its failure to adhere to true socialist principles. It was, he cried, 'being held hostage to the City and the International Monetary Organizations!' (as indeed it then was). On he went, getting ever more passionate, describing the role his father (Lord Stansgate) had played and how upset he would have been if he thought history was repeating itself.

Harold Wilson listened patiently and eventually the diatribe came to an end, without Tony having once declared his intentions. Harold (who quite likes to make a good story out of events!) said afterwards that at one point he panicked slightly, wondering if he would have to reshuffle the Cabinet all over again, and believing – so hidden were Tony's intentions in this cloud of verbiage – that he would have to find a new Secretary of State for Energy. However, as they said goodbye, Harold said, 'Well, are you going to accept Energy?', and Tony replied, slightly astonished, 'Yes, of course.'

Another famous 'lecture' occurred during the Opposition years in 1973, at a meeting of the Shadow Cabinet, of which Tony was a member. He was brimming over with what later became a full-time obsession: the idea of worker participation and co-operation. He talked excitedly about the underlying philosophy, while his audience sat silent, half-mesmerized, half-stunned. Eventually, after a lengthy description of a factory in his constituency where the workers had decided they ought to have the power to dismiss the entire management with one week's notice, Harold said quietly, 'But Tony, why give them as much as a week? Surely they could clear out their lockers in a day?' Even Tony laughed.

Much has changed since those earlier, happier days. But although Harold Wilson has been harsh in public comment, he has remained personally fond of Tony. One of his most quoted strictures, 'He imma-

tures with age', points up the irony that has caused this polarization
between the two wings of the Labour Party.

Most politicians, as they grow older and certainly if they have experienced office, became more rather than less moderate, more conscious of what is possible, the problem of putting the promise that
appeals to the electorate into hard performance. Not so Tony.

At around the age of fifty he realized that if he was going to acquire
power – power that would put his beliefs into practice – this would have
to happen within the next five or ten years. After that, the merciless
arithmetic of politics would ensure that he was too old to be the convincing leader of a new approach to socialist principles. He could not
risk waiting to see if events would mould the situation for him; he had
to do something himself.

If Harold Wilson had remained Prime Minister longer, Tony's
chances in the Leadership election might have been better. He would
still have been one of the younger men; he was clever, well-liked, the
label of 'extreme' had not been tied so firmly round his neck. But once
Jim took over, everything changed. The primary need was to keep the
Party in office, and the art of keeping the Party together slowly died.

As it must have appeared to Tony's logical mind, the natural successor to Jim would be considered to be Denis Healey – and by the time
Denis gave up being either Leader or Prime Minister, Tony himself
would no longer be one of the 'younger men'. He also knew that the
best time to make a challenge was during Opposition, when he had
more chance both of attracting the disaffected and of concentrating on
the necessary build-up of a solid body of support. Hence his comparatively sudden emergence as a would-be Leader.

One person who always believed that Tony would become Leader of
the Labour Party – and who stated it publicly in 1964 – is Mary Wilson.
Now, nearly twenty years later, it seems to me that if he had been born
a little earlier or a little later she would have been triumphantly right,
as his hairsbreadth defeat in the Deputy Leadership elections showed.
Policies apart – if he had achieved his present position during the days
when Hugh Scanlon and Jack Jones dominated the trades union movement, he would probably have been their man.

Who the unions favour depends on what condition the unions are in.
In the days of Arthur Deakin and Bill Carron they were very right wing:
Herbert Morrison and Hugh Gaitskell were their protégés. When they
were sitting on the fence between the wild Left and the more old-
fashioned Right, they looked for a middle-of-the-road candidate – and

from 1969 found one in Jim Callaghan. At that time, after their violent
internal swings in policy, there was a general desire for stabilization; in
addition, most union leaders wanted any candidate they backed to be
a substantial figure within the Party and one capable of attracting the
majority – in other words, a potential Leader. Which, at that time,
Tony clearly wasn't.

Again, if Harold Wilson had resigned during the Opposition years
after 1970, Tony, who had begun to emerge as an anti-Market champion, was one of the few national figures on the Left. Both John Silkin
and Peter Shore, who himself achieved prominence via the anti-Market
arguments in the 1970s, were at that time relatively unknown. As for
Michael Foot, although he was in the process of rising to the top of the
Shadow Cabinet, he had never actually held office before and was not
at that time regarded as a potential Leader of the Party. Whereas Tony
could have been seen as Leader material: his wilder streaks of conduct
and utterance were still in the future; the case he put against the
Common Market was both powerful and statesmanlike; and as a person
he would have appealed (to those sharing his views) as a young, passionate and attractive character.

Again, if Harold Wilson had remained in office longer, and if Tony
could have made himself toe the Party line more obviously and more
effectively until the Government's difficulties had resolved themselves,
he would have been a powerful candidate in any Leadership contest.
He would almost certainly have made a success of his part in any
subsequent election campaign.

Tony has the appeal of the visionary; what he promises is a better
future, in tones that ring with conviction. To the young especially, and
to those caught up in dreary and repetitious work routines, his can be
a siren call – especially as today the general run of politician is more
concerned with the present than what lies over the horizon. It is to
human nature that he appeals – but it is human nature, with all its
imperfections, that will sabotage his view of the Utopian socialist state,
where brother co-operates with brother, and self-interest is unknown.

Like all politicians, and despite his denials, he sees himself at the
pinnacle of this ideal system of government. It would be ludicrous to
pretend otherwise: any man with a political philosophy strong enough
to run counter to Party consensus and colleagues believes himself to be
the man to implement those policies.

In the event – not as unlikely now as it once seemed – that Tony Benn
did become Prime Minister one day, should we expect massive changes?

My own view is that they would be less dramatic than most imagine, if only because he would have to come to terms with the realities of what was possible. And the lines that circumscribe these realities are largely drawn up by the Civil Service – a Civil Service that has vastly increased in power since the days when he, as a Minister, saw its workings at first hand.

The difficulties would be twofold. First, there is the established machinery of government itself; then there is the fact that the changes Tony wishes to see would run straight into opposition from the – highly militant – Civil Service trades unions. He would have an extremely difficult task on his hands if he wished to change the system – and without changing the system, none of his ideas could be implemented. It would, I fancy, be a very different Tony Benn who emerged from Downing Street five years later.

He would certainly keep the staff on their toes. Tony is enormously enthusiastic, full of ideas and no regarder of time. He used to need very little sleep and would be at his desk very early, continuing to work when he went home. In the 1960s when he was a Minister, I was often woken by the shrilling of the telephone in the small hours, followed by the words, 'Are you awake?' As, of course, by the time I'd picked up the telephone, I was indubitably awake, I would hear him out on whatever thought or tremendous idea had seized him.

Along with the constant flow of plans and projects goes an unbounded enthusiasm for the process of modern communication – the whole technological bag of tricks, so to speak. Tony is fascinated by any kind of new technology; I have seen him like a child at a Christmas party over some brilliant new electronic gadget. Sometimes, I think, they were the cause of his late-night telephone calls; after those around him had disappeared to bed, he would resort to one of the recording machines on which he had stored the thoughts that came to him during the day – which would trigger off some fresh idea that had to be imparted immediately.

Two episodes always serve to remind me of both the endearing and the strange side of Tony Benn. The first occurred in 1964, when Labour was so newly in office that there was no proper Party Conference but merely a two-day weekend at Brighton in November. Tony had been appointed Postmaster General and, like the rest of the Government, was just working himself into the job. One evening, the Prime Minister said to me: 'Could you please get the Postmaster General? I want to see him urgently.'

I went off in haste, discovered Tony's room, knocked on the door, and told him when he opened it that the Prime Minister wished to see him. He asked me what about, to which I responded: 'I really don't know, but I think it's quite urgent.' 'Right!' he said, in his excited, rather breathless way, 'I'm coming at once,' and he pounded along the corridor behind me, full of excitement and anticipation written all over his face.

I could guess what was going on in his mind. The Prime Minister had sent for him – at this early stage that meant either that he was going to be asked to take on some new responsibility within the Post Office Department, or perhaps even a different job. So soon? Which was it going to be?

I knocked on Harold Wilson's door and said: 'Postmaster General for you, Prime Minister.' Upon which, Tony literally bounded into the room, eyes shining and beaming away in his enthusiastic way.

'So glad you could come, Tony,' said the Prime Minister. 'Want to see you, Postmaster-General, rather urgently.' By this time Tony was hanging on every word, so that he was all attentiveness when the Prime Minister continued, completely deadpan, 'It's my father's eightieth birthday – and I want to make absolutely sure that the telegram I send him gets there. I know what the Post Office can be like!'

I can only say that I had been just as taken in as Tony by this little joke. Not by a glimmer had Harold Wilson betrayed to me that the matter was anything other than urgent, so that I had arrived at Tony's door in the right state of breathless hurry – upon which his own natural enthusiasm had taken over.

Later on, when Tony was in charge of technology, I would quite often have lunch with him. My first visit to his office for the mug of tea and sandwiches that formed these luncheons was a sobering experience.

He had been given a huge room with beautiful windows and a view right down the river to Westminster. There was the Technology Minister sitting behind his massive desk, the usual enormous mug of tea in one hand, cheese sandwich in the other ... *and the map of Britain on his wall hanging upside down.*

I was mesmerized, but I hadn't the heart to ask him why – indeed, I was rather worried about what sort of reply I might receive. With his cheerful smile and in tones of utter reasonableness, he launched into an explanation. It made it easier, he said, to see that the South-East was not the centre of importance in this country. Then he said that if you turned the map of the British Isles upside down, it resembled the map of Italy and our poor areas were in the same position as the poor areas in Italy.

For someone like me, who can have difficulty telling sea from land on a black-and-white map, this short cut to working out the effectiveness of a policy on the redistribution of wealth and industry was entirely lost. But the memory of Tony Benn, political whizz-kid, technological addict, sitting behind his desk, eyes alight with his vision of the future, in front of the upside-down map of Britain, sums up for me both his eccentricities and his compulsive likeability.

Michael Foot, the man who surprised many by becoming the Leader of the Opposition, could, although he does not suffer from a split personality, be called the Jekyll and Hyde of politicians.

Nowhere is this more apparent than in those two important personality indicators: voice and manner. In private, and as a politician working among colleagues, Michael Foot is soft-voiced, a courteous, easy, light-hearted moderate, whose restrained manner makes him eminently likeable. But on a platform or in a similar public context it is a different story. He rants, he raves, he shouts; in short, he seems not so much transformed as possessed.

Once, of course, this style of oratory, with its dramatic declamations and gestures, was expected of public speakers. But today it seems curiously old-fashioned. True, two of Parliament's greatest speakers in the modern sense, Lloyd George and Aneurin Bevan, were the direct inheritors of this tradition. But in addition to this, these oratorical heroes of the recent past were also extremely funny, with a pungent turn of phrase and, always, a bedrock of powerfully reasoned argument, so that audiences were intellectually convinced as well as emotionally swayed; there was no attempt, as there often is with Michael, to hector the listener into agreement.

The same sort of dichotomy is evident in the discrepancy between the image Michael Foot presents to the world and the background he springs from. Admittedly – like Shirley Williams – he comes from that section of middle-class intellectualism where it is virtually an article of faith that the untidier you are, the more sincere are your beliefs. Mere physical appearance is, of course, as nothing when weighed against mind and morals (though it is arguable that a whole roomful of shambling, unkempt figures, however deep their sincerity, might depress the former and make one question the value of the latter); but it is doubtful if dishevelment to this degree is on target even politically. In my experience, the average Labour voter wants to improve his lot generally, and to ensure that his children learn more and earn more than he did himself; yet here is a Leader who appears to be trying to represent all that this voter wants to leave behind.

The key word is 'trying'. A genuine man of the people is one thing; the adoption of a 'working-class' image by someone from an obviously privileged background seems merely patronizing. It is no fault of Michael's that he has not had to claw his way up through scholarships, hard work, parental sacrifices to the distant goal of a university – as have many other leading Labour figures – and of course sincere and convinced socialists can be found in any walk of life. But somehow the effect does not ring quite so true when a deliberate shabbiness appears to have been adopted by someone who comes from a comfortable middle-class home, where everything from a public-school education to whisky in the drinks cupboard is part of an assured way of life. It is as though his outward persona was a disguise, a mask deliberately chosen to hide rather than a representation of the real man. For this appearance of simplicity – humility, almost – is in direct contradiction to the 'real' Michael: someone who is arrogant rather than humble, apparently lacking in self-doubt – a man whose whole outlook and attitude is coloured, albeit unconsciously, by the background of privilege from which he springs.

For years, Michael resisted office, saying that he wished to be free to express himself on Party policy without the hindrance of departmental or other chains. But after his great success as Secretary of State for Employment, after the taste of power within the Cabinet, his view most understandably changed.

His view, I believe, is that if Ronald Reagan can reach the White House at seventy – and furthermore, make a more dramatic impact on the course of American policy than many of his predecessors – there is no reason why he, Michael, should not become Prime Minister of the United Kingdom at around the same age.

But Michael's chance will have to come within the next year or not at all. This is in strict contrast with the average run of Opposition Leaders, one of the criteria of whose choice is that they will be able to lead their Party not only through one election, but quite possibly the one after that. On Michael's behalf, it is fair to say that we have been spoiled as a country in recent years: Harold Wilson was forty-nine when he went to Downing Street, and Margaret Thatcher only three years older. We have learned to expect our Prime Ministers to be young middle-aged, where the rest of the world seems perfectly accustomed to leaders of seventy-plus.

Michael's age, therefore, is probably an irrational barrier to viewing him as a potential Prime Minister; although it is one of the explanations as to why most of the Party view him in the light of an interim Leader. Although he is extremely popular with the left wing, who love not only his views, but his rousing, tub-thumping style of campaigning, I must confess that I was extremely surprised when he won the Leadership election: the Party as a whole is an extremely conservative (with a small 'c') animal, and tends to play safe in the sense of veering more to the right than the left of centre; so I am among those who believe that his election only represented a holding operation, until a final and collective decision had been taken not only on a candidate agreeable to the Party as a whole, but also on the machinery of election itself.

More serious in relation to any possible Prime Ministerial role is a fault that Michael shares with Jim Callaghan. Jim's major failing as a Prime Minister was that he never presented the nation with a view of the future – of what a Labour Government could, and would, achieve, given the power through co-operation to do what they wanted. Entering as we are with increasing rapidity the world of the micro-chip, vision and the ability to instil both hope and confidence are essential qualities in any future Prime Minister. So far, there is no evidence that Michael is the sort of original thinker who can initiate new policy, project current thinking in terms of future development in a changing society and, not least, present the whole package to the nation.

Michael Foot is a clever man – an intellectual and a fine writer. But that is not quite the same thing as having a good political mind. In the Party, his reputation was founded on his journalistic successes – among other posts, he was Acting Editor of the *Evening Standard* in 1942, and Editor of *Tribune* from 1948 till 1952; in many ways, he is still more suited to the trench warfare of Fleet Street than the battles of front-line politics.

Few politicians are responsible for individual acts that can be described as historical watersheds: acts that cause the whole flow of future events to take an altered course. Jim Callaghan is one. His sabotaging of 'In Place of Strife' meant an irreversible change in the relationship of the Government – any Government – with the trades unions, and a consequent shift of power that has written modern British economic and political history anew. If the corporate state had ever come into being,

Jim Callaghan could truly be said to have been one of its architects.

As for Jim himself, his personal watershed was his defeat by Harold Wilson when, along with George Brown, he stood for the Leadership of the Party in 1963, after Hugh Gaitskell's death. I do not think either George or Jim ever recovered from this; nor did Jim ever really concede defeat. A certain jealousy and envy coloured his whole relationship with Harold Wilson for the rest of their political lives, despite their regard for each other.

This was to surface in damaging form when Jim Callaghan became Home Secretary in 1968. As Chancellor, he had been a loyal and hard-working member of a team; then came the period of fiscal crisis leading to ultimate devaluation – and Jim had to make the decision as to whether he retired, went on the back benches, or stayed in government. Over and over again he had to face in his own mind the inescapable fact that it was Harold who had the power to reshuffle Jim from the Treasury to the Home Office, Harold who was the Leader. Unlike old loves or old griefs, it takes little to make an old jealousy resurface – even though Harold had acted generously in offering Jim a choice. After the devaluation catastrophe, another Prime Minister might not have thought in terms of a further Cabinet job.

The fraught and complex Harold–Jim relationship started even farther back than that first overt struggle for the Leadership. It began with the argument on unilateralism within the Party. Then (as now) there were three factions: those who followed Hugh Gaitskell's own very right-wing line, the left wing who wanted unilateralism, and those in the middle who did not want either to be unilateralist or to support the Americans to the death and who believed that there was a middle road in multilateralism that could form a compromise between Left and Right.

Jim had originally supported the left-wing line, as he had indicated in at least one Shadow Cabinet meeting. But he is, by instinct and inclination, a great Party politician. He can read the mood of the Party, he can sense which way it is moving before there is any apparent indication – and he has the agility to place himself with one bound at the head of the biggest column that is forming. Thus, he realized quickly that the big block votes of the trades unions would fall on Gaitskell's side (only one, Frank Cousins's TGWU, did oppose him). At the Party Conference that autumn, while Harold Wilson stood for the middle or multilateral line (a dual compromise on Polaris), Gaitskell wanted an independent nuclear deterrent for Britain. Agreeing with Hugh Gaitskell were not only Sir Alec Douglas-Home and Harold Macmillan but, most importantly in this context, the big right-wing trades unionists.

Jim, realizing that Hugh was going to win, threw in his lot with him. His price for backing Hugh and bringing with him valuable support from within the Parliamentary Labour Party was the political equivalent of demanding St John the Baptist's head on a charger. He wanted Harold Wilson's job and, like Salome, he got what he wanted.

It was not difficult to understand why he wished to exchange the job of shadowing Commonwealth Affairs for that of Shadow Chancellor. As a platform for making a personal mark as a formidable politician only one step from the throne, the job of Shadow Chancellor has no equal in Opposition. The Shadow Chancellor is the one who attacks the day-to-day running of government affairs as well as spearheading assaults on specific policies; he is always in the public eye and in the news; his speeches are widely reported and he is, more than any other single Opposition politician, the voice of his Party.

Harold Wilson, during the two or three years that he had been holding this post, had built up a great reputation for himself. He had started with every qualification for the job: he is a trained economist, having gained Top First in Politics, Philosophy and Economics at Oxford, and he is a 'natural' economist, in the sense that he has always been able to present economic arguments and monetary policy with clarity and distinction. And he was very funny. The combination of all these assets meant that his speeches were hard-hitting, witty and stylish. His performance in debate was relished by both sides of the House. His success at this difficult job not only caused dismay to the Government, but was a source of considerable irritation to his colleagues – until the Shadow Cabinet was reshuffled in 1961, just after the argument over unilateralism had died down.

'What went wrong, Harold?' asked Dick Crossman, when revealing to Harold Wilson that there was discussion in Gaitskell's circle about a reshuffle – including the question of what they would do with Harold Wilson. And Crossman added, 'I think you'll probably be made Shadow Leader of the House.'

The news that he might be moved was no surprise to Harold Wilson. Once he had come out against Gaitskell on unilateralism and the Clause IV issue in 1960, and stood against him for the Leadership – on the grounds that Gaitskell was dividing the Party – he knew the knives would be out for him.

That action in standing against Gaitskell was the action of a gambler, in direct contradiction to his reputation as an ambitious man who always played safe. He had no personal friends in the Gaitskell Shadow Cabinet to secure his position for him, but he expected some support – the votes of those who had polled for him in the Leadership election. What he did not expect was that Jim would come out against him, since Jim, he believed, was a left-of-centre moderate like himself, not a right-wing Gaitskellite.

He was aware, therefore, that the writing was on the wall, although he was ignorant of what it would spell out. Its first message was not unduly depressing. When it was suggested was that he would probably become Shadow Leader of the House, he laughed: although it was a poor exchange for the star job of the Treasury, it did at least mean much more contact with colleagues in the Parliamentary Labour Party. As he said at the time, 'It won't do me any actual harm, and by doing a good job it will give me a chance to work my passage back with those I've offended.'

His relief was short-lived; this was not to be. Instead, he was told that he was to be given the Shadow Foreign Office job. To this, his reaction was one of gloom: he realized that this was designed to put him in an office in which he could not possibly shine and, worse, where comparative ineptness might easily relegate him to the Second Division for good.

But disastrous as the Foreign Office was believed to be to Harold Wilson's chances of personal glory, his colleagues clearly did not think that his role there would be bad for the Labour Party. Otherwise Gaitskell would not have been confident enough to hand over this portfolio.

Once in the job as Shadow Foreign Secretary, luck played a part. The Foreign Affairs issues that came up during Harold Wilson's period as Shadow Foreign Secretary all had an economic content – and economics was his special field. One example was the Congo, with its copper and other mineral and economic resources, on which there was tremendous argument. Here, Harold was able to put the Left/Right arguments on the Congo into an economic context as well as taking a foreign policy line on it.

The result was that he made himself as effective a Shadow Foreign Secretary as he had been a Shadow Chancellor. But the sheer hard work involved necessitated one minor casualty. The sparkle and wit that he had been able to inject into his speeches as Shadow Chancellor, on his own subject, were temporarily lost – it is, in any case, difficult and often out of place to make knockabout political jokes on foreign affairs.

So Jim became Shadow Chancellor in 1961, in Harold's place. He had no academic qualifications for such a job and no real training for it. However great the determination and shrewdness that had caused him to rise in the Labour Party hierarchy, it was still no sort of preparation for entering a new and complicated world for which an economic background was considered extremely important if not essential, and for interpreting this world and his Party's views on it in the House, in the press and on television. Nor had he got the very clever mind of a George Brown – a man who substitutes for the formal education he lacks a natural high intelligence coupled with instinctive ability. To Jim, knowledge does not come easily, it is acquired only by dint of hard work.

All credit to him, therefore, that he set out to acquire the necessary training. For nearly a year he regularly journeyed to Oxford for tutorials at Nuffield College. Hugh Gaitskell was able to make these necessary arrangements for him not only with the help of right-wing economist friends but with the help of left-wing economists like Thomas Balogh and others, particularly when the Party switched its line on the Common Market.

Jim's lessons were, in fact, the only course open to him. Although it is possible for a Minister to bluff his way around almost any other subject from energy to employment until he has managed to acquire the necessary knowledge during the course of the job, with economics this is impossible. You either know about exchange rates and macro- and micro-economics – or you don't. It must have been irritating for him to see Roy Jenkins, who found it all so easy and effortless. Undaunted, Jim set out to equip himself for the job, a task requiring both application and something less commonly found: a realistic appreciation of one's own strengths and weaknesses. I can think of few potential Chancellors who would have gone back to school like this. It required application and enormous determination, and won him admiration and respect all round.

But when all this happened the Chancellorship was a long time ahead – as was Harold Wilson's switching of him to the Home Office. Although I say 'switching', the process was not as immediate as this verb implies: Jim did not instantly accept the offer of the Home Office in 1967.

Characteristically, he took some considerable time to make up his mind. For Jim, decision is agony; probably the main reason why, although he is a perfect Number Two (like so many who are marvellous deputies), he is not by nature a Number One. In that position, while he retained his acumen and his critical expertise, his previous instinctive 'feel' for the realities of the situation deserted him when everything, finally, rested on his judgement and not on that of the man above him. The most famous – and disastrous – example of this was the failure to make up his mind over when to hold a general election. Its continual postponement gave the Tories a chance to build up an unbeatable lead, and Margaret Thatcher in particular a chance to develop support within her own Party. It also disheartened his own supporters and backers.

Callaghan's mistake was in the first instance to allow the EEC to meet in a sunny paradise, Guadeloupe. He compounded that felony by staying on in a neighbouring sunny spot after the Guadeloupe meeting ended. After this, at a time when the streets here were icy and frozen with snow, and strikes were widespread from the non-collection of refuse to the non-burial of the dead, he returned to these shores querying the situation as one of crisis.

It was my view at the time that, when Jim Callaghan succeeded Harold Wilson in April 1976, he should have taken the earliest opportunity possible to go to the country and seek a new mandate, not only for the Labour Government but for himself as Prime Minister. Instead he chose the path of the Lib–Lab Pact and his position remained unconfirmed by the electorate.

Jim Callaghan is an extraordinarily able politician and his skill in this field seldom deserts him; but as a leader, the vital core of steely decisiveness is missing. He can be convinced, correctly, that a certain course of action is necessary, but he flinches from the equally vital corollary, that of setting it into motion. He can say to himself: 'I know that this is what we should do,' but not: 'Because I know this is what we should do, I shall see we do it – now.' So that while, in my view, he was extremely good as Foreign Secretary and as Number Two to Harold Wilson, once the latter resigned there was no one to take that final responsibility. It was now up to Jim – the real Jim.

I say the 'real Jim' because James Callaghan is not just an enigma, with or without variations; he is a contradiction. His public persona is quite different from the inner man. He looks kindly, genial, immensely reassuring, even gentle, but he is not necessarily just the warm, avuncular character he appears. Both he and Harold Wilson are extremely good politicians in the sense of being instinctive political animals; and they are about equal in their ability to manipulate and run a Party, the one intellectually devious, the other instinctively ...

This quality served Jim in good stead in the years of 1968 and 1969, when he realized that he and the trades union movement would together make an unbeatable pair. He supported them totally, stuck to them right through the Opposition years, became their spokesman and most loyal supporter even though this led him to a confrontation with the Leader of the Party.

At the time, Jim had a considerable band of supporters, who over-enthusiastically organized a 'Wilson Must Go' campaign, whose demand to this effect was signed by many of the Parliamentary Labour Party, mainly from the Right. Even Roy Jenkins was approached for his backing but so the story goes, he said, 'First tell me who they want to put in his place. If it's Jim, I don't want to be involved with it.'

After Jim, backed by his influential friends in Parliament and the entire trades union movement, had brought about the débâcle of 'In Place of Strife', his position, along with that of the trades unions, became even stronger. Now, the trades union movement and Jim went together like a horse and carriage – or hand in glove. Only Jim could deliver their vote – a vote necessary in the Opposition years to get the Common Market compromise formula through, to achieve unity in Parliament against Edward Heath's incomes policy or industrial relations. Now Jim was indispensable; and now, too, it was even more necessary to make sure that the trades union movement was 'kept sweet'. Without this support, Harold could not have survived in Opposition, and he depended on Jim tremendously during those years.

At the same time, Jim himself was taking a much less thrusting line. Just after we went into Opposition in 1970 he became ill and underwent a prostate operation, and he seemed afterwards to have decided on a quieter life. He would often make remarks like, 'I've been ill and I'm getting on. My only ambition now is to serve my Party and the country and to make sure the Party is strong and successful – everything else I'm content to leave to younger people.' He appeared to be turning himself into an elder statesman in front of our eyes. I myself had no idea of his ambition: I saw him as someone who had been defeated in 1963 and come to accept it, and who was a superb Number Two. Of course, like everyone else, I had heard about the intended coup to get rid of Wilson and replace him with Jenkins or Callaghan, but that kind of story is so much the stock-in-trade of every political scenario, irrespective of Party or country, that I was not greatly affected by it. So little, in fact, that when my book *Inside Number 10* was published in 1972, Jim's remark on it was: 'She's been far too kind.'

While it is absolutely true that the Labour Party originated from the trades union movement, Jim's definition is that it is, still and principally, the trades union movement; with the Parliamentary Party and the Labour Party in the country trailing well behind.

He has never made any secret of this belief; but I do not think that any of us realized the degree to which he would substantiate his credo in later years. His links with the trades unions brought him to power; he in turn was responsible for giving the trades union movement its powerful role in government. He would see his destruction of 'In Place of Strife' from the opposite viewpoint: that of rescuing the unions from an attack upon them, and then building them up into an indispensable arm of the Labour Party so that when election time came round again in 1974, they could work out the joint policy that was to become known as the 'Social Contract'.

The idea of deciding an economic policy solely on the contractual basis that if the Government's policy seems right and acceptable the trades unions will agree to deliver certain commitments in terms of pay restraint is perhaps possible in an ideal world where the trades union movement can control itself; so far, the TUC has not achieved the power to dictate to its own members. The legacy that Jim left was that, today, anyone who leads the unions does so from behind.

Jim remains one of the outstanding figures of the post-war years and is a remarkably adroit politician.

The key to Denis Healey is Marxism. That is to say, although he left the Marxist ideology a long time ago, when he left the Communist Party, he still thinks like a Marxist. Although over the years he has moved steadily away from his far-Left beginnings to stand now on the right wing of the Labour Party, his thought processes still have that relentless, almost predetermined, step-by-step Marxist flavour about them.

Face him with a problem and he will pursue its solution through to the ultimate, logical conclusion without allowing himself to be diverted – as most people can be diverted – by any considerations, however important they seem at the time. It is this quality that once caused Harold Wilson to use a Nye Bevan saying to describe Denis: 'He's like one of those Trojan cars, boy – once they get on the tramline they go straight back to the depot.'

With Denis, logic rules, to the extent of taking a sledge-hammer to crack even a small political nut. It is partly this that has given him the justified reputation of being a political bully – a reputation he jokes about. He once looked across a lunch table at me when he was talking to his neighbour and said, 'Marcia thinks I'm a political thug.'

He was right – but I also think that he has the best brain in the Party. Not only is he extremely clever, but he is also a very cultivated man. Add the ambition that is common to every politician and which Denis has in large measure, and you begin to wonder why Denis is still – well, Denis Healey, also-ran, when he should by all the laws of averages have become Leader of the Party.

Although he was the natural successor to James Callaghan, by the time the Leadership election came round opinion within the Party had changed so dramatically that Michael Foot attracted more votes.

But Denis Healey does not have the obvious defect of his far-Right, Marxist/Rand Corporation approach. He is not inflexible. When we went into Opposition in 1970, for instance, everyone thought that Denis would take a pro-Market line; instead he was prepared to vote for a compromise in order to keep the Party together. He has got the intuitive knowledge essential to every Leader of exactly when you have to be flexible in order to survive as an individual or as a Party – and which is possessed by very few on the far Right of the Party.

Denis Healey's great strength is the forceful logic that is the legacy of his Marxist past, backed up by a powerful personality that does not hesitate to bludgeon through some course of action that he feels to be necessary or right. A clear argument put in a simple way, with great conviction, is always persuasive; in politics especially, where so many areas are 'grey', where so often the individual politician is uncertain whether he believes in this or that aspect of Party policy, it is doubly attractive. The person who, like Denis, has the gift of making his argument so logical as to seem irrefutable can naturally steamroller the objections of others – as Denis has done on many occasions.

Political bully Dennis may be but, unlike most bullies, he does not lack courage. He is never frightened to say what he thinks. In contrast to most other politicians, who may have equally strong views but who water them down to avoid giving too much offence when it comes to a confrontation, Denis does not mince his words. If he thinks an argument is weak, he says so; if he thinks someone is being disingenuous, he will not hesitate to accuse them of dishonesty. He never flinches from being unpleasant when he thinks it is necessary – though in ordinary conversation he is cheerful and friendly – and he is always perfectly prepared to stand up for himself in the face of hostility.

One of the most typical examples of this latter trait came after Labour's defeat in 1970. It was the day after Polling Day, and the Cabinet was to meet for the last time at Number 10. Outside, a large crowd had gathered, a 'guillotine crowd'. In days gone by, they would have been the ones who came up to Tyburn for the spectacle of a public hanging; now they were intent on watching the execution of a government.

That day, it was boiling hot (as it had been throughout the campaign), so that a feeling of general irritability was ready to ignite into something uglier. Though there were tourists among the crowd, the main body of people were there to gloat and give vent loudly and unrestrainedly to their feelings. It was also seeded with a number of Tory cheer leaders; I recognized people who had jeered and booed outside on various crisis occasions.

As each Member of the Cabinet arrived, he or she had to run the gauntlet of terrific cat-calling and booing. It was rather horrible. We saw it all from the second-floor windows above the front door. All of them came in with their heads bowed, looking a bit shaken at such fiercely expressed hostility.

All except Denis, that is. He got more noise than anyone. His response was to turn to them, smile and put up two fingers. Immediately, they all burst out cheering, and the atmosphere became quite different. Simply by facing them out, showing them he didn't care and was prepared to answer them back in the same spirit, he'd forced them to change their attitude. This was Denis at his most effective.

This direct, rather jokey retort was not only brave but typical of him; he has a reputation for the non-stop playing of jokes and tricks. At one time this cost him the chance of becoming Opposition spokesman on Foreign Affairs. Denis's habit of turning everything into a joke had been taken amiss by some of his socialist colleagues in Europe and America, who thought he went too far, and reports to this effect flowed back to Hugh Gaitskell. In a personal sense, his humorous approach is appealing: he cheers you up and makes you feel amused and jolly – after probably first giving you an intellectual trouncing!

Like Jim Callaghan, whom he resembles in no other way, there is a discrepancy between Denis's external appearance and his personality. No one would suspect that this big, bulky man with his florid complexion and bushy eyebrows is the cultivated person he is, with interests ranging from intense musicality to films and photography.

To look at, Denis may be the sort of colourful character who is a cartoonist's dream, giving an impression of solidity and warmth. But scan him more closely and you see that the cosy glow is an illusion – rather like the flicker-without-heat of a simulated log fire compared with the leaping flames of the real thing. The laugh is more contrived than ready, the eyes appear a little too sharp the longer you look at them, the cutting edge shows through the simple phraseology with which he woos the television public.

In Denis's case, I think it is almost possible to say that without his eyebrows, he would not be the popular figure he is today. Trivial as this may seem, it is nevertheless true that the attentions of cartoonists and impersonators do make politicians much more widely known. Denis's eyebrows, voice, mannerisms – the way he puts his head on one side and disparages opponents in phrases like 'silly billy' or 'foolish' – make any imitation of him instantly recognizable. When Mike Yarwood put him up on the screen, he became a national figure of a kind different from his colleagues – a part of everybody's family life. He was not, however, able to capitalize on this exposure as much as he should have (although he realized its importance) because he had not worked out how to. The greatest gift any politician can be given is to be able to make people identify with him, and usually this is something that happens at an instinctive level. But with Denis, the human element in his personality is not as strong as the cerebral. First and foremost, Denis is an intellectual – an intellectual who wants to be in politics, who is extremely ambitious, who adapts as well as he can to his political environment but who does not have that bit of the actor in him that virtually all Leaders need. To go the whole hog politically, you need a bit of the ham.

Roy Jenkins is a man who has succeeded in politics without having the personality of a politician.

He is shy, a trait that makes him unable to relax to the point of being totally himself; and he is still, even now, nervous whenever he is going to speak in the House or take part in a television debate or interview, or even make an ordinary platform political speech.

This diffidence, compared to the arrogance – often cockiness – of many politicians, is something that I personally find appealing. There are those who think that *au fond* Roy is an intellectual snob; I think it is rather that his intellectual interests mean that he is often out of touch with the more down-to-earth tastes of the 'ordinary' man. Add to this his general aura of having stepped straight out of an After-Eight Mints advertisement and it is possible to see why his success with the Labour

Party faithful was wafer-thin. To the average voter, it is more important that any potential Leader understands the realities of life in a semi than that he appears able to find his way round the intricacies of a wine list.

Nevertheless, Roy is a man of the strongest principle. If he were not, if he did not feel burningly about many issues, would he be in politics? The answer, I am sure, is No. He is an historian, a man of great achievement, an author who has written a number of extremely important and excellent books – a man, in short, who could make a happy and satisfactory life for himself quite outside politics.

But certain political issues have dominated Roy's life – the chief one being, of course, the Common Market. He has always been a devoted Marketeer and until 1970 this was in line with Government policy. In Opposition, though, after Britain had yet again been rejected by the French, the Party swung round to a position that was officially anti-Market.

Roy was faced with the alternatives of either swallowing the new policy whole, or sticking to his guns and resigning. As a man of principle he chose the latter option, giving up his post as Deputy Leader. Fortunately, he was not too high-minded to agree to the compromise formula later worked out, which involved the renegotiation of the terms of entry coupled with the agreement of the electorate, via the ballot box, either through a referendum or an election.

I say 'fortunately', because one of the main tasks of the Opposition years was to reunite the Party – which included bringing them together on the issue of the Market. Before this compromise had been worked out Roy voted with the Tories for entry into Europe.

At heart, Roy is a liberal Whig, of the sort quintessentially found in the eighteenth century, with their belief in a sane, ordered and civilized society dependent in its turn on the fundamental decency of human nature.

This attitude found expression in his term at the Home Office, whither he went to 'free Britain' from what he regarded as the restrictive legislation then prevailing. The phrase, 'the civilized society', he used to describe his introduction of various progressive social measures – on divorce, abortion, homosexuality and the rest – has dogged him ever since. *His* intention was to remove the veil of hypocrisy from our attitudes to these matters, making plain, open, safe and accepted what was already practised in secret, in conditions ranging from squalid to dangerous. What he did not expect was the Permissive Society, with its interpretation of his reforms in a less than 'civilized' way.

At the time he went to the Home Office this type of change seemed inevitable. The basic attitudes of society were shifting, the country as a whole was more prosperous, expectations were higher, new areas of life had opened up, old beliefs were being overturned. A general relaxation of the tight disciplinary framework of the law was felt to be necessary. Roy was the architect of this liberalization; a comprehensive and difficult task that he performed brilliantly.

Nevertheless, after nearly three years at the Home Office, Roy was probably lucky to have been transferred to the Treasury. By that time there was little left for him to liberalize in this way; and public opinion, with one of its pendulum swings of mood, was ready for a more conservative Home Secretary – one who would hold the line rather than seek to push it forward. In Jim Callaghan, they got one.

Once in the Treasury, Roy had to work extremely closely with Harold Wilson; especially so, as he became Chancellor in the aftermath of the difficult financial period that culminated in devaluation. Harold Wilson's prior attitude to Roy had been one of slight suspicion – Roy was well to the right of him politically – in which was mingled a strand of envy for Roy's more reflective, leisured approach to politics; an approach which he, as Leader of the Party, could not afford. But their relationship flowed smoothly; there is a Downing Street adage that the temperature of the relationship between a Prime Minister and his Chancellor can be gauged by whether the door of the connecting corridor between Number 10 and Number 11 is kept locked, unlocked or open. When Roy was at Number 11, the door was always unlocked, and very often open; he and Harold maintained a continuing dialogue. Whereas when Jim Callaghan was Chancellor, the door between Number 10 and Number 11 was usually closed, though never locked, and he and Harold met only at times of crisis.

Part of the reason for this can undoubtedly be found in the personality of Roy Jenkins. Opinions on anyone's outward appearance vary: Roy's lisp makes him seem rather effete and languid to some, his glasses – and the way he wears them – make him look slightly aloof. He is elegant. One of the most attractive things about him is his rare, rather shy smile, and he is well known for his genuine kindliness among his colleagues. To me he was always very friendly and nice, in his rather shy way. I recall one occasion that was both memorable and typical. When Harold Wilson resigned, Roy made a speech at the Parliamentary Party meeting that was touching because of its honesty and genuine feeling. 'Every-one knows that I have not always been Harold's warmest supporter,' he said, 'but now I want to say thank you for all he has done.'

The generous and spontaneous gesture is one of Roy's most attractive characteristics. Once, when Chancellor, to mark some occasion he gave Harold a record of Asquith making a political speech. Any record made as long ago as that, and on such a subject, must be extremely rare; to Roy, a man who fervently admired Asquith, it must have been something very special indeed. To give a present like that is true generosity.

It is not surprising that, in contrast to many senior politicians, Roy is a man with friends. People like being near him because they enjoy his company; as they get to know him, he inspires great loyalty, affection and warmth. Most of those close to him now have been his friends and supporters since the days of Hugh Gaitskell, from whom he inherited the more successful of the Gaitskell right-wingers.

When it came to the 1976 battle for the Leadership, therefore, Roy had considerable potential support, which might have become increasingly evident. He would never, I think, have been a strong enough candidate to gain an outright majority, but I believe that in time, with a position as strong as his, he could have 'written his own ticket' in terms of the job he wanted.

Without doubt, this was the Foreign Office that went to Tony Crosland. It is equally true to say that Jim would not have wanted to place a potential rival in such an important job, and one in which he would undoubtedly have shone; as it was, Jim was quite ruthless about sacking or reshuffling those who already held jobs in order to replace them with his own appointees. With Roy, as with Barbara Castle, whom he sacked immediately after coming to office, there was the additional reason that they were two of the three originators of 'In Place of Strife' (the third, of course, being Harold Wilson himself).

Roy, well aware of all these overtones, or undertones, had already decided to accept the European job. But if he had taken the alternative course of remaining, Jim would have found his own life much more difficult: instead of a relatively smooth passage on most questions, Roy's would often have been a strong dissenting voice that he could not afford to ignore.

Roy's wish to accept the European job put Harold Wilson into something of a quandary at the time. When Harold Wilson came to tell him that it was on offer and Roy then said to him that he would like to accept it, Harold did not want Roy to think that he, Harold, wanted to get him out of the way and off to Europe in order that Roy could not have either the Foreign Office or any other senior appointment in any reshuffle. Nor could he tell Roy that it would not be he but someone else who did any reshuffling. The only surprising thing is that Roy himself did not say, 'If I stay, I would like to think that I could get to the Foreign Office.'

Anyone else of Roy's ambition and ability would have fought like a wildcat for the Foreign Office. But that is not his style. 'The only thing Roy has ever fought for in his life is a table at the Mirabelle,' remarked a colleague, with a certain amount of truth at the time, though since dramatically confounded by Roy's efforts in Warrington and Glasgow Hillhead.

For Roy, the world of politics as it is today is still too rough; his attitude is Asquithian: he believes that life should be leisured, dignified and well-rounded. He slightly despises the politician who eats, speaks, drinks and talks politics and can think of nothing else. For Roy, meeting friends, discussing serious questions quietly and enjoyably over a meal, are more important than battling in committees, working on speeches, addressing rallies, arguing with Party officials. He believes there is more to life. I agree with him.

Of all the present leading members of the Labour Party, Peter Shore is probably the one who has been closest to Harold Wilson for the longest time.

When Harold was Shadow Chancellor, it was Peter's responsibility as Head of Research at Party headquarters to provide him with any necessary research. This laid the foundations of the excellent relationship they enjoyed when Harold became Leader of the Party.

In the months leading up to the dramatic 1964 election that first lifted Harold to victory, a decisive role was played by Peter, as one of the small inner circle around Harold, consisting of Dick Crossman, Tony Benn, Thomas Balogh, George Wigg and Dick Plummer.

Once Labour was in power, he became Parliamentary Private Secretary to Harold, working in Number 10. Unlike some Parliamentary Private Secretaries, who do most of their work in the House of Commons and just look in at Number 10, Peter treated it as a base, and consequently became very much part of the team. He was most successful at managing to be where the Prime Minister needed him – usually at

Number 10 in the morning, and at the House in the afternoon and evening where he could liaise politically between the Prime Minister and the Parliamentary Labour Party.

It was no surprise, therefore, that eventually he was given a government job. But even when Secretary of State for Economic Affairs, it took a long time for him to live down the title of 'Mr Wilson's Poodle' which had resulted from his close attendance on the Prime Minister. This tag irritated Harold just as much as Peter. The Prime Minister believed rightly that those who had worked for him as Parliamentary Private Secretaries or in some other personal capacity (Gerald Kaufman and Eric Varley are other examples) rose to Ministerial office not because they were his protégés but because the reverse was true: he had singled them out because of their intrinsic merit. With Peter, as with the others, the proof of this is that he has been regularly elected to a high position on the Parliamentary Committee of the Labour Party.

Whether or not he will become Leader of the Party is another question. Intellectually, he has all the necessary qualities; in addition, he is a very good, instinctive politician, with that most valuable of gifts, a great understanding of ordinary people and what they need. As a friend, he has a warm and kindly nature. Politically, he is very aware: a shrewd operator who knows what modern politics is about, who understands the importance in today's world of the right presentation of policies (though sometimes he forgets this on his own account), and who is conversant with the whole apparatus of the Party machine.

To me there remains a nagging doubt partly caused, I am sure, by that well-known quirk of the human mind: always thinking of someone as they were at the stage in their career when you knew them best. For me, this means that the young, junior and relatively inexperienced Peter Shore whom I worked alongside is a more familiar figure in my mind's eye than the senior political figure he now is.

Discounting this, though, I still feel that there is some slightness about his public persona that is more than merely the reflection of his youthful image. This is enhanced by a physical appearance that, with his height, slimness and pallor, makes him look less solid than other public figures.

However, Peter's understanding of presentation has resulted in his putting in some hard work on his own image, with the result that he is now less the impoverished professor, more the well-presented parliamentarian.

What seems to be emerging is a British de Gaulle. One discrepancy remains: his rather plummy voice, which irritates colleagues (and probably the ordinary Labour voter) in the same way as does Roy Jenkins's inability to sound his 'r's'. It was a source of some amusement to me many years ago that Peter, unaware of his distinctive tones, was continually surprised that he was immediately recognized on the telephone before he had time to announce who he was.

But these are minor points; and far outweighed by his intellectual ability and political acumen. One example of this was on the occasion when Margaret Thatcher became Leader of the Conservative Party. I arrived at the House of Commons just as a meeting of senior Cabinet Members was breaking up. I remember they were all laughing, joking and slapping each other on the shoulders with remarks to the effect that all was now well. 'That's it, we're home and dry,' was the general tenor. 'No need to worry about the next election. It's a foregone conclusion. Well, how could the Tory Party – the Tory Party – possibly win with a woman at the head?'

Peter came up to the sofa on which I was sitting at the end of the room, waiting to clear some work with the Prime Minister, and sat down beside me. 'What do you think?' he asked me. 'I don't believe what they're saying is right,' I replied. He said quietly, '*I* think it's going to be extremely difficult to beat her.' Instinctively, and because of his own attitude to the whole question of women's rights, he had seized on one vital point: that the women's vote, which is of extreme importance in any election and often a pointer as to the final result, could be brought very powerfully into play by Margaret Thatcher.

Peter is unfortunately not typical of the Labour Party as a whole in his view of women. Many leading Labour figures have an attitude to women's rights completely opposed to the whole spirit of a movement that believes expressly in equal opportunity.

Like Harold Wilson, Peter recognizes the power of the whole feminist movement, and the need to have more women, where they are so qualified, in positions of importance. Of all the senior Labour figures – Neil Kinnock excluded – he is the one with the best chance of mobilizing women's votes. This is hardly surprising from someone with a wife who has risen, as a doctor, to a very senior position in the Department of Health and Social Security.

The junior members of the Gang of Four can both be unequivocally described as good-looking. David Owen was the matinée idol of the Labour Party, and Bill Rodgers is handsome in a saturnine and sinister way that is in keeping with the general 'blankness' (the only word I can find) that surrounds him.

Bill is not exactly mysterious (though his politics are difficult to understand: beyond the fact that they are right wing, and that he likes and admires American politicizing, with its primaries, conventions and general razzmatazz, there is nothing clear-cut about them), it is just that too little is known about him by the general public. His good looks are implied rather than obvious: he could be preserving some deep secret for highly laudable reasons, or he could just have emerged from a conspiracy.

Along with this, he is not well-known personally, partly because he is not a very good mixer – nothing like as good, for instance, as the other three SDP leaders. Within his own small group, he is popular, even though argumentative and aggressive. He is very sure of himself – and his ideas – so can appear rather off-hand, even slightly rude in manner, to those he doesn't know well.

His ability is undoubted. He is very clever, very able, and undoubtedly invaluable to the SDP from the point of view of actually getting things done: recruiting support, raising finance, mobilizing the key influential people in every area – and keeping intelligent and precise records of the whole process.

Despite these invaluable gifts, I do not see him as a Leader. There is a certain quality essential to the would-be Leader that can fall anywhere between full-blown charisma of the John Kennedy type and the ability to get on with, and handle, people. Unless you are, as the Americans call it, 'personable', it is very difficult firstly to become a Leader, and secondly to be an effective one. This is what Bill Rodgers lacks; though his other qualities ensure that he could be a superb Number Two.

David Owen, on the other hand, although not as clever as Bill Rodgers, does have this necessary quality. He has great charm – when he wants to use it; he is a hard worker and a fighter, a man of strong convictions about which he is prepared to be aggressive. An example of this was his hard-fought battle to retain his seat in a marginal constituency, a campaign which he handled brilliantly.

David, like Bill, is a very able administrator; this accounted in part for his great success at the DHSS – a success which was not reflected in his career as Foreign Secretary. To jump so quickly and so early into a senior Cabinet post was a little too much for him; if he had approached it more slowly, perhaps via a senior post in the overseas area, he would have achieved the necessary experience and skill.

As a person, David is extremely kind and genuine, with the ability to mesh successfully with those around him. His only 'personal relations' problem seems to be with those on a much lower level than himself. He is, for instance, one of the very, very few Cabinet Ministers who (while at the Foreign Office) changed his driver almost as often as he changed his suit. Or rather, they changed him: none of them could cope with the job – the dashing about from one end of England to the other at short notice, the abrupt manner. But without the stress of office, he is certainly more relaxed about this – as about other things – and has grown in stature and qualities during the Falkland Islands crisis.

Furthermore he has a keen radical mind and a killer instinct which few of his colleagues possess. But much more, his timing is good and he is young enough to survive successfully the confrontation with his new leader, Roy Jenkins.

During the 1960s the very talented group that emerged on the Right of the Party, of which David Owen, Bill Rodgers and the late John Mackintosh were members, included two other notable figures – Roy Hattersley and Brian Walden. All became leading figures in the political world by the late 1970s. Roy Hattersley's progress was to be more flexible than any of the other members of the Group.

After Harold Wilson left Number 10, he was heard to mutter frequently that he would not have selected for membership of a Cabinet some of the people Jim Callaghan had chosen. The criticism was aimed at, among others, Roy Hattersley. As he watched Roy, however, in the posts he was given both in Government and Opposition, Harold Wilson changed his view and acknowledged Roy's many qualities.

Roy has all the physical advantages a politician can hope for in the UK. He has a rounded comfortable figure, a pleasant face and, of course, a northern background with the reassuring, dependable Yorkshire accent, suggesting good down-to-earth common sense. And this is certainly one of Roy's strongest characteristics. If he adds a slightly *staccato* style to his speech, then that merely suggests another Hattersley facet, as if the chopped-off brusque phrase and a shake of the jowl can add verisimilitude to the philosophy expounded. The style, however, is somehow too contrived and studied.

Roy Hattersley is a man of many talents, an agile and adept politician who can, in the way Jim Callaghan could, trim his sails according to the winds, showing a talent by no means to be underwritten or undervalued. He writes with elegance and charm and could quite easily have made a separate and distinctive career for himself as both an author and a journalist.

If the smile is less than warming it is only in the manner all northerners have of never overdoing anything – or in political parlance what is so often described inelegantly as 'over-egging the pudding'.

The old Labour Party might well have found it safe and easy to opt for Roy as Leader: a Leader for all sections of the Party. As it is, the present Labour Party may find something profoundly unattractive about someone who has a flexibility that leaves him unadopted as the champion of any large grouping or major Party crusade. Roy has, I suggest, at the end of the day far fewer friends in the Party than he has enemies. It is ironic that in fact, if selected, he might well make a Leader to give the Party electoral victory and the support of the mass electorate which, at the moment of writing, it so sadly lacks.

In politics there are always the outstanding figures who 'might have been' – the lost Cabinet Ministers and great political personalities: Brian Walden is one such. I was always deeply impressed in the 1960s by Roy Jenkins, who in 1964 refused Harold Wilson's offer of the Department of Education and Science on the grounds that he knew so little about either. He thereby gave up an early place in the Cabinet of the time and had to serve as Minister of Aviation outside the Cabinet until he became Home Secretary. Looking back, his decision was clearly right.

Brian Walden similarly impressed me by refusing Ministerial Office later, on the grounds that he simply could not afford it. For personal reasons he needed a big income and a Minister's pay was just too tiny to meet his needs. When he refused he must have been very aware that such an offer would have been the beginning of a distinguished political career and eventual appointment to the Cabinet.

Of the group on the Right, Brian, while philosophically committed to the policies they represented, never allowed his feelings to degenerate into the bitter personal criticisms of Harold Wilson in which some others indulged.

Since he left Parliament he has become one of the most outstanding personalities on television: a clever, acute and incisive interviewer; he possesses to balance it a gentle, courteous and kindly manner that allows the most penetrating and relentless questioning.

I suspect he is also a man of some spirituality whose view of the human condition and all its complexities, its sorrows and joys, permits him to stand back far enough from events to judge them in a far longer perspective than would have been possible in politics. Indeed this very attribute, I suspect, was always perhaps the one priceless gift he possessed which made politics a career he should always have avoided. And yet that gift would in certain cases have been an equally priceless and unusual asset in a Cabinet Minister.

If any man in the Wilson years deserved the title 'Mr Nice Guy' it was surely George Thomson, now Lord Thomson of Monifeith. He had a highly regarded and very worthy career as a Cabinet Minister before leaving for Europe and the post he was to hold there as one of Britain's Commissioners.

A close friend and confidant of Jim Callaghan during the 1960s and early 1970s, he was by 1974 an outstanding figure in his own right, a man liked by the majority of Labour MPs, no matter to which part of the Party they belonged. His greatest contribution was, in my view, to the Rhodesian dialogue, which had been bitter and often sour and needed the very qualities possessed by George Thomson, the quiet, courteous and patently honest archetypal Scotsman.

I have no doubt that in his present role as Chairman of the IBA he will be just as popular and successful. His appointment coincides with a massive expansion in television technology and communication. There are some controversial years ahead for the visual media, and I am sure that George Thomson's particular gifts as a political diplomatist will stand him and the IBA in good stead.

While I have no doubt Alasdair Milne at the BBC will prove an outstanding success in the Reithian mould for the Corporation, he will have his work cut out to cope with the combined force of George Thomson and John Whitney at the IBA.

Roy Mason could have been Leader of his Party if the circumstances had been right. Timing, and events, are political incalculables; all that can be spoken of with certainty is calibre. And here Roy scored.

Roy Mason was regarded very highly by Harold Wilson, who thought at one point that he might prove the one candidate upon whom people from centre Left, Right and the large centre area of the Parliamentary

Labour Party would be able to agree. Roy seemed to have all the qualifications: a trade unionist who had himself worked in the mines, he represented a mining constituency, had been educated at a grammar school, and came from a traditional Labour background in a traditionally Labour area in the North. His personality is overwhelming, confident to the point of cockiness. He is a trifle brusque and peremptory with those around him. His strong point is a great streak of common sense which amply substitutes for any lack of intellectual quality that his critics might complain of. This ability to see things as they are means that he has a great understanding of the world of business and the way in which Britain must earn her living.

This basic clear-sightedness and good sense, allied to his solid roots and his traditional support for policies that he regards as being correct, is one of the reasons he was sent to Northern Ireland – and why he was popular with the Northern Irish (though not necessarily with everyone in his own Party). His time there has, unfortunately, left him with a rather grim legacy: spending his life now with the Special Branch protecting him at all times.

Roy would be a 'natural' as Chairman of the Coal Board. Like Alf Robens, whom he greatly resembles, he is ideally suited to this post, and like Alf, too, he is a leader who never made it. Both had the potential, but their timing was wrong and their following small when needed, larger when the moment had passed.

On a higher note he leaves a legacy for which he may be remembered by many long after his contribution to Labour politics has gone into the political shadows. He is an expert and imaginative creator of tie designs including a rather splendid one for Chequers, and there are many more to his credit with Westminster and Whitehall associations.

Like Roy Mason, Eric Varley – also a potential Leadership candidate – comes from exactly the same sort of background: both come from mining areas and both have had experience of working down the mines. Jokingly, I often suggested that Eric's experience was of the tongs and coal-scuttle variety rather than faceworking, but this was untrue and unfair – Eric has direct experience of mining as well as a great knowledge of the industry.

He too has an instinctive understanding about the Party in the country, in industry and in Parliament; but he has had to learn the hard way. He has an extremely good mind and a very attractive character.

By nature he is kindly, quiet and reserved and, although he is now more gregarious and easier in manner, this was not always so. It took him some time to adjust to parliamentary life and metropolitan politics – to the requirements in terms of wining, dining and socializing that go with being a leading politician and a Minister.

Eric started off too in the post that can traditionally be the road to high office: that of a Parliamentary Private Secretary (if you are lucky) to the Prime Minister, or a Cabinet Minister or leading member of the Government, which can be equally rewarding. Peter Shore trod this path, as did John Tomlinson, Harold Davies, Charles Morris and Ken Marks. Eric Varley served as Harold Wilson's PPS for two years before being promoted, quickly rising then to senior office.

By 1974, Harold Wilson's third term, Eric was made Secretary of State for Energy, then became Secretary of State for Industry when Tony Benn was moved sideways to take over the Energy portfolio.

Eric is someone who has not yet achieved his full potential. The Party's present state makes any form of prediction about the political potential of individuals extremely difficult; what is certain is that Eric has not yet 'peaked'. The moment of truth will occur when Michael Foot finally decides to retire. If he does so before the next election it is unlikely that Eric will be ready. He may well be a candidate, but he would face stiff opposition.

Nevertheless, all the makings of a Leader are there. I am not one of those who believe that his quiet, aloof, slightly withdrawn manner means that he is unwilling to express an opinion – or even lacks one. I think his views are strong and definite, but that he prefers the silent approach to life – something which brings with it its own danger. Eric needs to be encouraged, not to say prodded; if this forceful support is available from family, friends and colleagues, he may go a long way. But if it is at any point withdrawn he could, like the Dormouse, very well retire into a corner and go to sleep.

What I am certain of is that he would make the best possible Deputy Leader of the Party to any of the Leadership candidates and provide the much needed balance that comes from a trades union background.

I first got to know John Silkin in 1963, when Dick Plummer's death left vacant the seat in Dulwich which John Silkin eventually won. At the time, John was not regarded as belonging to the 'acceptable' Left; rather he was, to most, just a rich solicitor whose representational stance

was difficult to identify, but who was clearly unlikely to follow in Dick
Plummer's political footsteps. Added to which, Dick's supporters in
Dulwich were very much hoping that the seat would go to Frank
Beswick (later to go to the House of Lords). John worked hard at
winning them over, and in the end secured first the nomination and
then the seat.

From then on, he adopted the position in which he was happiest: left
of centre. In his case, this meant, in those days, somewhere a step or two
to the left of the usual left of centre position held by Clem Attlee – a
position which would probably be regarded as reactionary Right by
today's left-wingers.

John Silkin is a charming, personable, likeable man with a kindly
and avuncular manner; he is talented, witty and an effective speaker
both on a platform and in Parliament. He is fairly expert in the troubled
waters of inter-Party politics, understands the mechanics of running the
Party, and was a good Chief Whip. As Chief Whip he gained a reputation for being rather soft, although he was in many ways much
tougher than his successor Bob Mellish, who had the reputation of being
tough but who could, in fact, be extremely soft.

When Chief Whip, John worked closely with Dick Crossman, who
was then Leader of the House. They did much innovative work, especially in inaugurating those committees that involved Members with
the work of the House. This evolved from an idea of Harold Wilson's,
as a means of managing a very large parliamentary majority – something almost forgotten in the age in which we now live. (Macmillan's
majority in 1959 was 106, and in 1966 Harold Wilson's was 96.)

Inevitably, such a large parliamentary majority led to restlessness.
Few of those who enter Parliament with high hopes and aspirations
want to become mere 'Lobby fodder', there simply to vote government
legislation through. This restlessness and frustration increased to the
point where many of them became extremely difficult and independent,
often actually obstructing legislation. The House of Lords Reform Bill,
something that would have been eminently desirable in the late 1960s,
was held up in this way. There were difficulties, too, on other issues,
such as the boundary changes, immigration, and on incomes policy and
economic policy generally.

One of the devices which Dick and John brought into play in the
House to keep Members occupied was a very full use of Select Committees, and the introduction of new ones. The present much-enlarged

system owes a great deal to their action during that period.

By the time an attempt was made to see if the Industrial Relations Bill could be pushed through Parliament towards the end of that Government, John Silkin had been moved to a different job. There were those who felt that MPs had enjoyed too much liberty during the Crossman–Silkin years, and that consequently this Bill, like others, would never go through; even though Bob Mellish, as the new tough Chief Whip, took over, still the legislation was not passed. In my view, the Crossman–Silkin axis, if retained, might well have proved effective.

For John Silkin, this was a key period. He learned much about the standing of the Party in the country via MPs aware at first-hand through their constituency work of reactions to Government policy. He also received a training invaluable to anyone who wishes to be Leader of his Party. The post of Chief Whip (also held by Edward Heath) is un-equalled as a method of learning about both the running of Parliament and the running of one's own Party in Parliament. (Francis Pym may well prove another beneficiary of this training-ground.) Much of the burden of being simultaneously Prime Minister and Leader of the Party is removed if you are completely at home with the mechanics of Parliament and Party alike.

Why has John Silkin not achieved higher things? There seem to me to be two reasons, the most obvious being that he is, quite simply, still seen to appear too lightweight. Despite the fact that he was Minister of Agriculture during Common Market negotiations in the late 1970s, the jobs he has held have not been of the kind to give great weight to a parliamentary figure. Apart from Agriculture and the post of Chief Whip, he has held only one other that could be so called: Minister of State for Housing in the Environment Department.

The second, or 'x', factor, is that there is an erratic streak in him – a streak difficult to identify or isolate. His political reactions are sometimes too dramatic and overdrawn, and over-reaction is something no one who aspires to be Head of his Party can afford.

But I am reluctant to write him off in this role, however, fearing that the prophecy of an Indian fortune-teller might well prove correct. When John was once on a visit to India some years ago, he was accosted by a seer who told him that he would be the leader of his people. John with his great good humour tells this story as a joke, but, as a great believer in astrology and clairvoyance, I wonder.

*   *   *

The Ministers whose performance in the last Labour Government (under James Callaghan) rated much higher than expected were Albert Booth and Stanley Orme. The latter, incidentally, from the Left of the Party, gradually moved to a left-of-centre position, particularly after his years in Northern Ireland.

Although it seems unlikely that either Albert Booth (whose name rather militated against him) or Stanley Orme will reach higher office in any future Labour Government than they have already held, this cannot be said of certain other members of the Front Bench – should the Labour Party as we know it survive.

I would pick out the following: David Ennals, of course, for his proven ability and centre stance; John Smith, who did distinguished service as Secretary of State for Trade; Neil Kinnock, now a leading member of the National Executive Committee, notable for charisma, intelligence, ability as a communicator and left-of-centre appeal; Stanley Clinton-Davies, a lawyer, who has evinced first-class administrative ability, and now a capacity to deal not only with domestic but – more recently – with overseas policy: his appearance as a Party spokesman on the Falklands crisis has been impressive. Then there are other worthy and outstanding men, such as Christopher Price, Frank Field, Geoffrey Robinson, Jack Straw, Stuart Holland, John Golding, Norman Buchan, Philip Whitehead, Andrew Faulds, Charles and Alfred Morris, Austin Mitchell and Michael Meacher, to name just a few of them.

However, the person who has for me perhaps shone most in Opposition, after proving himself extremely able in Government, is Gerald Kaufman. He has what most of the others (with the exception perhaps of Neil Kinnock) lack: a forceful and persuasive House of Commons manner. This shows in his debating skill and his ability to present a powerful case.

The art of debate, and of both putting forward and sustaining a reasoned argument on some particular point, is something that has fallen into disuse over the last ten years. Gerald has had the good political training that comes from fighting unwinnable seats (including that of Harold Macmillan), and has shown repeatedly in the House of Commons that he was well able to rally his own side in debate. This is a valuable talent: such a person serves at once as a standard-bearer and a symbol of strength to his Party. He is also an extremely impressive performer on television.

Gerald is yet another of a number of distinguished MPs and Ministers who in turn acted as Harold Wilson's Parliamentary Private Secretary in Number 10. Among them, as I have said, were Peter Shore and Eric Varley, John Tomlinson, Ken Marks, Charles Morris and Frank Judd, and in earlier years, Ernie Fernyhough, Harold Davies, Bill Hamling and the lovely Joe Slater, who had previously served as PPS to Hugh Gaitskell.

Gerald came to Number 10 in the first instance as Political Press Secretary to the Prime Minister (when that was a separate post to that of Downing Street Press Officer). To join us, he gave up his job as Political Correspondent of the *New Statesman*; prior to that he had spent many years working for the *Daily Mirror*.

This experience, along with his spell in Downing Street from 1965 to 1970, had given him a high degree of knowledge and insight into the workings of government, and the Prime Minister's office in particular; equally importantly, he had learned a very great deal about the work of an ordinary Member of Parliament. It must never be forgotten that Prime Ministers are also constituency MPs, and must give a high priority to this part of their duties.

Gerald had a training unique and special and he took full advantage of it, studiously learning all he could about all three roles. When Gerald was appointed a Minister in 1974, he was well equipped and, without too much difficulty, quickly adapted to the life and work of a Minister. After the defeat of 1979 he put this knowledge to good use by writing an amusing and informative book about a Minister's life.

It seems virtually certain that in any future Labour Government he will be one of the most successful senior members.

Nothing can rival the portrait of Tony Crosland that emerges from his wife's memoir of him; nevertheless, it would be quite wrong of me to talk about leading Labour figures during the Wilson years without mentioning Tony. His intellectual quality was, of course, his most striking attribute, but it was combined with a gift possessed by few Labour politicians: the ability to talk to those less intellectually endowed without appearing condescending.

A story told to me by Bill Blyton (now Lord Blyton) bears this out. Bill, a former MP for Blythe, a miner from a mining community, a shrewd and intelligent man but with little formal education, had often sought Tony's advice on the more intricate aspects of the Party's financial and economic policies because, as Bill remarked, he and his friends felt perfectly comfortable with this middle-class Oxford-educated politician who was known for the brilliance of his intellect.

For those who were his intellectual equals, this image of Tony as teacher and adviser to socialist colleagues hardly rang true – yet it was one for which he was admired by many in the House who knew him well. It was, moreover, in direct contradiction to one of the accusations most often levelled against him, as against other Gaitskellites: he was, it was said, too often condescending and arrogant towards those who had not had his advantages.

Tony was a democratic socialist in the best sense of the word; moreover he was at ease with his Party, unlike many of his friends on the Right. Roy Jenkins never felt really at home with his Party nor did he have, as Tony had, goodwill and warm affection either for its rank and file or its officials.

Tony was a right-wing moderate able to see the other's point of view, strong and firm on unpopular policies which he felt to be right. I can recall him arguing very strongly and persuasively in favour of higher taxation to pay for the social wage which everyone increasingly accepted as of right, as their expectations rose. Crosland made a lengthy speech one summer at Chequers, arguing this case passionately at a Socialist International conference, and greatly impressing his colleagues. He was to repeat it often in the years that followed. Where other Labour politicians would retreat in the face of electoral unpopularity, on this Tony stood firm, believing rightly or wrongly that if the case were presented honestly and straightforwardly to the electorate, the electorate would respond equally fairly.

These qualities of intellectual brilliance combined with courage would, I believe, have made Tony Crosland a first-class Chancellor of the Exchequer. Indeed, he was one of the two candidates for that post – the other was Shirley Williams – most in Harold Wilson's mind before his retirement in 1976.

In my view, as Foreign Secretary Tony was less able to show his true worth; the Foreign Office is a considerable strain with its enormous workload, the wide spectrum of issues involved, the number of people to be seen, visits to be made, the continuous moving around, and the cruel demands it makes on personal lives. I am sure Tony enjoyed the Foreign Office. I am equally sure that he would have found the Treasury both more challenging and more rewarding, and less intrusive. Emotionally and temperamentally he was more suited to it; it would have encouraged and enabled him to develop his whole political 'personality', including those qualities that cause many to believe him a lost Leader of the Party.

Could he have made it? In any election for the Leadership after 1976, he would have done extremely well. He might also have failed to put himself to this test.

He, I think, rather than Roy Jenkins, was the true heir of Hugh Gaitskell. In retrospect, it was a pity Tony was not moved to the Treasury in the reshuffle of 1975. From there he might have found the necessary ambition to press his own claims.

Leading Labour Personalities: Women

Harold Wilson, in my view, and indeed in the view of many women in Parliament, was the one post-war Prime Minister who did most to encourage women and bring them into government. Even so, the record is slight. Today there should be far more women in Parliament as a whole and an identifiable number of outstanding women serving in government. In fact the numbers on both counts change little, and Margaret Thatcher has made no effort even to match what Harold Wilson did.

He himself never claims that he consciously brought women on. When questioned he merely states that he went for the best people. That in itself says a great deal about him. Many men – and most leading male politicians – do not feel so unfettered by sexist prejudice.

Men, of course, in general are not compatible with intelligent women. The majority of women politicians are intelligent. It takes a special sort of man to like the company of intelligent women and a very special sort of male politician to like the company of intelligent female politicians.

Leo Abse, of course, would be able to explain this away in terms of breast-fed or bottle-reared male politicians as babies and their relationships with their mothers. If life were only that simple a national campaign launched by the COI and a Government Health Warning against baby milk powders would solve humanity's problems overnight. World resources might remain the same and limited, but human nature would be so transformed that all problems would be benignly and intelligently resolved.

In the last twenty years there have been some – though few in number

– outstanding women in the Labour Party. Of these, Barbara Castle is, to me, pre-eminent.

I should explain that I am talking here of those who are household names. There have been many talented and capable women in the mould of Eirene White and Joyce Butler, respected and popular within the Party but not national figures – former women MPs like Alice Bacon, Elaine Burton, the colourful and controversial Bessie Braddock who made Liverpool her own, today's Joan Lestor, Ann Taylor, Jo Richardson and Betty Boothroyd. The two latter started their careers as secretaries to Labour MPs – Betty for Harry Walston and Geoffrey de Freitas, Jo for Ian Mikardo.

The outstanding women have all served on the National Executive Committee of the Party. Three achieved this via the Women's Section of the NEC, for which union support is necessary. One of the few in Labour's history to be elected to the Constituency Party Section of the NEC in the same way as Harold Wilson, Denis Healey, Jim Callaghan and Michael Foot, was Barbara Castle. In other words, she competed on equal terms with her male colleagues.

As a Cabinet Minister she has also been, measure for measure, the equal of those same colleagues. She was a brilliant administrator: as a Minister, or Head of Department, she has not only understood the workings of that Department (no mean feat in itself!), but been able to cope with departmental problems as well as her own departmental work. Straightforward as this may sound, it is often quite the reverse. A Member of Parliament can be a superb politician but prove to be a bad Minister, rather in the way a journalist can be a brilliant writer but a bad editor. Barbara was both able politician and first-class Minister.

As a person she is friendly, easy to get on with and, as they say where she comes from in the North, has 'no side to her'. Her flaming red hair may represent her left-wing views; the way it is styled represents another aspect of Barbara: her essential femininity.

She likes pretty clothes and has an eye for fashion. Her nails are always polished, her hair beautifully done. A lot of women MPs are well turned out, but in a classic dateless style; Barbara adds fashion details: the frilly blouse, large floppy bow and the right contemporary accessories.

Barbara's clothes were also responsible for the 'dressing' of one of the chairs in the Cabinet Room in Number 10. When we were there in the early 1960s, none of the old furniture had been repaired or refurbished – let alone replaced. The legs of many of the chairs round the Cabinet Table were time-worn, with roughened surfaces or splinters that laddered Barbara's stockings. When she emerged at the end of a Cabinet meeting with yet another ladder, which she either had to repair with the emergency tactic of nail polish or suffer all day, she made a fuss. Either, she said, she ought to have a special 'stocking allowance' – or something should be done about the chairs. By the time we left government, she had won. The Civil Service, with the whole-hearted support of the Prime Minister, had agreed that to do nothing would amount to sex discrimination. Accordingly, one chair was clothed with frilly little Victorian drawers, to save Barbara's most un-Victorian legs from splinters.

Despite their totally different temperaments, Harold Wilson and Barbara have always enjoyed an extremely good relationship. Part of this, undoubtedly, is due to their similar beginnings: both come from the North of England, both went to Oxford, both have first-class academic minds that make them intellectual equals, both entered Parliament at roughly the same time, both were left of centre in the Party – though Barbara would certainly regard herself as still to the left.

At one point their careers flowed jointly. When Harold became first Overseas Secretary and later President of the Board of Trade, Barbara was his Parliamentary Private Secretary for a time – Harold inherited her from Stafford Cripps. This speaks much for them both: to have a woman PPS in that early post-war Government was an innovation.

Harold Wilson likes women, their approach to policy and their company. Barbara has always been very much a woman; in those days she was an extremely attractive young woman with her petite figure, beautiful pink and white complexion, and gorgeous auburn hair. She looked dainty and feminine – but she had this razor-sharp mind and powerful personality – a colourful person thrown into sharp relief by Harold Wilson himself. In those days he was, by his own admission, 'a bit of a pudding', with his addiction to detail, facts, figures – a character whose greyish tones contrasted sharply with Barbara's brilliant hues.

Both of them enjoyed a joke. Apart from the general banter that was part of their relationship, I remember one incident in particular. This concerned Barbara's spaniel, bought in the early 1960s at the time of the great disarmament campaign and christened 'Aldermaston' after the marches.

She took this beguiling little puppy with her when she and Harold were travelling by rail together to a political rally. She was not, however, watching Aldermaston as carefully as she might have been because, unknown to Barbara, the puppy answered a call of nature immediately outside the compartment door. When Harold, who decided that he wanted a breath of fresh air, got up and left the compartment in his turn, he slipped and skidded down the corridor. Barbara's only comment was, 'Aldermaston's the only living creature who's put the skids under Harold Wilson' – a remark which removed what annoyance he might have felt.

All in all, Barbara's friendship with Harold Wilson, like their political relationship, dates back further than that between most leading political figures. In those early, flexible days they got to know each other's strong and weak points, methods of working, motivations; something that stood them in good stead for the rest of their working lives.

Perhaps I should say here that I never saw that famous temper of Barbara's exercised against Harold or anyone else; when she got angry, as she quite often did, it was because of some political argument and never on a personal basis. The result was that, whatever the differences between them, she was able to maintain friendly relations with almost all those with whom she came in contact. But because she was a woman, this emotional expression of her feelings was invariably described as 'temper' or a 'tantrum'. Harold Wilson's phrase was much milder: 'Barbara was giving me stick again,' he would say.

With Jim Callaghan, Barbara's relationship followed a declining curve – a curve that ended in a sudden abrupt drop. It is difficult now to remember that Jim was once considerably to the left of centre in the Party, but when Jim, Harold and Barbara were all young this was at times indeed so. Barbara knew Jim well and, although she never actually worked with him in a Department or on some joint project, they got on well without being especially close. She gave the impression of understanding him or, as she put it, she could 'see him coming'. This facility served her in good stead because her working relationship with Jim Callaghan has been more a history of debate than (as with Harold Wilson) co-operation: she was never part of his Treasury team or involved in Home Office or foreign affairs when he was Home or Foreign Secretary. Only on the National Executive Committee did they serve together.

But argument is one thing, sabotage another. What James Callaghan did to 'In Place of Strife' not only ultimately damaged the Labour Party, it did irreparable harm to his relationship with Barbara – for which Barbara, later, was to suffer.

Hostility against the industrial relations proposals contained in the Bill was inevitable. Barbara had been prepared to face the wrath of the trades unions, the cries of outrage from her own left-wing colleagues. She believed strongly in what she was doing and, as with any measure that ran counter to the political opinions and interests of one section of the Party, would have been surprised at a meek acceptance. Jim's orchestration of the opposition, his overt support for it culminating in a breach of that fundamental tenet of constitutional faith, collective responsibility – this was something quite different, about which she felt very strongly indeed. This was to be a source of bitterness between them from 1969 onwards.

Nor did Jim forget. Harold, as Prime Minister, was almost above danger; Barbara was not. When Jim succeeded after Harold's resignation, his first act as Prime Minister was to sack Barbara, who found herself in the ironical position of being asked to make way for a younger person by a man who had just done the reverse – *succeeded* a younger man. Barbara herself was at the same age – sixty-seven – as Michael Foot when he later became Leader of the Party; and she was acknowledged by all to be a highly competent Minister.

A point in her career that contrasts with those of many other women in politics is that only one of her senior posts was specifically 'female'. As Harold Wilson has often joked, women rarely make it to the top jobs because the Home Office lives in the past, the Treasury contains too many Mandarins, and the Foreign Office has been too greatly influenced by Lawrence of Arabia and the years the officials have spent amongst the Arabs. Certain Ministries – Consumer Affairs, Education and Science, and the Social Services – are tacitly acknowledged to be the province of the statutory woman in Cabinet. Barbara's first job, Overseas Development, was none of these latter, and her second (she became Minister of Transport in 1965) is widely regarded as an essentially male job – as was her third, Secretary of State for Employment.

As Transport Minister, Barbara overcame the seeming handicap of being a non-driver by claiming that it was actually an advantage: she had no prejudices or hang-ups, she declared, from either driver's or pedestrian's point of view. As a non-driver she was also able to put over great conviction in her view of public transport. Her brilliant handling of this job was helped by her flair for public relations: she got transport into the news, she fought hard for it, she presented it well in Cabinet.

Her third job during those first two Governments was the spectacularly difficult one of Employment – described by her predecessor, Ray Gunter, as a 'bed of nails'. In any Government, this is not only a difficult but a sensitive post, involving as it does the Government's relationship with the working population as a whole, inclusive of its most powerful elements in the shape of the trades unions. Precisely how testing this post can be has been shown even more forcibly in the past few years. Barbara is the only woman to have held this extremely taxing Ministry; it can be seen as yet another proof of her equality in all senses with her male colleagues.

To me, amongst the women Judith Hart is the great enigma. There is something unapproachable, almost mysterious, about her. Over her career, too, hangs a question mark: this talented, ambitious woman, with a long record as a leading figure in the Labour movement, who has served on the National Executive Committee, has never yet held a senior Government job such as the Secretaryship of State for Home Affairs, Trade, Environment, or others at that level. Only once, as Minister for Overseas Development, has she attained Cabinet rank.

In her early political life Judith was, of course, in competition with Barbara Castle; later she was overshadowed by Shirley Williams. The DBE awarded to her by Jim Callaghan in his outgoing Honours List was seen by many as his way of compensating her for this lack of higher office.

Judith herself has always said that she got on extremely well with Jim Callaghan – better, in fact, than she did with Harold Wilson, although it was Harold who made her early career possible by first making her Minister for Overseas Development, then giving her a Foreign Office appointment on the Commonwealth side. Later on, during the 1975 re-shuffle, he tried to persuade her to become Minister for Transport; but because this was not at that time a Cabinet job, she refused to accept it. Instead she resigned from Harold Wilson's Government; it was left to Jim Callaghan to bring her in again later, for her second 'shift' as Minister for Overseas Development – this time as a Member of the Cabinet.

Judith has always been unequivocally to the left of the Party. Despite her cool and businesslike exterior (it is easy to imagine Judith as managing director of a large company, or head of a nationalized industry), when she feels strongly on a political issue she becomes, on a public platform, strident, aggressive and often more extreme in her views. Above all, she seems to have a bitter edge to her politics that is totally absent in the other ladies.

Judith is very feminine, with a penchant for elegant clothes that are fashionable as well as being smart; they are well chosen and often, like the accessories, expensive. Her colour sense is good and her jewellery special.

I saw Judith most frequently in the late 1960s; she belonged to a small group who at that time were pressing the Prime Minister hard to take some positive action on the devaluation question. Judith was the link between this group and Number 10, and as the Prime Minister's Political Secretary I was responsible for transmitting to him many of the views she put forward on behalf of her similarly minded colleagues. So we saw a good deal of each other.

Her relationship with Harold Wilson, which had become closer during that period, was very understandably somewhat marred by a security muddle that happened during the 1970s. Judith herself believed – at first quite wrongly – that it was the reason she was not given a Cabinet appointment at the beginning of the 1974 Government.

This episode occurred through a truly extraordinary coincidence. Judith Hart, so the story ran, was a possible security risk because she had once been a member of the Communist Party and had, in addition, travelled frequently to Moscow and Eastern Europe. Only when the matter was pursued further did it transpire that Security had got hold of the wrong Judith Hart – the other Judith Hart was a lady who not only had the same name but whose career had been similar. More than that, the 'wrong' Mrs Hart was married to a man who bore the same Christian name as Judith's own husband!

Despite the depth of Judith's left-wing convictions and the burning convictions of her political utterances and writings, she lacks the common touch. Her public persona is characterized by a certain aloofness. Nevertheless, she is a very effective platform speaker, though in the House of Commons she is much less impressive. Yet she is a substantial figure and has made her own very formidable contribution to the role of women in politics, and in particular to Labour politics today.

The last of the trio of women who were Labour's greatest female stars in the 1960s and 1970s is Shirley Williams, whose star is temporarily in eclipse. Shirley is someone who, in addition to her other undoubted gifts, is endowed with a quality that few male and even fewer female politicians possess. It is an ability to project an idealized version of herself, a myth in which all those around her believe gladly and whole-heartedly.

Like all myths, it fits where it touches. Shirley *is* extraordinarily competent; Harold Wilson viewed her as a potential Chancellor of the Exchequer (the job he eventually wanted her to hold): he felt that her intellectual qualities, combined with the strong common sense that is an element of her character, would bring a new dimension – that of the reality of everyday living – into what is usually a detached, almost arid, area of government.

But so far, Shirley Williams has not performed in a job that would, usually, go automatically to a male member of the Cabinet; she has only held the 'female' posts of Consumer Affairs and Education and Science.

This, combined with her rumpled-schoolgirl air, gives the impression – underlined by her warmth of manner – that she has a nature both feminine and soft. Beside her informality and casualness, the clothes put on apparently at random and the hair that appears innocent of any acquaintance with brush or comb, the 'feminine' attention to grooming and detail of Barbara Castle – and for that matter, Margaret Thatcher – appears businesslike, cold, precise, and with a certain kind of hard-edged ferocity. (My own belief is that the reverse is true: both Barbara Castle and Margaret Thatcher are extremely feminine women under a tough exterior.)

Many men find Shirley irresistible. To some, her very untidiness seems a challenge. They realize, correctly, that her attitude to life is almost totally cerebral, they listen to that soft, seductive voice – and they feel that if only they got the chance, they could introduce her to a whole new world.

She is much better looking than in her photographs; as a young girl she was beautiful enough to have been considered for the lead role in *National Velvet* – it was only when Shirley (Catlin, as she was then) could not take it that the part went to Elizabeth Taylor. I remember Dick Crossman rushing into Number 10 once, to say that he'd had the most fantastic journey back from Bristol, mesmerized, as he put it, by this marvellous woman with a fabulous sexy voice. 'Who was it?' we all asked; and when he replied 'Shirley Williams', there was general amazement – we in the office had seen Shirley in many roles before but never that of fascinator. But as the 1970s wore on it turned out to be quite a common phenomenon.

This power of attracting, together with her general niceness – it is not, I think, going too far to describe Shirley's nature as 'lovable' – makes it easy to see why she has an enormous following. People become absolutely devoted to her – rather in the way boys or girls at school become devoted to the Captain of the first xi. Add to this her charisma, the mesmeric aura that surrounds her, and you have this quality that compels belief – the 'myth' factor. I am sure she knows she has it – though perhaps not why – but I do not think she exploits it. Essentially she is a private person, with an instinctive aversion to being taken over either by a cause or a machine.

In every other way she is Prime Ministerial timber, but unless she can resolve that conflict sufficiently to allow herself to become part of a collective exercise she lacks the strength of a Margaret Thatcher to carry the office on her own. She is strong, she has a certain steeliness, but she lacks that absolute, total dedication that makes other politicians allow the whole of their lives to be absorbed. I do not think Shirley would sacrifice all of hers – unless she had a guarantee that in the end she would make it. She would not allow herself to be packaged in the sense that Margaret Thatcher was packaged – which would, in turn, allow a Kennedy-style exploitation of her 'myth' quality.

As it is, while Margaret Thatcher is saying figuratively 'I am what I am, and you take me or leave me', Shirley is ... whatever you have decided in your own mind you want her to be. A myth, especially to those around the ikon, is both enjoyable and compulsive, but it does not always take its subject further forward. And that is Shirley's problem.

Of the present lady Members on the Labour Benches, a number are outstanding: Joan Lestor, Betty Boothroyd, Ann Taylor, Shirley Summerskill and Gwynneth Dunwoody.

Gwynneth is particularly notable because of her recent great success within the Party, her election to the National Executive Committee. She is a clever, able and forceful woman, and an articulate and doughty fighter – unsurprisingly, in view of her parentage. She is the daughter of the late Morgan Phillips, a former General Secretary of the Party and one of the cleverest Labour politicians of the 1940s and 1950s, who carved a career as distinguished in international politics as in those of the United Kingdom; and whose interpretation of the role of General Secretary made this post as key and essential to Party politics as that of the Leader himself and his senior colleagues. Morgan Phillips spoke for the Party with a degree of authority that has never been reached by any General Secretary since.

Gwynneth is an obvious 'chip off the old block': she inherits her father's political leanings and his expertise, adding to these the advantage of a Cambridge education and the experience of representing Britain in the European Parliament (before the days of elected members). Her election to the National Executive Committee is another facet of experience that will prove invaluable to her in the years ahead.

Colourful, earthy, with a direct and forceful manner of speaking, she has a strong streak of common sense inherited from her mother (now Lady Phillips, Lord Lieutenant of London). Gwynneth is young enough to be central to the Party in the future and, I anticipate, a senior member of any future Labour Government.

TWENTY-EIGHT

Changes in Parliamentary Techniques

Sitting in the Strangers' Gallery or listening to broadcasts of 'Today in Parliament', it is sometimes difficult to imagine how polite – there is no other word – was parliamentary debate in the immediate post-war years.

Although the exchanges were often much sharper, and certainly much funnier and wittier, than today, there was no underlying malice or ill-will. There was healthy, robust cut and thrust, telling blows were given and received, but the whole level was higher and there was a basic respect for the views of an opponent, whoever he might be, as from one professional to another. Along with this went a respect for and an understanding of the traditions of the House, and a desire to ensure that these should be preserved and maintained. In this atmosphere, people could argue fiercely opposed views within the Chamber, yet form friendships outside it.

But during the 1960s – and to a greater degree the 1970s – the whole climate of parliamentary debate began to deteriorate. Personal confrontation, and the denigration of the opposing Party, its members and its policies, became the order of the day.

Usually, a change in attitude can be traced to the top of whatever pyramid – whether that of organization, office or family – is concerned. In Parliament, a confrontation – not to say a ding-dong battle – was gradually building up between Edward Heath and Harold Wilson. It was often referred to as a conflict similar to that fought in the previous century by Disraeli and Gladstone; it was, in any event, quite different in tone and essence from the exchanges between Harold Macmillan and Harold Wilson, which were relished by both.

At the same time as these changes were occurring inside Parliament, the social climate throughout the country was also altering. The general liberalization of thinking and customs, the upsurge of rebellious independence in young people, produced an attitude at once more cynical and less deferential towards both Government and Parliament. When two leading parliamentary figures were seen to be, figuratively speaking, at each other's throats, people's suspicions were confirmed and the general level of public respect for parliamentarians dropped.

Some of the generally lowered prestige of Parliament is undoubtedly due to those social changes: a cross-section of all Members in the House today reveals quite a different mix to those of pre- or immediately post-war years. In the 1940s and 1950s, well-off businessmen, gentlemen of private means, professional men (in particular lawyers) and Labour intellectuals from comfortable backgrounds were in the majority, with a strong minority of trades unionists and others – miners representing mining constituencies, for example; common to almost all of them was that respect for their particular tradition which was in itself a discipline that made for more efficiency in the working of the organization concerned, and a belief that if the outward trappings of respect were abandoned the institution itself would break down. This philosophy is today seen most obviously in the almost mystic regard in which the British monarchy is held, and in the whole effectiveness of uniforms generally; politically, the Americans have brought to a fine art the principle that no matter what the politics of the person addressed, the office they hold must be respected.

By the time of the first 1974 election, then, both sides were sitting down in their respective headquarters to discuss how to avoid putting over the image of constant confrontation between Heath and Wilson, which was what the media seemed determined to project.

One of the reasons for the undoubted Wilson/Heath hostility was, strangely enough, their similarity. Both were lower-middle class; boys who had been to grammar schools and achieved their position by dint of native intelligence and sheer hard work rather than through money or influence; each has strongly held beliefs, but in direct opposition to the other.

A further exacerbation was that Edward Heath was, in terms of image, the Tory Party's answer to Harold Wilson: Harold Wilson, who had been so enormously successful with the electorate immediately he took over, was a man with whom they could identify, a man of the 1960s who represented technological and social change, a man whose career could serve as an example to their sons. The Tory Party, conscious of the sociological changes that were taking place and the emergence of the new mass of the lower-middle class, felt that they should fight Labour on their own ground. Hence Heath.

In my view, this was a profound mistake. I have always thought that one of the most difficult Prime Ministers to fight was Sir Alec Douglas-Home. He was only narrowly defeated in the 1964 campaign – a campaign in which he was extremely successful simply because he was himself: he represents a strain in Conservative politics with which they are naturally at home. He is an aristocrat, with the best of the aristocratic qualities: he is completely natural, at home with anyone of any class, background or occupation. Because he does not have to 'put on an act', he never has to be trained, schooled, directed or briefed; and because he is an extremely nice man, this quality of being himself is doubly effective.

But once Sir Alec, a much under-estimated holder of the office of Leader of the Conservative Party during the difficult years after Harold Macmillan's resignation, lost the 1964 election, the knives were out. They allowed themselves to be influenced by various jibes in the media and from Harold Wilson that having a 14th Earl to lead the Conservative Party was antiquated and fuddy-duddy and that they should modernize not only their Leader but the process by which they chose one. This meant election, rather than the selection which – to the Conservatives – is much more natural. The result was that they came up with a man who was almost a blueprint of Harold Wilson, but who was out of context because the Party he was leading had *not* changed.

One aspect of the remoulding of the Prime Ministerial role inaugurated by Harold Macmillan was the introduction of Prime Minister's Question Time – a quarter of an hour set aside twice a week at 3.15, at the end of Question Time, for the Prime Minister himself to answer questions. It was yet another line underscoring the fact that the Prime Minister, as Macmillan saw it, was not only the head but the focus of Government.

Initially, the questions put to the Prime Minister were confined to specific subjects and were those to which only he could give an answer. From his point of view, this system had a further recommendation: all the questions for the Prime Minister were brought together during these fifteen-minute periods rather than being taken piecemeal throughout the daily Question Times Sessions. This meant, in turn, that if necessary the Prime Minister could confine his appearances in the House to Tuesdays and Thursdays, thus allowing him more time for the growing volume of work at Number 10.

But gradually this admirable system changed, and the work of the Private Secretary at Number 10 responsible for making sure that the Prime Minister was fully briefed for his twice-weekly sessions became infinitely more complicated. From 1974 onwards, questions began to be used not as a means of eliciting information but as devices for putting the Prime Minister 'on the spot' on issues that he might find awkward to discuss, and for scoring points off him on some subject on which he had not been forewarned and therefore briefed.

This change did not, of course, happen overnight. Gradually questions changed from the straightforward to the trap. Where once Harold Macmillan would have been asked: 'What is the Prime Minister going to do about the unemployment situation in West Yorkshire?', now the question put down for Margaret Thatcher is 'Will the Prime Minister visit Leeds when she is in my area in the month of March?' with the real dynamite in the follow-up question; for example, 'In view of the fact that she is not coming, can I ask whether she has plans to counter the threat posed to engineering workers in my constituency by the import of Japanese motorcycles?' In the ordinary course of events, a question like this that relates to employment or industry would be transferred to the responsible Minister: now it can creep in on the coat-tails of an unrelated and seemingly harmless query.

From a Prime Minister's point of view, all this makes for nervous work. First, there is the increased and infinitely more complicated work for the briefing secretary or secretaries. In the 1964–70 Governments, an extraordinarily efficient cross-referencing system was developed at Number 10 under the then Private Secretary Peter Le Cheminant (who went on to a distinguished career at the Home Office). He was followed by equally expert successors, who built on his work so that now there is a complete and comprehensive record stretching back over the years on what must be just about every subject under the political sun.

The Private Secretary responsible for briefing must also take note of the parliamentarian who is asking the question. Many MPs have special interests, others have what can best be described as special obsessions; whatever they may be – British Honduras, the Thames flood barrier or security – be sure that they will be dragged into the supplementary question.

Here there are two choices open to the Prime Minister. She (or he) can say 'I need notice of that question,' or she can say 'I have no plans to visit Leeds.' In the latter case her questioner will then say, 'But is the Prime Minister aware that . . .' in his supplementary; in the former, she may be laying herself open to a danger of another kind. 'Prime Minister Refuses to Comment on Tragic Error' is the sort of headline she doesn't want screaming out of the next morning's papers. So she has to make an instantaneous judgement as to whether it is worth while slapping her questioner down – or whether she should respond in order to put across some point that the national press, and perhaps television, will pick up.

All in all, the two fifteen-minute periods between 3.15 p.m. and 3.30 p.m. every Tuesday and Thursday, when the House is sitting, are dreaded by most Prime Ministers. The cut and thrust of debate is one thing; being responsible for the sole handling of some question to which the 'wrong' answer may produce embarrassment, humiliation, triumph for the Opposition or a major internal Party row, or a field day for the press, is enough to strain the nerves of the coolest performer.

Harold Macmillan himself confessed that he used to feel physically sick before Prime Minister's Question Time; and towards the end of his last term of office Harold Wilson confessed to steadying his nerves with a small glass of brandy. As for Margaret Thatcher, it is impossible to judge from her demeanour whether she suffers from this political version of stage fright. Here, at least, she is the Iron Lady.

TWENTY-NINE

The Civil Service and the Prime Minister's Department

Writing at the end of the Labour Governments of 1964–70, I said that whatever failings there had been during that period could largely be attributed to defeats of the Government on two separate fronts. The first was in the continuing battle against the Civil Service, the second was the failure to achieve a workable prices and incomes policy agreed with the trades union movement.

In 1976, when Harold Wilson resigned, the situation was entirely different. A voluntary prices and incomes policy was well on the way to being hammered out between the Government which James Callaghan had inherited and the trades union movement. Since his defeat in 1979, however, the problem has returned and the need for a solution is even more acute after the Thatcher years, for Labour, than it was after the defeat of Heath in 1974. As for the civil servants, there had been a sea change for them as much as for the Labour Ministers who took over in 1974. However, I believe that the battle to establish the precedence of the elected Government over a non-elected Civil Service has still to be resolved.

It is a problem from which all Governments and all Prime Ministers seem to retreat nervously, with the result that real power still remains with the civil servants who sit permanently in Whitehall rather than with the politicians who come and go with elections.

There are, of course, exceptions to this rule. Many distinguished Ministers have taken on the Civil Service at its own game and won; as for the Civil Service itself, since 1970 it has received far more attention than ever it had in the preceding twenty or thirty years. There have been investigation, scrutiny and enquiries, not only by politicians but by the media and by academics, all in search of the solution as to how you can marry the unelected with the elected.

Today, too, the electorate in general is far better educated and informed about the Civil Service than it ever was before. To a great extent, this new knowledge is due to the attention focused on the Civil Service by the media – not only in serious and informative articles but also via the vehicle of comedy. *Yes Minister*, on which many who have experienced the Civil Service at first hand, including myself, have had the pleasure of giving advice, shone the spotlight on its senior echelons in an extraordinarily accurate though amusing fashion.

Today, therefore, most people can differentiate between the mass of civil servants who administer the various government departments throughout the country, and the highly qualified men and women who act in a special capacity in Whitehall. They are aware that the power lies in the hands of a small group known as the Administrative Class, headed by Permanent Secretaries and their deputies – the so-called Mandarins.

Despite the scrutiny to which it has been subjected over the last ten years, the Civil Service has changed little either in the way it organizes itself, or in the way it selects those who will staff the administrative grades. These, the powerful élite, still come mainly from the same backgrounds – the public schools and Oxbridge, from the South of England rather than the North.

Nor have the greater proportion of reforms recommended by the Fulton Inquiry of 1969 yet been carried out. The one major change that did come about – the removal of the Civil Service from the aegis of the Treasury to a separate independent existence in its own Department responsible for itself – has been reversed. Control over the Service has passed back to the Treasury, the most powerful Department in Whitehall with the exception of the Foreign Office.

Few would suggest that the Civil Service is neutral. The questions posed by the Fulton Inquiry ten years ago still remain. When Labour took over in 1964 I remarked then (and again in 1970) that the Civil Service administrative grades were in the main pro-Conservative.

I believe I was wrong for the right reasons. How could they be anything else? They came from backgrounds and families which were usually Conservative, they moved in the circles where Conservative politicians moved and Conservative politics were the order of the day.

Their politics and inclination tailored them for service with a Conservative rather than a Labour Government. By 1964, thirteen continuous years had been spent in servicing Conservative Administrations. The violent change was traumatic for them, much as they had tried to prepare themselves for the incoming socialists and despite the isolated individuals – some distinguished ones in the Treasury – who welcomed Wilson's victory.

Despite the failure to reform the Service, it is now obvious that it has changed. As the methods of selection have remained the same, this alteration is not so much due to any greater objectivity on the part of the selectors as to the changes in society that have occurred as a result of reforming Governments (both Labour and Conservative) over the last thirty years.

My guess is that those who now staff the Administrative Class of the Civil Service are more likely to be potential SDP and Alliance supporters. The switches in policy between Left and Right, especially since 1964, have deeply affected attitudes in the Civil Service. This, together with changes in society since the war (and particularly since the 1960s), has produced civil servants from a different sort of background that is, in its turn, politically tuned in to the changing political scene – a background which, in my view, produces people more likely to be interested in the new Alliance Parties than the old regimes.

Any middle-of-the road Party must surely have a natural appeal for civil servants, who, by their very nature, dislike change. What they like is to see the machine tick over; their *raison d'être* is that they are the continuing presence in national life and at the heart of government. Politicians come and politicians go (rather too frequently these days), but the civil servants go on for ever. For this very reason, they tend to resist switches in policy; indeed, the experience of both Labour and Conservative Governments over at least the last twenty years must throw up all too many examples of where policy changes outlined in the election manifesto have been successfully resisted by the civil servants after the politicians who promulgated them took office.

Prior to 1964, the civil servants had become used to a long period of Conservative Government. Unlike the present Conservative Government, and its Labour predecessors, it was in no sense a radical Government of change, but a consensus Government. Perhaps I should make clear here my belief that a radical Tory Government can be as unpopular and meet with the same resistance from the civil servants as a Labour Government; what they dislike is change, whether it comes from Left or Right. Indeed, the moves by Mrs Thatcher to appoint sympathetic people to the top key jobs in Whitehall stems from her awareness, I believe, of this dilemma. In addition she is building up a formidable personal team of advisers in Number 10 to act as a further buttress to her authority.

The emergence of the Alliance and the SDP, combined with the social changes that have produced civil servants from a more politically liberated background, seems to me to suggest a situation where there is a political Party tailor-made to the traditional attitudes of the Civil Service. The SDP and the Alliance give them a political choice that caters to their most salient characteristic: the desire to avoid violent changes of policy.

The slow move back to consensus is being carried out not via the Conservative Party – the old progressive Conservative Party of Harold Macmillan and Rab Butler – but through the central grouping of the Alliance, headed by Roy Jenkins, David Steel and Shirley Williams.

Today's Conservative Party, just as much as Labour, is antipathetic to the Civil Service. Its 1979 manifesto declared a need for radical alterations in how the country is governed equal to any suggested in Labour manifestos – exactly what the Civil Service fights against. Both the leadership and the constitutions of the two main Parties spell conflict with the Civil Service.

These charges may sound strange in the light of the efficiency with which after an election the Civil Service produces the legislative programmes that give substance to the manifestos on which the political Parties have contested the election. But it is a different story once the victorious Party is in government; then, the Civil Service seeks by every means available to halt or amend what it regards as ill-considered or difficult to achieve. It is a tribute to their efficiency – and I am convinced they are the most superb bureaucratic machine in the world – that they are able to do this so successfully. A critic I may be, but I also have the greatest admiration and respect for their ability and efficiency.

The office of Prime Minister is uniquely lonely. To be thrust into this world from the hurly-burly of politics is a traumatic experience for any Prime Minister, however seasoned a politician he or she may be.

All other Ministers have senior advisers and specialists in their Departments as well as colleagues close at hand the whole time, who not only channel information but help their Ministers formulate ideas, assess cases, arrive at judgements. The Prime Minister is alone in Downing Street; there are neither senior political nor official colleagues in Number 10.

To some extent, the Cabinet Secretary fulfils this role – although this is not the same as having advisers and colleagues virtually within earshot, as were Thomas Balogh and the Special Policy Unit under Bernard Donoughue, which certainly helped to fill this gap for Harold Wilson and James Callaghan.

Equally there is a strong case for a special cadre of senior people trained as advisers to be incorporated into Downing Street; such a group undoubtedly adds to the effectiveness of both the Prime Minister and the Government – and obviates some of the difficulties that do occur. It curbs the tendency of the Civil Service to force the hand of the Prime Minister and prevents it from acting alone – of which there have been all too many instances, especially on the Foreign Affairs side: from the Soames affair in the 1960s and the argument over *détente* in the 1970s to the Falkland Islands crisis in 1982.

There is in my view a case for going even further: to the establishment of a special Prime Minister's Department, designed to cope not only with this specialized side of his or her life, but also with the increasing volume of work that the office entails. Many of our institutions, founded or amended in the nineteenth century but neglected since then, are now – for want of a better word – creaking; there is a case, I believe, for examining the possibility of the need for a Prime Minister's Department within the context of an overall study of governmental practice and organization.

It might help too to separate the Prime Minister's place of work from the Prime Ministerial residence: a special building for the Prime Minister's Department would take away from that office the trappings of power which, in any case, give a misleading impression of what can be done independently of Government or Party. Perhaps in more anonymous and workaday surroundings, without the glamour and history of Downing Street and the special aura that surrounds the office of First Minister, the job itself might become, if not easier, then at least more straightforward. Let Number 10 remain a residence for our Prime Ministers, but let them carry out their working duties elsewhere.

As I have argued elsewhere, the Prime Minister is not only Head of Government but Leader of his or her political Party; he stands at the peak of both and both roles must be catered for – separately. Although Harold Macmillan managed this by integrating personal and political appointees within the Civil Service staff, it seems to me obvious that this can be done more effectively by means of a separate political presence in Downing Street. The job of those who staff the Political Office runs largely parallel to that of the Private Office: namely, servicing the Prime Minister with political information, apprising him of what is happening within his Party, advising on the possible reaction among his colleagues or the country to certain policies, and keeping him in touch with his political colleagues in Parliament and the regions.

Prime Ministers who ignore the need for information of this description and this service do so, in my view, at their peril. I also happen to believe that, as civil servants are trained at the Civil Service College, there should be training facilities and provision for all potential political assistants.

Ignorance of how the administrative machine works causes many difficulties for those drafted into Number 10. Douglas Hurd, who became Head of Edward Heath's Political Office, pointed out in his book on the Heath years that one of the advantages he had was his service in the Foreign Office, which had given him a thorough knowledge of the machinery of government. It meant, he said, that he could work much better within Number 10 than someone who came in from outside (as I had done in 1964).

A training in administration as well as a political background should be a necessary part of the equipment of the political assistant, or aide, and would enable them to function more efficiently in servicing their Leader. This could be achieved if, as happens more or less everywhere else in the western world, political parties were financed by the State. Ensuring that our politicians receive the best possible advice in the performance of their duties will not only oil the wheels of the State machine but, more importantly, benefit the country as a whole – particularly now, with political changes ahead.

Quite apart from the rethinking involved by the arrival of a new and strong political grouping, there remains – for any progressive Party – the question of its relationship with the trades unions. In such changing times, it seems to me dangerous to the Labour Party to be left dependent on trades union financial aid. This may well suit the Conservatives, but it is no service to democracy.

Ahead lies a new and unknown industrial world, shaped and powered by microchip technology at the inevitable expense of human labour. The trades unions themselves may well become redundant in due course. Should not our political institutions take note of and make provision for such changes?

The question, 'Who runs Britain?', was originally posed with the unions in mind. It could be directed just as accurately against the Civil Service as against the trades union movement – and in the years to come, probably against the media more than either. With all that new technology means in terms of communications – with satellite and cable TV, video and improved terrestrial broadcasting – the power and reach of the media will become even greater, and their influence more pervasive.

These problems and others will face those who enter Downing Street in the 1980s and 1990s; to seek to solve them with today's machinery will be to invite trouble. What will be needed then – as has been needed for the last twenty years – is some degree of equality in expertise, experience and balance between the political presence in Whitehall and the administrative machine, incorporating those who have a direct connection with the outside world, and in particular with the new areas of influence and power as they open up.

It is an exciting prospect, which seems to me admirably suited to any Party that is truly progressive and reforming. Since 1950, we in this country have been passing through a period of dramatic change, brought about not only by technological developments, but also by increased affluence and massive social legislation. It has been a period presided over, for much of the time, by Harold Wilson.

THIRTY

The Future of the Labour Party

Will the Labour Party be the reforming, progressive Party presiding over the next leap forward? Is it too late to correct what is happening to it? Schisms, disarray, disaffection are damaging and dividing the Party; sometimes it seems that every fresh public issue forms a further occasion for disagreement. But it is *not* the first time, and it has recovered from earlier spasms.

It is true that the Labour Party has always been a ragbag – a coalition – of different views; it therefore follows that any Leader of the Party must be able to gather these diverse threads into his hand while urging the Party in the way he wishes it to go. The nearest analogy I can think of is the man driving a team of huskies which, if released from the traces, frequently hurl themselves at each other's throats. Or, as Harold Wilson put it, a stage coach in which everyone sits either happily or being sick while it rattles along, but when it comes to a crossroads, all the passengers get out and start to argue over which way to go.

Of past leaders, Attlee managed to control the Party successfully until forced by ill-health to go to the country when he lost, Gaitskell did not, Wilson and Callaghan both managed it, but Michael Foot has apparently failed. The moral seems to be that only a man from the centre, acceptable to both wings of the Party, succeeds, whereas a man recognizably from either Right or Left will fail.

The miscalculation over the last election, the crippling blow dealt by Jim Callaghan's 5 per cent pay offer in October 1978, followed by the winter of discontent and the subsequent defeat, hastened what was inevitable: the process of disaffection. Even more to the point, the electoral pact that was struck with the Liberals did two things that left

the ground ripe for the seeds of an SDP Party: it angered and disheartened those of the Left who were not militant, forcing them to take a side
they were not prepared to take; and by its cynicism it disillusioned those
supporters throughout the country who had always suspected that those
in Westminster were more interested in power than in the policies they
had promised to carry out. If Jim Callaghan had asked the country for
a mandate after he took over in 1976 he would, in my view, most
certainly have been given a strong one.

Before the Callaghan/Steel alliance in 1977, most Labour politicians
regarded the Liberal Party as very little different from the Conservatives
– and indeed in many cases more reactionary. So the pact that was
cobbled together in order, as Jim Callaghan justifiably saw it, to keep
Labour in office, gave the final and greatly accelerated impetus to new
political arrangements.

If Hugh Gaitskell had not died in 1963, a realigned Labour Party
might have arrived on the British political scene much earlier. If Hugh
had lived, and succeeded in his attempt after the 1959 election defeat to
swing the Labour Party right, hiving off the large left minority, this
might have led to the emergence of a Social Democratic Party – the
forerunner of which was the then Campaign for Democratic Socialism.

The Labour Right were deeply unhappy with the then hard Left.
Douglas Jay even sought to change the Labour Party's name because
he felt it gave the wrong image to what he and fellow-Gaitskellites
wanted – a Party that was democratic and progressive but that did not
suffer from a 'socialist' tag. Few now remember the long and acrimon-
ious debate – comical as it was – about what the Party could be called
instead.

These arguments of the 1950s and early 1960s could have left the
Conservatives in office for very many years. Sad though it is to say, it
was the death of Hugh Gaitskell that saved the old Labour Party as
such: with his successor, the ordinary voter found a man with whom he
could identify, and the Party a Leader under whom they could all unite.
The counter-argument that the Party would have been better off if high
noon had been fought out with the Left then and resolved is one of the
'ifs' of history.

THIRTY-ONE

Final Days

The Farewell Party is no less a tradition in Number 10, Downing Street than in any other office in the land. For the Prime Minister, in his role as Prime Minister, the Farewell Party as an entity proliferated into a number of official or semi-formal functions to mark his resignation. Among them were dinner with the Queen and the informal dinner given to the Cabinet.

But no specific function had been arranged to mark his quittal of the most important position in the Labour Party: that of Leader. In the great wave of shock and surprise that swept the country on learning of Harold Wilson's resignation, it was not always easy – even for those around him – to remember that, as far as the Labour Party was concerned, he was standing down from an equally important role.

The sad task of arranging some suitable gathering fell to me, as head of the Downing Street Political Office. Along with Transport House (many of whose staff would be guests) the date of 29 March was chosen for a reception starting at 6.30. Although this was officially supposed to end at 8.30, we all knew from past experience that the party would go on longer.

Everyone who had worked for Harold Wilson directly was asked. This meant not only those at the top: heads of departments, the General Secretary of the PLP, the National Agent, the Directors of Publicity and, Overseas Research, the TV Officer and the Meetings Officer (responsible for the countrywide arrangements of public meetings), but everyone with whom he had a personal connection, such as the Whips, the Whips' runners, the Parliamentary Private Secretaries, the various committee clerks and secretarial staff.

All the same, it wound up a much larger affair than the original estimate of fifty to sixty people: the guest list was added to until the last minute and, naturally, the staff from Number 10 looked in as well. Unlike other Downing Street parties, no single person was responsible for sending out the invitations for this one – rather, they were added to the list throughout the period prior to the party by personal members of the Prime Minister's staff and others close to him, as they thought of someone else who ought to be there. The mechanics of arranging it were handled by the Civil Service girl who had become, in effect, Social Secretary in Number 10.

Because of the significance of the occasion, rather than any feeling of jollity the whole evening had an undertone of sadness. There was, however, music, in the shape of a small group – piano, bass and drums – laid on by Albert Murray, who also suggested that, in view of the fact that it was a purely private occasion, Joe Bulaitis (a photographer whom we all knew) should take pictures privately so that we would all have something for our own records to remind us of this very poignant occasion. Professional and generous as always, Joe covered everything from the arrival of the guests onwards.

Three-quarters of the way through Harold made a brief speech thanking everyone for what they had done for him, and saying how sad it was to be saying goodbye. At that point one of the PLP staff looked at me and murmured agreement with the words, 'It's not just goodbye. It's the end of an era.'

Standing in the circle of those who had remained until the last, one hand grasped by David Frost and the other by Harold Wilson as we all sang 'Auld Lang Syne', I felt this strongly. All of us were very moved.

My feelings were somewhat different, however, when pictures of the party began to trickle out into the world's press; someone had not resisted the blandishments of the media. What was most distressing was that because the photographs were naturally concentrated on groups, those who were talking together, the animation of a toast of thanks being drunk rather than the still faces of those listening sorrowfully as Harold bade us all farewell, the evening came across as a jolly little knees-up rather than what it was: a genuinely moving few hours.

A side-effect for me is a reluctance to put on the dress I wore that night again. Every time I open my wardrobe this spectacular black caftan embroidered in gold, made by Arab craftsmen in Israel and bought for me by a friend in Jerusalem, reminds me of an evening that was, for me particularly, so poignant. Nor did the endless reproductions of the picture of myself in it, standing there singing, make me more enthusiastic about it!

Of course, at the time – and as always when among friends – it seemed enjoyable. I particularly relished a triangular conversation between Tony Benn (who had happened to be in the building and had therefore decided to look in), Jim Callaghan, only that day elected as Leader of the Party in succession to Harold, and myself. Tony, an entertaining talker in private, had remarked, in jest but straightfaced, to Jim, 'You do know, of course, that Harold doesn't have to resign as Prime Minister?'

Strange as it sounds, this was constitutionally correct, because Harold, although no longer Leader of the Labour Party (which role he had resigned earlier), was still Prime Minister: he had not formally handed his resignation to Her Majesty so she, in turn, could not send for the new Leader.

'What *would* happen, Jim, if he doesn't hand in his resignation?' Tony pressed. Deadly serious, Jim replied, 'Mary would never allow that.'

Index